# ORWELL IN ATHENS

INFORMATIZATION DEVELOPMENTS AND THE PUBLIC SECTOR, 3

*Previously published in this series*

Vol. 1. P.H.A. Frissen and I.Th.M. Snellen (Eds.), Informatization Strategies in Public Administration

Vol. 2. P.H.A. Frissen, V.J.J.M. Bekkers, B.K. Brussaard, I.Th.M. Snellen and M. Wolters (Eds.), European Public Administration and Informatization

# Orwell in Athens

A Perspective on Informatization and Democracy

Edited by

## W.B.H.J. van de Donk

*Tilburg University, The Netherlands*

## I.Th.M. Snellen

*Erasmus University Rotterdam, The Netherlands*

and

## P.W. Tops

*Tilburg University, The Netherlands*

1995

**IOS**
Press

**OHM**
Ohmsha

*Amsterdam, Oxford, Tokyo, Washington, DC*

ISBN 90 5199 219 X (IOS Press)
ISBN 4 274 90044 4  C3034 (Ohmsha)
Library of Congress Catalogue Card Number  95-075769

*Publisher*
IOS Press
Van Diemenstraat 94
1013 CN  Amsterdam
Netherlands

*Distributor in the UK and Ireland*
IOS Press/Lavis Marketing
73 Lime Walk
Headington
Oxford OX3 7AD
England

*Distributor in the USA and Canada*
IOS Press, Inc.
P.O. Box 10558
Burke, VA 22009-0558
USA

*Distributor in Japan*
Ohmsha, Ltd.
3-1 Kanda Nishiki - Cho
Chiyoda - Ku
Tokyo 101
Japan

LEGAL NOTICE
The publisher is not responsible for the use which might be made of the following information.

PRINTED IN THE NETHERLANDS

# Table of Contents

CHAPTER 5     Laying Down the Infrastructure For Innovations
                      in Teledemocracy: The Case of Scotland                                61

*J.A. Taylor, B. Bardzki and C. Wilson*

CHAPTER 6     Community Information Systems:
                      Strengthening Local Democracy?                                             79

*C. Bellamy, I. Horrocks, with J. Webb*

# CHAPTER 1

# Orwell in Athens

*A perspective on Informatization and Democracy*

Wim B.H.J. Van de DONK, Ignace Th.M. SNELLEN and P.W. TOPS

> 'What are often taken to be 'mere' tools and instruments are better seen as political artifacts that strongly condition the shared experience of power, authority, order and freedom in modern society'. (Winner, 1987)

Newt Gingrich, who recently was elected Speaker of the U.S. Congress, enthusiastically supports initiatives for an 'electronic democracy'[1]. 'CyberNewt' also promotes the idea of a virtual Congress, through which 'ordinary citizens' can participate in the democratic process. Like many other politicians, citizens and scholars, he expects that information and communications technologies (ICTs) can be of great help to restore some of the ideas that Herodotes, some 2500 years ago, defined as essential characteristics of a democracy: that issues regarding the public domain should be openly and freely deliberated by its citizens, who, furthermore, should be able to control those who hold the offices to govern the public domain.

A review of the literature concerning the relationship between ICTs and democracy which is presented in chapter two of this volume, makes clear that the first experiences in using ICTs to enable that kind of democratic capacities and practices, like the *Hawaiian Televotes* and the *Columbus Qube Tube* (Ohio), have already existed for a decade or so (see van de Donk and Tops, chapter two). Since then, the stormy development of information and - especially - communications technologies, has increased drastically the possibilities to use ICTs to support democratic decision making practices. The infrastructures and communication standards that facilitate the use of all kinds of applications (cable, ISDN network, telecommunication networks) have, and are being realized at a great pace. Political leaders, notably in the United States of America and the European Union, have made statements about the role that

---

[1] For more information about his statements: GEORGIA6@HR.HOUSE.GOV. Gingrich is one of the 50 members that actually participates in the House of Representatives Constituent Electronic Mail System (CEMS) that facilitates direct interactions among congressmen and constituents. Although often presented as a means to make politicians more responsive, one should realize that those systems are operated with help of software that uses an artificial intelligence rule-based system to filter the incoming messages. Their filtering rules include the subject matter of the message, the identity of the sender, the date of the message and cost-benefit considerations that indicate whether there is some reason to think that the information benefit will exceed the cost of reading or answering it (Rocheleau 1994: 90).

national information infrastructures and digital superhighways can play in empowering citizens in Western democracies. Although most of their statements about the future of telecommunications and informations infrastructures still mainly concern the significance to the economy and the market (see chapter thirteen), some of the things they say, do reveal that they acknowledge that ICTs are also - at least potentially - challenging existing relations and positions in the political system. They seem to recognize that ICTs can play an important role in shaping the body politic of society, like other technical systems and infrastructures have done already, (e.g. Winner 1987, Sclove 1992). The question as to what extent democracy can and will be enhanced is one of the most intriguing.

In several countries, projects that use ICTs to rejuvenate democratic practices have been or are being introduced and developed. Although earlier speculations about a *living room democracy* are still far from being realized, citizens are offered many new devices to participate in democratic decision making procedures (e.g. Public Access Terminals, Public Bulletin Boards, Online Voter Guides). And although ICTs are often associated with internationalization and globalization, many projects that are considered as promising instruments to promote and restore citizen's involvement in public affairs can be found at the level of local democracy, i.e. in municipalities and counties. In some cases (e.g. the contributions from the UK to this book), these projects mainly regard the citizen as a consumer of public services. In other cases, however, the renewal and reform of democratic politics, is an explicit aim of these projects (see for instance the chapter on *free-nets* and *digital cities* by Schalken and Tops). In the Netherlands, the use of ICTs has, already and for some time, a prominent place on the political agenda concerning the renewal of local democracy (e.g. Depla 1995). Various applications of ICTs are used to arrange a variety of projects which support different democratic routines or capacities (e.g. informing, debating, voting and organizing). Many of their projects explicitly try to persuade Joe Citizen - the desinterested 'Couch Potato' - to come back in the democratic arena and to participate in public life. That is not an easy task. For past years a large number of American citizens avoided to go to the ballot box. In Europe also, many citizens turn their backs to the public domain.

Politicians like Gingrich suggest that ICTs could and should be used as a crowbar for dismantling the ossified 'democratic' institutions that are now dominating the public domain. In the eyes of both the American and European electorate, these institutions have indeed lost much of their lustre. They have become symbols of 'syrupy' decision making by people, who are hardly recognizable as genuine democratic representatives. Some authors even claim that so-called representative democracies are neither representative nor democratic any more (Ellul 1992).

Against this background, ICTs are both praised and welcomed as a strategic opportunity to strengthen the power of the 'demos' which has long been neglected by traditional politicians. It is probably highly symbolic and no coincidence that people like Silvio Berlusconi and Ross Perot - who claimed to be 'real' democrats -

have extensively used ICTs in their political campaigns. Some other politicians, however, explicitly warn against electronic democracies.

Gingrich's counterpart in the Netherlands, Wim Deetman, chairman of the Second Chamber of Parliament, is reacting more reservedly towards projects in which ICTs have been used for electronic referenda and other forms of direct democracy. Some of his arguments have accompanied those kinds of projects since the earliest stages of computer democracy. He fears that electronic instant referenda will lead to a kind of permanent electioneering, resulting in incoherent, fragmented policies dominated by continuously changing, conflicting, individual and short term interests of the citizens. He expects that politicians and political parties will be reduced to 'electronic ears' without a programme of their own. Consequently, they will have great difficulties to propose and pursue policies that are inspired by their own political ideas and philosophies about a just and good society (Deetman 1995).

Some other authors doubt whether the introduction of digital democracy will provoke more citizens to participate in democratic decision making. Winner (1992), one of the leading writers about the significance of new information and communications technologies for democratic developments, doubts whether the widely felt mood of alienation that characterizes the 'demos' of the Western democracies is, if at all, a fruitful basis for developing more direct forms of citizen participation with help of ICTs. 'If politics in its minimal definition is of little concern to people, what real chance is there to broaden the horizons?' (Winner 1992: 4).

But, whatever the opinion of politicians and expectations of philosophers may be, various applications of electronic information and communications technologies, are very likely to play an increasingly important role in democratic politics. For some time now, various applications of ICTs are more or less successfully used by different actors in the democratic polity such as interest groups, politicians, representative bodies and individual citizens.

It is quite reasonable to believe that ICT applications will not only be of significance for existing actors, institutions and practices. They certainly can support existing practices and procedures of democratic rule, i.e. congressional oversight. However, one may not *a priori* neglect scenario's according to which ICTs facilitate the establishment of new conceptions and arrangements for democratic decision making. The advent of telecommunication infrastructures like the digital superhighways, which will further enable the use of all kinds of interactive facilities, is considered to be an important step towards a more participative democratic political system.

Since the beginning of the nineties, a new generation of initiatives and projects have been set up in and around public administration. A common feature is their ambition to renew democratic decision making structures and practices with help of information and communications technologies. Various applications can be found: public bulletin boards, community information systems, electronic town and village halls in which electronic town meetings are organized, public access terminals. One can even visit *digital cities* where political debates are organized in virtual pubs. The digital superhighways revive ancient dreams of more direct and participatory modes of democratic decision making. Free-nets and digital cities are set up by people, some of whom are ideologically related to projects that tried to realize kinds of participatory communities in the sixties and seventies. During their fact-finding mission in the digital cities, Schalken and Tops found out that the population of these digital cities shows some striking similarities with the population of ancient Athens, where democracy started to develop (see chapter ten). Highly educated political representatives of 'Groen Links' (ecological, left wing) are the most serious and active *citizens* in digital Athens.

However, it may be far too early to conclude that ICTs will enable and facilitate, or even provoke, the renewal of democratic political decision making practices, let alone whether or not that would bring us a kind of digital Athens. The way in which democracies will be affected by ICT applications, is highly dependent on the role of the bureaucratic organizations. These organizations, which do not get any significant attention from those who are describing the new democratic computopia's, usually have an impressive experience in using computers. Although many of these organizations are still mainly associated with large mainframe computers, they are very successful in using the newer generations of this technologies. The older generations of computertechnology were effectively used to automate and rationalize their internal affairs (Frissen 1989, Brinckmann and Kuhlmann 1990). The newer generations and applications like, interactive networks, datacommunication and telematics (Taylor and Van Every 1993, Zuurmond 1994) play a crucial role in two priorities that are warmly supported by their political masters: improving services to citizens and fighting fraud. In order to be able to realize these new priorities, and to contribute - in a more general sense - to an effective and efficient bureaucracy, ICTs are used for a radical transformation and reorganization of existing administrative work processes (see also Vintar, this volume).

In many Western bureaucracies both political and technological opportunities arise for re-arranging external relations with other bureaucracies - by coupling and integrating their databases, and with the citizens, now often regarded as 'clients', who have to be helped as efficiently as possible. Many new projects to create public bulletin boards, one stop shops, public access terminals, intelligent and interactive software, chip cards etc., are being started to improve existing services. Furthermore, devices are developed to monitor and analyze citizen's preferences, opinions and interests. Very likely, these devices will increasingly be interactive, which already is the case in some of the projects to be presented in the following chapters.

From an analysis of these projects it becomes clear that ICT applications are particulary reinforcing bureaucracy's capabilities to play a dominant role in the democratic polity. By using (interactive) applications of ICTs, bureaucracies are able to gather more and better information about the preferences of the citizens. These data are used by them as a source of anticipatory, instead of participatory policy making. In doing so, they tend to put aside the elected politicians and representative bodies, who have difficulties to compete with the quickly expanding information processing capacities of bureaucracies. Zuurmond (1994) has shown that informatization facilitates an informational integration by inter-organizational standardization and datacommunication. Through such an integration, traditional bureaucracies are being transformed in highly efficient and effective *'infocracies'*. By integrating and coupling their databases, these bureaucracies are able to develop and defend a dominant view of their own on societal problems. This view will be derived from the data they obtain as a result of the 'informating capacities' of all their transactional or electronic tracking systems and focus on analysis of preferences of citizens who leave their digital 'footprints' behind while using their administrative chip cards.

Do the developments contradict earlier expectations regarding the democratic potential of ICTs? Authors who concentrate on the potentialities of ICTs for bureaucratic organizations don't hesitate to speak of Orwellian forms of surveillance and control. Even if one does not agree with the oppressive surveillance described by their scenario's, one can clearly see that developments will potentially endanger some of the rights that - in a democratic Rechtsstaat - traditionally protect and preserve the autonomy and freedom of the citizen towards the state. According to Westin, the (...) strong citadels of individual and group privacy (...)' that '(...) limits both disclosure and surveillance is a prerequisite for liberal democratic societies.' (Westin 1976: 24). It is not surprising to see that Zuurmond uses a comparable metaphor just the other way around. He speaks of 'virtual fortresses' to describe the power of the bureaucracies that more and more successfully use ICTs to monitor and control various aspects of the behavior of their 'clients' (citizens as well as private organizations) (Zuurmond 1994). Poster even speaks about a 'Superpanopticum', a system of surveillance without walls, windows, towers or guards that will be the result of the 'circuits of communication' and the databases they generate (Poster 1990: 93).

In this book, the claim that ICTs can support those who are trying to reform or strengthen democratic politics is explored and discussed both at a theoretical and empirical level of analysis.

In the first chapters of this book, the relationship between ICT applications and democracy is explored at a general level. In chapter two, Van de Donk and Tops will present a general overview of the literature on this relationship. They conclude that, until now, the debate about the meaning of ICT applications for the future of democracy has been dominated by two extreme positions, represented by Orwell and Athens. Both positions are based on a highly speculative, rather one-dimensional assessment of the charactistics of the technologies involved. One group of authors considers ICTs as a set of technologies that tend to promote decentralization, transparency, interactiveness and freedom of information. Consequently, ICTs are seen as an inherently democratic technology. In their publications, they tend to focus on the role that ICTs can play in making representative democracies more responsive or in restoring ancient dreams of more direct forms of democracy. Their projections and speculations usually are confined to one kind of actor in the democratic process: the citizens. They mostly neglect the role of bureaucracies and other institutions in the democratic arena. Another group of authors, on the contrary, tends to overemphasize the role ICTs can play in making bureaucracies more effective. They consider ICTs as a technology that is strongly biased towards extending all kinds of political and organizational control and surveillance.

Van de Donk and Tops claim that the projects which are now being started will enable empirical research which endeavours to evaluate the role of both citizens and bureaucracy. That will also enable us to transcend the classical, disjunctive position: Orwell or Athens. Moreover, the existing positions, mostly speculative in the estate, were biased by a view on the nature of ICTs, which could be characterized as a kind of technological determinism. Van de Donk and Tops conclude that the dominance of these two positions in the debate for a long time obstructed a more empirical approach of the relationship between ICT applications and democracy. Since an increasing amount of practical experiences can be studied, a much more complete but also much more complex and ambiguous image of this relationship comes to the fore. ICTs seem to be successfully used in projects that are based on conceptions of democracy that previously were neglected.

In the next chapter, Edwards elaborates some conceptions of democracy and their relationship with ICT applications. He makes a distinction between a populistic, a liberal and a republican view of democracy. He investigates the relationship between democracy and informatization by looking into the fundamental assumptions these views of democracy entail for the role information is playing in the democratic process. ICTs' influence on the functioning of democracy is investigated analytically by looking into the information and communication aspects of two crucial demo-cratic relationships, that between electorate and representatives and between represen-tative bodies and government. Edwards' framework helps to make explicit some of the basic assumptions that are underlying the projects in which ICTs are used to enhance 'democracy'. The framework also can be used for a systematic and strategic reflection on exactly what kind of democracy one wants to support with such a project.

As Snellen points out in chapter four, a confrontation of the normative assump-tions of democratic theory and the reality of informatization in the democratic arena makes clear that a 'cultural lag' exists between democratic reality and democratic theory. While ICTs increasingly facilitate possibilities for channeling democratic influence through bureaucracies, these possibilities are not recognized in conceptions of democracy theory. ICTs contribute to an erosion of some of the basic assumptions of democracy theory. The possible democratic role of a representative bureaucracy, which is strengtened by ICTs, will have to be 'ratified' by democratic theory. According to Snellen, the actual situation gives, in fact, an easy alibi to public sector managers who are responsible for ICT applications to restrict their responsibility for these projects to technical and organizational aspects which obscures their democratic aspects.

The following chapters present an empirical analysis of various concrete projects is given. Such an analysis brings up a lot of other aspects and problems that will have to be considered when projects are developed which introduce ICTs into the democratic arena.

In chapter five, on the deployment of infrastructures for teledemocracy in Scotland, Taylor c.s. show that these infrastructures are a boundary condition of the development for innovative projects that support local councillors, local communities or some form of direct democracy. As a consequence of economic competition between those who have to supply the technical infrastructure for that kind of projects, these projects actually are unevenly and patchily spread over the different parts of the country. By explaining these differences by pointing at the role of economic competition in national telecommunications policies, they have determined yet another factor that seems of great relevance for the occurrence of innovative projects in this field.

In the chapter on the role of Community Information Systems (six), Bellamy c.s. have developed a more general typology of projects that aim at improving the exchange of information with the citizens. Their research on the development of Community Information Centers made clear that not only the competitive relationships on a market, but also the larger political and cultural context ('supply-side politics') are crucial motive forces behind these projects. In this respect, the specific state of local democracy in the U.K. is held responsible for the rather technocratic character of the projects that have been developed. Most of the projects reflect a major (sic!) orientation on economic and technological values like efficiency and professionalism.

In chapter seven, Vintar stresses that in those societies where democratic routines and cultures still have to be settled, the practical level on which the quality and accessability of all kinds of public services has to be assured, is a promising field for using ICTs. A research project that has been carried out at the level of local authorities in Slovenia, makes clear that organizational models based on the use of Computer Supported Cooperative Work Systems can bring about many changes in the functioning of Slovenian local democracies that will contribute to its democratic character.

In chapter eight, Frokjær c.s. report on the introduction of Computer based Tools for Cooperative Work among Politicians and Officials in Ravnsborg, a municipality in the northern part of Denmark. The system was introduced to support an important reorganization aimed at a reinforcement of political control of politico-administrative processes in this municipality. Although some interesting observations could be made, the results of the evaluation are still somewhat inconclusive as to the question whether these kinds of systems will contribute to a strengthening of the democratic character of municipalities like Ravnsborg.

In chapter nine 'Democracy Denied. The Political Consequences of ICTs in UK Local Government', Pratchett draws upon both deterministic (explaining the anti-democratic character of current ICTs) and constructivist (the specific political culture of British local democracy) explanations of technological change to explain why the democratic potentials of ICTs are usually neglected in British local government. Pratchett's principal argument is that those ICTs which have found their way into British local government are not inherently flexible and variable in their effects. Rather, he claims that the dominant features of currently used applications of ICTs - like standardization, the integration of databases, the pressure to use similar data-definitions a.s.o. - have contributed to a rigidity in local administrations that make them much more technocratic and authoritarian, but less democratic in their dominant orientation.

In chapter ten, Schalken and Tops report on the 'Digital City' in Amsterdam. Like many free-nets in the U.S., the project tries to establish a virtual community in the city of Amsterdam. They present some technical and organizational features of this project as well as some results from a survey among its digital inhabitants. As we already indicated before, the population of the Digital City resembles that which was gathered regulary in the agora of ancient Athens. Although the digital city theoreti-cally provides an excellent infrastructure for teledemocracy in the real city of Amsterdam, for the moment most of the debates are being organized in and about the digital city itself. Some existing political parties try to use the digital city to explore whether these kinds of systems could help them to regain their position in the democratic debate.

In chapter eleven, Depla en Tops explore how traditional political parties are preparing themselves for the digital era. Political parties have - in the perspective of this book - an interesting commonality with bureaucracies: they are both a blind spot in democracy theories and very active in developing and using ICTs that can help them to defend and even reinforce their position in the democratic arena. Depla and Tops present an overview of the various applications of ICTs that political parties are using, and how these are affecting their position and role in representative democra-cies. The question whether the traditional mass parties that traditionally fulfilled an intermediary function in a representative democratic system, will have a chance to survive (or even reinforce their position) in the political arena of the information polity is still very difficult to answer. Depla and Tops discuss some possible scena-rio's that can be discerned with regard to the question of how ICTs will affect their internal organization, their relationship with the electorate and their strategic position in representative democracies.

The extent to which a political system is a democratic system must also be determined by looking at some of the fundamental, constitutional rights that are attributed to each of the individual members of the polis. In chapter twelve on the meaning of informatization for the openness of government, Zouridis explores the ways in which ICTs can help them to find and use governmental information. He presents two systems in which applications of ICTs are used to support citizens to find their way into the governmental dossiers they need for an effective participation in the democratic debate. In this respect, ICTs notably seem to facilitate the possibilities citizens have to access and retrieve governmental information.

As a consequence of ongoing informatization, many dossiers are available in an electronic format. Therefore, existing laws that regulated citizens access to governmental information have to be adjusted to this new situation to prevent gaps in the public access laws. Applications of ICTs can also contribute to the development of navigating systems that - more or less actively - show citizen's what kind of information is available for them. Zouridis concludes that a greater transparency of government, although desirable from a democratic point of view, does not automatically get a lot of attention by those who are responsible for the development of administrative information systems. In order to prevent ICTs from mainly being developed and used as a 'technology of secrecy' he claims that the design of governmental information systems should be seen - and discussed - as a set of policy choices that regard the openness of government.

Another important right of the individual members of the demos is the right to be let alone, as some have described the right of informational privacy. Raab investigates the claim that protecting informational privacy is a roadblock that some people want to put at the electronic superhighway. In chapter thirteen, he extensively describes the proposals for 'information superhighways' in the United States, Canada, the United Kingdom and the European Union in terms of their perceived implications for democracy and the protection of privacy. He concludes that, for the moment, Information Superhighways are being developed primarily for their likely benefits to the economy and the state, and to the involvement of the citizen/consumer in both. The improvement of democracy is important as well, but it is more a side benefit or luxury than a motive force for ISH infrastructural development. Democratic goals only seem to play some part in the public statements of higly involved politicians. Instead of roadblocks, Raab concludes, a certain degree of informational privacy protection seems to be a precondition of success, in that it enhances the acceptability and legitimacy of ISH applications.

In chapter fourteen, Bekkers and Van Duivenboden zoom in at the citizen's role as a client of public organizations. In this role, citizens are more and more confronted with public administrative bodies and organizations that are using modern generation ICTs for an extensive coupling and integrating of their databases. Bekkers and van Duivenboden explore both threats and opportunities this could bring about for four major democratic principles that protect the democratic citizen from arbitrary and capricious behavior of the state: legal equality, legal security, the rule of law and the principle of checks and balances. They discuss how different forms of datacoupling (Computer Aided Front End Verification; Computer Matching; Computer Profiling) could bring both threats and opportunities for both governmental organizations and their clients.

In the final chapter of this book, Van de Donk and Meyer present an explorative investigation into the impacts of informatization for political decision making processes. While most of the research and debates regarding the relationship between ICTs and democracy is focused on voting, elections, political parties and the meaning of ICTs for different views on democracy, the role of ICTs in the 'daily life of democracy', political decision making, tends to be neglected. From a democratic point of view however, these decision making processes are equally important as campaigning and electioneering. Also in the context of concrete decision making processes, functions and characteristics of democratic politics can be recognized. Informatization is playing an important role in these processes. In this chapter, it is asked to what extent that role is strengthening or weakening the democratic nature of these processes.

Van de Donk and Meyer suggest that ICTs are affecting political decision making processes by affecting information properties (like accessability), aspects of information processing (like aggregability) and information behavior (like tunnel vision or myopia) in political decision making. In two explorative case studies, they investigate how the use of a certain application of ICTs are affecting two kinds of political decision making processes: political agenda building and allocative policy making. Although their observations do certainly reflect the specific applications of ICTs that were studied, it is clear that it is far too early to champion ICTs as a democratic technology.

The Orwellian impression the theoretical and empirical studies in this book leave about the relationship between ICTs and democracy is, that ICTs are a technology that fits especially bureaucracies best. Bureaucracies have a relatively strong position vis à vis representative bodies. They dispose of full time highly trained professionals. They discovered the potentialities of Information and Communications Technologies much earlier than their counterparts, the people's representative bodies.

Because the chapters that follow demonstrate that ICT applications in a democracy tend to strengthen the relative power position of the buraucracies, we see the results of our study as a corroberation of the 'reinforcement theory' developed in Irvine (Danziger et al. 1982, Kraemer and King 1994). According to this theory, ICT applications tend to be deployed to improve the power positions of the more powerful actors at the expence of the less powerful ones.

So ICTs tend to be used to build in bureaucratic Orwellian positions in democratic Athenian environments.

As to the title of this book we could choose between 'Orwell and Athens' as contrary positions, and we could have added a question mark to the title: 'Orwell and Athens?' On the basis of the material presented in this book we decided that it had to be 'Orwell in Athens', because - although ICTs clearly do support the revival of some Athenian characteristics of democratic decision making - the Orwellian potentialities of ICTs are becoming well entrenched in Western democracies.

## Acknowledgments

The editors of this book want to thank the Chairman of the European Group for Public Administration, professor Hugo van Hasselt, for enabling its permanent study group on Informatization in Public Administration, to meet each other annually and work together on several projects. A common meeting of the contributors to this book in Bad Tatzmannsdorf (Austria), in September 1994, was crucial in the process of making this book. Mrs. Cathérine Coninckx helped us to make these meetings as efficient as possible.

The earliest ideas for this book and some of the chapters in it were born during a sabbatical stay at the Netherlands Institute for Advanced Study in the Humanities and Social Sciences (NIAS) of the first and second editor of this book. Some other authors also stayed there for a sabbatical leave or to participate in one of the conferences that were organized by the nucleus on Informatization in Public Administration. Both editors and these authors gratefully acknowledge the hospitality and the excellent provision of services by NIAS.

For reviewing and correcting the use of the English language of some of the chapters, we want to thank our colleagues and friends Christine Bellamy, Ivan Horrocks, John Taylor and William Webster.

Manon Hornesch assisted the editors by correcting typoscripts, summarizing chapters and producing the indexes. Kees Schalken did a great job restyling the figures and tables.

The office of Guus Donker at the Erasmus University in Rotterdam was the real, virtual, but in any case very effective αγορα where chapters, corrections, telephone-calls, faxes, floppies, files and email messages came together to decide that they were going to be this book.

# CHAPTER 2

# Orwell or Athens?
# Informatization and
# the Future of Democracy

*A review of the literature*

Wim B.H.J. Van de DONK and Pieter W. TOPS
*Tilburg University, PO Box 90153, 5000 LE Tilburg, The Netherlands*

**Abstract.** The authors present a review of the literature regarding the threats and opportunities modern information and communications technologies (ICTs) bring about for several aspects of political democracy. They conclude that two 'classic' scenario's, 'Orwell' (surveillance bureaucracy and disappearing political freedom) and 'Athens' (electronical forms of direct democracy) dominated the (often highly speculative) literature. Recent empirical research seems to confirm that the characteristics of ICTs are relevant for democratic and political life. ICTs can support different views on political democracy. ICTs can help to make representative democracy more responsive. Some forms of direct democracy can now be realized with help of ICTs. New forms of political and social participation can arise by introducing ICTs in issue groups and social movements. New media, like computer conferences and interactive cable TV can enlarge the amount of people involved in public decision making. On the other hand, however, there are some threats: alienation of 'citizens' in a 'push button' democracy, in which political parties and traditional social institutions like unions and private organizations will no longer be able to integrate different views and interests.

## 1. Introduction and Thematization: Where did Orwell go wrong?

With regard to the feasibility of democracy in the information society, two extreme positions can be recognized. One position claims that the 'electronic revolution' will realize the digital superhighways that will result in a more democratic society and a drastic renewal of political culture and structure (Etzioni *et al.* 1975, Becker 1981, Hollander 1985, Barber 1988, Abramson *et al.* 1988). Others believe that the electronic revolution is primarily a technocratic revolution, which will automatically and inevitably result in Orwellian surveillance and control of citizens and employees (Thompson 1970, Rule 1974, Martin 1978, Ackroyd *et al.* 1980, Burnham 1983, Will 1983, Sterling 1986, Laudon 1986, Morris-Suzuki 1988, Zuboff 1989).

Reviewing the literature, one clearly observes that much attention has been paid to the question: *Orwell or Athens?* Between 'Orwell' and 'Athens', however, there exists a large number of intermediate positions, often based on research on a more moderate scale or explicitly focussed on one actor in a democracy, such as parliaments or political parties (e.g. Frantzich 1982, 1989). In this chapter, we give an overview of the literature regarding the meaning of informatization for democracy[1].

We will start our review with a short exploration of some characteristics of information and communications technologies (ICTs). Some of them (like interactivity, decentralization and increased possibilities for controlling information flows for both senders and receivers) make ICTs very relevant for several aspects of democracy and political decisionmaking.

## 2. Computer, Information and Communications Technologies: What is New about It?

ICTs are referring to computers, communication-software and -devices, satellites and cable networks, but also video cassette recorders and glass-fibre cables. Consequently things like direct mail, electronic mail, video-, computer- and tele-conferences, instant polling, computer-assisted telephone interviewing, teletext, on line databases and interactive television have become possible. Abramson, Arterton and Orren (1988) simply refer to them as new media, that enable new methods of gathering, processing, conveying and storing information which fundamentally affect communication processes between various actors (e.g. Van de Donk and Meyer this volume). In this survey, we will not discuss precise definitions. According to Abramson, Arterton and Orren, new media have at least six specific characteristics which make them of special interest to politics and democracy (1988: 32-66).

In the *first* place, the new media enormously increase the quantity as well as the accessibility of information for politicians as well as citizens.

*Secondly*, the new media accelerate the processes of gathering, distributing and storing information. Time and place (distance) are hardly restrictive factors. Information about political events is virtually immediately available at large distances for everyone who has a need for it. Politicians have increasingly less time to react to events. The opinions and reactions of the general public are more and more readily available as well (e.g. by means of advanced forms of instant polling, (see McLean 1989 and Moore 1992).

A *third* characteristic is that the new media (by means of a larger amount of possibilities of selection) enable the receivers of information to exert more control over the information.

---

[1]   This chapter is a slightly adapted version of an article the authors published in 1992 (Van de Donk and Tops 1992). Some new publications in the field are discussed. Some of them are only present in the - updated - bibliography. The original article was written in the framework of a larger research project on 'democracy and the information society' that was sponsored by the Dutch Organization for Technology Assessment (NOTA).

A *fourth* characteristic is that new technologies make information targeting by the sender of information possible; the information can be geared to ever more specifically defined target groups. Besides talking about broadcasting we can now also increasingly talk about narrowcasting. Politicians may, for instance, use new media to compose very detailed profiles of groups of voters and subsequently approach each group in a specific way (direct mail, video tapes) and with a specific message. Opposed to possible advantages, such as a deepening of information and a better fulfillment of people's needs there are possible disadvantages, like a reinforcement of fragmentation and of opportunities for manipulation.

A *fifth* feature concerns the tendency to decentralization which would be incorporated in new technologies. However, this feature is not completely unambiguous and according to Abramson *et al.*, it would be sensible to make a distinction between ownership and use of new media. The ownership of new media becomes more and more concentrated in the hands of a few media giants (see also McLean 1991). However, decisions about their use, that is about the question what is recorded and broadcasted by new media, can be taken at a more and more decentralized level. As far as the application of computer networks is concerned, this tendency to decentralization remains controversial. In computernetworks, decentralization always takes place within a framework of centralization: due to the transparency of such networks, central supervision on decentralized processes remain possible, in many cases it is even more effective than it has been ever before (see Sterling 1986, Snellen and Van de Donk 1987, Zuboff 1989).

The *sixth* and last feature of the new media is their capacity to bring about interaction between sender and receiver. It is by this interactivity that the old media (such as TV, radio and newspapers) are most sharply contrasted with the new media. It enables viewers and other receivers of information to react immediately to what is presented to them. They are no longer passive receivers of programs made by others, but active participants who can also exert influence on the content of programs. Abramson *et al.* state that interactivity is still the least developed feature of the new technologies. This can be explained by the costs that go with it, but also by the adaptations it requires to existing habits with regard to the use of media. Since they wrote their seminal book, however, the information superhighway, by means of which a lot of people have various possibilities to interact by electronic mail, the feature of interactivity is rapidly developing.

It is particularly this possibility of interactivity that has resulted in wild speculations about the possible impact of new media on the functioning of democracy. The central point is the idea that new life could be breathed into the long cherished ideal of direct democracy by means of interactive media. As will turn out later, very particular views of democracy appear to play an important role here.

## 3. Old Ideals and New Technology: Direct Democracy

Many authors suppose that the ideal of direct democracy can finally be realized by means of new technologies. Particularly futurologists like Naisbitt and Toffler have high expectations of the possibilities of self 'representation', which new media would make possible (Naisbitt 1982, Toffler 1980, Hollander 1985 and Masuda 1985). These media would create the technical and organizational opportunities for individual citizens to participate directly in political decision making. Because of this the *raison d'être* of representative institutions - to make democracy possible in large-scale societies in an organizational way - expires, so they argue. Technology makes it possible to list the opinions of individual citizens in a short period of time and at a low cost. Due to this, intermediary organizations, such as political parties and pressure groups, will loose their function and representative institutions may disappear. Citizens can become self-governing and will no longer need to transfer decision making power to political representatives. A direct, plebiscitarian democracy becomes feasible when the 'demos' (that can be defined and selected easily for the problem that has to be decided upon) can come together virtually. Concretely, such a plebiscitarian democracy can be depicted as a system in which issues are presented to citizens, for instance via interactive television that enables electronic voting by means of a connected telephone or a special keyboard. In this manner many instant referenda can be realized at relatively low costs of participation for citizens (Martin 1987, McLean 1989 and Van Dijk 1991).

As far as we have been able to gather, electronic plebiscites with formal decision making power have not been carried out anywhere yet. In the seventies and eighties some experimental projects which have been inspired by this concept of democracy, but without formal decision making power, were started in the United States. Famous examples are the *Hawaiian Televotes* and the *Columbus Qube Tube* (Arterton 1986, 1987, Becker 1981). Experiences in the United States show that participation in these forms of opinion polls is relatively low (Abramson *et al.* 1988: 169). Although the participation rate is still higher than in more traditional forms of participation via hearings and surveys, the assumption that new media will breathe new life into the ideal of direct democracy is by no means justified. Anyhow, the instant referendum does not appear to be the practical and time-saving alternative to political participation in which Joe Citizen - 'bored with baseball and too broke for video gambling' - would like to take part (see also Eulau 1977 and McLean 1989).

Besides the instant referendums just mentioned, the opinion polls and the influence they exert on the behavior of politicians are by some authors also called a form of electronic plebiscitarian democracy. Abramson *et al.*, for instance, argue that at this moment the ideal of direct democracy finds its greatest triumph in American politics by the influence of opinion polls on the behavior of politicians (1988: 20, see also Roll 1982, Moore 1992). And McLean alleges that an inherent relation exists between direct democracy and random selection (selection determined by lot), as was understood in ancient Athens. Today this form of random selection has been reintroduced by means of opinion polls; after all citizens' opinions are listed by way of random sampling. Due to the increase in quality and velocity of the polls, the impact of these opinion polls on the behavior of politicians has increased more and more, says McLean, who considers this an element of direct democracy in an otherwise indirect system of democratic decision making. Following Burnheim he talks about a system of demarchy, a combination of (statistical) democracy and anarchy (McLean 1989: 130).

These concepts of electronic plebiscitarian democracy have been critically received in literature (Laudon 1977, 1980, Eulau 1977, Grewlich and Pedersen 1984, Calhoun 1986, Arterton 1987, Abramson, Arterton and Orren 1988). They would, for instance, reduce the role of a political citizen to that of a passive person who pushes a button or fills out a questionnaire. This *push button* democracy undermines active involvement of citizens with policy making and implementation. In the plebiscitarian version democracy is reduced to the passive recording of points of view. Because of this the risk of instant-decision making arises, whereas one of the merits of the democratic system is that in a relatively long process the advantages and disadvantages are considered and that all interested parties can make a contribution to the discussion.

Moreover, electronic plebiscites (certainly when they are confined to simple consultation and are not organized within a framework of a broader social discussion) would have an atomizing effect on the political behavior of citizens (Laudon 1977). They assume that political opinions are formed in an isolated way in private situations (at home in front of the TV). However, research proves that political views are often formed in the context of organizations of which people are a part (work, neighborhood, club). If the setting of the formation of political views shifts from group settings to isolated citizens, the protective and stabilizing function of such groups would disappear, says Laudon. Subsequently the mediating and informing role performed by these groups will disappear. This could, among other things, result in individual citizens becoming more accessible to and more mobilizable by political bureaucratic elites. The atomization of society and the elimination of intermediate organizations may make the masses into objects of manipulation by politicians and their advisors. When used in this way, information and communications technologies will contribute little to the organizational and political competence of citizens.

The electronic plebiscites do not only enhance citizens' control over decision makers, but also the decision makers' control over citizens; it is the (political bureaucratic) elites that decide on the questions, determine the information channels and decide what happens to the results.

## 4. More Responsive Indirect Democracy

For many authors representative democracy is not 'a sorry substitute for the real thing', i.e. direct democracy, but an authentic and even superior form of democratic decision making. Direct democracy, they state, does not come with merely practical objections. The most important objections are matters of principle and always have to do with the observation that in a system of direct democracy decisions are too easily made by applying the majority rule. Consequently the functions that are also considered to be essential for a good democracy, such as the protection of minorities, the correcting effects of checks and balances, the restraining influence of deliberation and compromising and the arbitrating and informative effects of intermediate organizations, do not come out well enough in forms of direct democracy.

Of course representative democracy has its problems as well. Many of these problems have to do with the question to what extend there is a congruity between the views of the representatives and the views of the voters. This question has a normative as well as a factual component. The normative component refers to the question to what extend there has to be congruity. Must the MP follow the views of the electorate in everything or does he have room for personal considerations? If so, how much room? (OTA 1987: 7). The factual component concerns the question in what way congruity can be accomplished between the views of representatives and the people they represent. Which institutions, procedures and codes of behavior can contribute to that? This is where ICTs come in.

First of all they enable the MP to be informed about the opinions and views of his electorate in a relatively simple and accurate way. By regularly conducted opinion polls the MP can more easily be kept informed about the preferences of his electorate. These polls can provide an important supplement to the relatively primitive information channels that are often dominated by party activists, which a MP has at his disposal.

At the same time a normative problem emerges here as well, as Roll observes (Roll 1981, also see OTA 1987). Does the introduction of all these forms of instant polling not in a way undermine the MP's autonomous position (Williams 1982)? What in fact remains of his constitutional obligation to make decisions without any assignments or instructions? It becomes increasingly difficult for him to ignore the results of opinion polls with impunity. Will there be a point at which this technologically induced conception of democracy (the OTA study speaks of 'instructed representation') can no longer be brought into line with a MP's constitutional position? What is still a point scored from the point of view of direct democracy (see the previous paragraph, seems to be a loss from the perspective of representative democracy, at least beyond a certain point.

A second contribution of the new media to a more responsive representative democracy lies in the fact that it makes more, and more direct forms of contact possible between a MP and the people he represents. An example of this form are the telephone and multipoint videoconferences, in which a parliamentarian can communicate with citizens. In the United States such forms of contact between voters and representatives are rather popular (Abramson *et al.* 1988: 141). Furthermore direct mail and video facilities enable the MP to inform his electorate about his parliamentary activities and the positions he takes in them more frequently and livelier than in the past. In addition direct communication lines arise between representatives and voters, with elimination of the filtering effect of the official media (Frantzich 1982, Alexander 1995).

The use of new forms of information and communications technologies in support of existing systems of representative democracy has up to now expanded enormously in the organization of election campaigns, which occupy an important place in a representative democracy. Abramson, Arterton and Orren give some fascinating examples (see also Berkman and Kitch 1986). One of those refers to the way in which the Republican Party developed a database containing information about the opponent of the Democratic Party, Walter Mondale, in the campaign for the presidential elections of 1984. During the election campaign a data file of about 75,000 items was built up containing 45,000 quotations of Mondale, which covered his entire political career. At the height of the campaign the database was updated every 24 hours. Each time when Mondale made a statement about a certain topic, his earlier statements about the subject were consulted, which allowed the Republican Campaigners to immediately confront the Democrats with any inconsistencies. The easily accessible database was available on a decentralized level by using computer networks. Because of this database, among other things, the Republican Party managed to keep the initiative during the election campaign of 1984 and undermined the campaign of the Democrats on numerous occasions (Abramson *et al.* 1988: 92/93, see Berkman and Kitch 1986, Broder 1987b and McLean 1989 for other examples).

## 5. Democracy as Active Citizenship

In a number of discussions about the relation between new media and democracy a third conception of democracy plays a part, beside the plebiscite and representative variety. We are talking about what Abramson, Arterton and Orren call the *communitarian democracy* and Barber refers to as *strong democracy*. In this approach active citizenship and participation of citizens in the public debate are the key issues. It is consultation and persuasion that leads to a collective definition of general interest. Here democracy is not only a method of decision making, but especially 'a course in civic education'. Whether the decisions are in the end made via a system of direct or indirect democracy is a matter of secondary importance. Essential in this conception is the active participation of citizens in discussions about affairs that are of general interest.

ICTs can, according to some, contribute to the realization of this ideal of democracy (Becker 1981, Barber 1988). For instance, cable television, modern telephone networks and computer networks create several kinds of possibilities for active and interactive discussion among interested citizens. In this respect electronic town meetings or *the electronic commonwealth* are sometimes mentioned. The new media can see to it that information about political matters are accessible to everyone and that it is geared to the need for information of specific groups. At the same time they can considerably increase the scale on which town meetings take place and so the number of participants. Consequently the somewhat parochial character, sometimes attached to this idea of communitarian democracy, can be broken with (Abramson *et al.* 1988: 280).

Well known examples of the use of new media in the United States are the *Berks Community Television (BCTV)* in Reading (Pennsylvania) and the *Public Electronic Network* in Santa Monica (California). In a lot of cities in Northern-America and some cities in Europe, the so-called Free-Nets have come into development. Free-Nets are computernetworks that simulate the real world; they are virtual communities. Via Internet they are connected to a world wide network of computers (see the chapter of Schalken and Tops in this book for a more detailed description of the Free-Nets).

Laudon, by whom in 1977 a very critical study was published about the relationship between communication technology and political participation, is rather positive about this application of ICTs. It can be used, he argues, to stimulate processes of opinion forming and of participation and to leave behind internal oligarchy in political and intermediary organizations. An important condition is that the technology connects as good as possible with existing democratic procedures and institutions (add on strategy). One should not want to create new technology induced institutions. Furthermore, it is only possible to a very limited extent to establish a political community, which did not exist before, by technology alone. On the other hand new groups, such as the disabled and the elderly, can more easily take part in a political debate (see also Pedersen 1984).

A problem with the electronic town meetings is the supervision of the agenda. Who determines what will be discussed? Teleconferences are relatively easy to manipulate by lobby (groups) and interest groups. In the Netherlands several experiences show that even a *moderator* not always succeeds in maintaining the (democratic) quality of these digital debates. That is why it would be naive to suppose that the electronic town meetings automatically lead to a greater equality of and admission to participation possibilities (Abramson *et al.* 1988: 184, see also McLean 1989 and Arterton 1987). On the other hand, Barnouw (1982) and McLean (1989) point at increased possibilities some groups will have to place their '*buried issues and hidden agendas*' on the political agenda.

## 6. Intermediary Organizations

In the previous paragraph it has been mentioned that information technology can also have various consequences for intermediary organizations between government and citizen. Among these organizations both social connections (such as organized interest groups and social movements) and political parties are to be considered. Investigation into the application of new technologies in these organizations (which many authors think are invaluable for a stable democracy) is actually still in its infancy, and was somewhat pushed into the background by all the attention that has been given to the significance of informatization for political democracy.

### 6.1.　Issue and Pressure Groups

In an investigation into the sociological aspects of the discussion about abortion in the United States it turned out that modern technology enabled many volunteers to contribute to the activities of the (pro-life) movement, while simply staying at home (Luker 1984). Via personal computers in which address and telephone lists were kept up to date, a large number of letters could be sent in a relatively short time from a number of different homes to politicians. A switchboard system on the organization's telephone automatically put incoming calls through to the private telephone of one of the many volunteers who made themselves available at certain hours. Technology, in short, made it possible for many people to be active in the pro-life movement (with an average of ten hours a week), while attending merely four meetings a year. On top of that the investigation proved that a relatively large number of pro-life activists came from groups with a low social status. That is why the use of the new technologies contributed to an 'external democratization' of the pro-life movement. As a result the nature of the participation changed greatly, say Abramson *et al.* (1988). Activities are after all developed by isolated and autonomous individuals, who seldom have direct contact with each other or exchange and test opinions and information. In order to (be able to) function people are also strongly dependent on the information that is provided by the movement's leaders or administrations.

### 6.2.　Cybertribes

Electronic communication differs largely from face to face contacts: citizens are approached individually, they do not receive the political information in a social context, the opportunity to communicate directly with other members of the group is lacking, and the differences in status and power with political leaders are often rather great (Abramson *et al.* 1988). This causes a quite radical change in the bases of participation. The new technology - e.g. the virtual issue, and special interest groups that are active on the internet - mobilizes more or less isolated citizens instead of groups of citizens with a collective identity and a mutually shared system of meaning. 'Call them cybertribes: bands of like-minded citizens 'threaded' together instantaneously, specifically, globally, sometimes obsessively - eager not just to find and reinforce each other, but to influence real events' (Fineman 1995:30). As a result rather loose and flexible organization patterns arise in which the quantitative size of the mobilized group is not infrequently the most important criterion. The 'membership' of such an 'organization' has a very transitory nature. Instead of activities meant to tie the members as much as possible to an organization the leadership will more likely make use of marketing techniques from time to time in order to activate as many people as possible. The larger the amount of people they can bring together (in a 'virtual' organization), the greater their political influence.

Laudon (1977: 112) too, made some interesting remarks about the application of ICTs in issue groups and social movements (see also Neustadt 1985 and Montes 1986). The often flexible 'structures' of these movements may prevent a frequent application of ICTs. But according to Laudon real barriers are especially present in the tradition of acting collectively on the basis of ideological certainties. He assumes that particularly the symbolics of many activities of this type of political movements will not be easy to replace by electronic interaction with the action computer. He sees possibilities for umbrella organizations. But the use of ICTs enforces some structuralization of connections and communications, which will make them more easily recognizable for authorities, which can also implicate a threat to their identity.

## 6.3. Political Parties

On the basis of developments in the United States, Abramson, Arterton and Orren argue that the new media will further strengthen the already existing tendency towards a more and more direct relationship between political leaders and individual voters. 'The politicians reach the people via television; the people reach the politicians via polls' (1988: 90). The influence and role of political parties and other intermediary organizations between government and citizen is pushed back more and more. Benjamin (1982) directly relates technological development with disintermediation, which he considers to be an important characteristic of informatized political systems. Just as the local shop disappears and is replaced by electronic shopping, the new technology can excavate other intermediary structures (Pedersen 1984, Everson 1982, Benjamin 1982, Frantzich 1989). But, naturally ICTs can also work the other way round, and create new possibilities (Benjamin 1982, Bogumil 1987, Bogumil and Lange 1991). However, Bogumil and Lange, who investigated the use of ICTs in German political parties and trade unions, observe that the new possibilities (the use of modern telephone switchboards for a direct, intern democracy, opinion polls and the like) often still come to a standstill in existing structures and interests. English political parties seem to be more creative (McLean 1989). In their contribution to this volume, Depla and Tops offer a more detailed analysis of the impact of ICTs on political parties (see chapter eleven).

In an electronic democracy politicians chiefly have the role of popular leaders, and much less the role of a representative of a political movement. The voters are mostly addressed as atomized individual media-users, and hardly (ever) as citizens who are actively involved in the developments in their country or municipality. The media play an increasingly important part in activities which used to be (part of) the exclusive domain of the political parties. For example selection and spotting of 'high potential' candidates is becoming an increasingly important, almost autonomous criterion which can only partly be influenced and controlled by political parties. Information about the views of the electorate no longer reach the party leadership primarily via the reports from party channels, but via coverage in the media and polls of opinion agencies. The (new) media are in a way becoming competitors of the political party organizations as connecting links between political parties and their voters. In the long term this will undoubtedly have great consequences for organization and functioning of the political parties. For the national party organs the necessity to maintain an extensive (and expensive) network of local departments can increasingly decline. A part of the functions which make these departments so interesting for the national party leadership (like obtaining information about the views of the electorate) is more and more taken over by the new media.

## 7. The Transparent and Fragmented Citizen

Laudon (1984) warns for utopian fantasies about the relationship between informatization and democracy. Through fine-grained registrations of all kinds, the citizen becomes more easily an object of surveillance, as all forms of behavior - even phoning to a certain government agency - can be registered. Every act that is mediated or supported by an application of ICTs is registered, and completing a kind of societal deoxyribonucleic acid (d.n.a.). that makes individual citizens and groups of citizens more or less fully transparent, and expose them to commercial and political forms of *demographic, sociographic and economic stereotyping* (Meadows 1985). Here too, technological development is to be considered a potential threat to public liberties (Winner 1986). Sterling points out that two important landmarks have been passed on the way to a more important role of surveillance bureaucracy, namely the possibility to link extensive files by so-called universal identifiers and the established effectiveness of surveillance to trace fraud or, on the contrary, problem groups who need extra attention from government (Sterling 1986: 31). There is a threat of a movement which will likely reinforce itself: information systems enable politicians to zoom in on problems of certain groups in society, and to urgently request the issuing of rules or financial aid. Groups which are largely dependent on government regulation and support will be far more extensively registrated than other groups, and are probably also more vulnerable to illegal invasions on their privacy (and public liberties) than others (see Eulau 1977, OTA 1987).

As a result of the extension of the supervision and of options for recipients of information and the reinforcement of the 'targeting' possibilities for senders of information, the public can be divided and defined into distinct groups. '*Mr Average*' will get company, because he will turn out to represent too many rough mazed categories for the purpose of an electoral strategy.

Especially in electoral systems in which they have a clear, territorial electorate, politicians increasingly possess of computer based census profiles which enable them to become acquainted with policy preferences and probable reactions to policy initiatives which fit the characteristics of their electorate (Martin 1987, Benjamin 1982, McLean 1989).

Moreover, these groups will get almost exclusively information (through forms of computer based vote-targeting) which confirms their own world view. Some say this will lead to a further 'balkanization' of the electorate.

Abramson *et al.* observe in this connection that the general, national (old) media can be looked upon as an important source of general 'civic culture', in which a collective political vocabulary, a common political agenda and a homogenization of the public opinion are stimulated. The rise of the new media puts this function under pressure. In a *livingroom democracy* the voters' attention can be drawn to - what already has been defined as - their interests. Politicians can conveniently make use of this by showing, by means of *direct mail*, to a certain part of the electorate that they struggle for their interests, without having to inform other groups with opposite interests (Burnham 1983). Sterling sees possibilities for political parties as well. He expects that better insight in policy preferences and opinions in various parts of the electorate will enable political parties to include '(...) more divergent positions into a party structure and of holding them together in a coalition' (Sterling 1986: 28).

Politics is becoming a matter of intelligent direction rather than of ideology. Further on we will see that this also becomes important on the level of the skills of the individual politician.

### 7.1.    'You only go Duck-hunting Where the Ducks are.'

Not only the own electorate, but also the electorate of the political rivals can be adequately shown by means of the new technology. Opinion polls and political marketing lead to a *transparent electorate* which can be intelligently manipulated (McLean 1989). In the United States *political marketing, campaign management, geodemographics and lobbying* are subjects which already have an important place on Graduate Schools for Political Management. The means (addresses, profiles and the like) for a digital election strategy are for that matter often provided by specialized companies and *direct mail consultants* (Everson 1982, McLean 1989). This type of companies helped American politicians, but also trade unions, win elections in a remarkable way (Burnham 1983: 92).

In the United States direct mail is also used successfully to finance expensive election campaigns. Legislation (Federal Election Campaign Act) has imposed a limit to the contributions of individual sponsors. That is why campaign strategists needed a means that enabled them to reach larger groups. Direct mail proved to be an effective means with an unexpectedly high response (McLean 1989: 65). By means of a database with addresses and information about earlier contributions to campaigns, voters are humored with 'personal letters' which are composed of well chosen *canned paragraphs*.

Admission to data files in the executive not only leads to a better *'oversight'* of the executive (see paragraph 9), but also creates new possibilities for political marketing for the members of the American Congress. When a certain subsidy is decided upon, partly owing to an initiative of a certain politician of a certain state, he is allowed to inform the interested parties in his constituency about it: the address files of the government bureaucracy make it possible to circumvent the politically not always easily passable road via the media (Burnham 1983). The new technologies create *unmediated media* (Abramson *et al.* 1988). The arbitrating and filtering effect which the established media, such as newspapers and the TV, have on the data transmission between government/politicians and the citizens is under great strain. The new media enable politicians to have direct contact with their electorate on a large scale, and get round what they not infrequently experience as an annoying and negative influence of reporters. In the United States Congressmen make, for instance, their own news reports, which are transmitted to local TV stations in their own states via satellite.

## 8. The Broker in Majorities: the Electronic Politician

Potentially, the new media also have great consequences for the characteristics of the political trade. In concise terms: data analysis would take the place of gut-feeling, quantitative calculation would replace political intuition (Eulau 1977, Pedersen 1984). Eulau exposes the concept of politics which is - sometimes implicitly - held by 'supporters' of electronic politics. They look upon politics as the search for truth and politicians as information recipients. Then ICTs would make a form of rational administration and democracy possible, in which the 'irrational' element of political decision making is eliminated. In this conception the specific role and contribution of politics - making decisions on the basis of ideological meaning - is based on an 'information shortage'. ICTs will assure that this information shortage is canceled out which causes rational decision making to become 'perfect' and politics to become superfluous (see also Frissen 1991).

That the complex process of political decision making on the contrary is more than rational decision making and looking for truth, and that it is particularly the challenge and assignment to always consider and choose between different interests and opinions, is forgotten in this approach of politics. More information is often not desired at all, and it often causes more inconvenience instead of adding anything to the political process of wheeling and dealing (Eulau 1977: 19).

The swiftness with which the media report on political events has reduced the time politicians have to react and to form a measured opinion. More and more often they have to give 'instant reactions'. The direct media coverage not infrequently turns small events into great incidents. A slip of the tongue can have great consequences. The time and space to negotiate, deliberate, form compromises and form effective coalitions comes under pressure. The polling-politics push political leadership and discussion and deliberation - two important components to come to consensus within the political community - to the background (McLean 1989). In connection with that the long term perspective, which is already under a great strain, disappears as well (Roll 1981). Partly under the influence of the new information technologies political decision making is more dominated by more or less coincidental ad hoc coalitions in which other changing political majorities occur. The role of the politician becomes the role of a 'broker in majorities' (see also Albeda 1992). Reagan, for example, did not accede to power by a majority based on consensus, but by a coalition - partly thought out by computer strategists - of many related 'single issue groups'. Sailing on unstable coalitions is of course also possible without computers (Roosevelt, Mitterrand), but the new media give a headstart to politicians and parties that know how to use (and can afford) the new possibilities well. In itself all this does not necessarily mean that the political process changes fundamentally, but the new media reinforce the already present tendencies to a staccato-like democracy, in which short term decisions tumble on top of each other: this contributes to the vulnerability of existing political systems as Depla and Tops argue in chapter eleven.

## 9. The Electronic Agora: Informatization in Parliament

In several publications the meaning of informatization for the functioning of parliament and other representative organs is more specifically investigated (Chartrand 1968, Steinbuch 1978, Gau 1980, Rose 1980, Frantzich 1982 a and b; Breman 1983, Kevenhörster 1984, Kraemer and King 1987, OTA 1987, Snellen et al. 1989, Van de Donk, Frissen and Snellen 1990). There is paid much attention on the possibilities which informatization offers to reinforce the position of power of the representative body in relation to the executive. We also find publications in which an account is given of empirical investigations into the consequences of parliamentary informatization for the internal functioning of the representative body. In this paragraph we give an account of the most important views, results and conclusions with regard to the internal and external dimension of parliamentary informatization. We start off with a survey of the most important applications of this technology.

## 9.1. Applications of ICTs in Parliament

From publications by Chartrand 1962, 1982, Saloma 1968, Chartrand and Borell 1981, Rose 1980, Frantzich 1982, Segal 1985 and Ditlea 1986, we can infer that the American Congress started to apply several forms of information technology much earlier than the parliaments in Europe did. Particularly the increasing growth of legislative work (size and complexity), the considerable growth of the members' contacts with their grass roots supporters and the growing informatization in the executive were reasons to invest in information systems. These are of a rather varied nature which can, according to Frantzich, be accounted for by Congress's heterogeneous need for information. There is a need for systematically accessible parliamentary documentation, which also in the Dutch (Breman 1983), French (Gau 1980) and German parliaments (Kevenhörster 1984) was realized first. Systems which provide insight into the progress of parliamentary activities can usually be linked to it. In Frantzich's *Computers in Congress* (1982: 145) a large number of the parliamentary systems is extensively described (e.g., the 'Geographic Reporting System' (GRS), which shows the distribution of federal funds over the various states and districts graphically and/or in accessible tables).

Decision making procedures (legislation) in the American Congress could be followed electronically already in the seventies (Rose 1980, Frantzich 1982). The increased possibilities for datacommunication have especially been important to the opening up of bureaucracy, but are also used by members of the American Congress for internal communication (electronic mail) and for gaining access to datafiles of various social groups, professional organizations and interest groups. For the preparation of opinion forming and decision making several (external) files can be consulted.

But also in parliamentary decision making (voting) information technology plays an important part. In 1973 an operational electronic voting system was introduced (not without fierce resistance, see Frantzich 1982: 91) which can quickly registrate the votes given and - we will see this further on - make an instant-analysis as well. This instant-analysis already stimulates interventions during the voting procedures in order to put members who have not yet voted under maximum pressure to obey the leadership.

## 9.2. The External Dimension of Parliamentary Informatization

In surveys on parliamentary informatization the parliament's relative position in the trias politica gets much attention (Gau 1980). The informatization arrears which Congress had in respect to the government bureaucracy was increasingly seen as an information arrears. In the U.S. they have chosen a triple fold strategy in order to make up for the arrears.

First of all Parliament can block the development of important informatization projects in the executive during the budget debates. When blocking is impossible there is still a whole series of delaying tactics available (Kraemer and King 1987: 95).

The second strategy is more important. Many times members of parliament (or parliament committees) successfully attempted to gain access to data files of the executive (data on progress, statistical information on various fields of policy). Especially Frantzich (1982), and to a lesser extent also Gau (1980), Kevenhörster (1984) and Kraemer and King (1987) give a fascinating account of the *access wars* that accompanied it. Sometimes services and departments were unwilling and access could only be got by appealing to the Freedom of Information Act. Sometimes those parliamentary information requests received a warm welcome: the agencies saw a good chance to bring their programs and policy projects to attention. Miewald and Mueller (1987) warn for a possible blurring of the different positions which a representative body and an executive are supposed to have.

A third strategy concerns the construction and the extension of its own informatization resources. The development of its own information systems, analysis and calculation models was a necessary step for the reinforcement of its position. A good example of this is the Congressional Budget Office (CBO) which was given authorization to develop its own fiscal calculation models after a collision between Congress and President Nixon (who, according to the congress, fiddled with the calculation models of the American Tax Authorities). On top of that these models were more geared to the needs of the Congressmen, who were henceforth able to 'compute politically'. The consequences of fiscal policy proposals could be visualized per (election) district (see also Nathan 1987).

The balance of power between legislative and executive had been disturbed by the computers in the executive, but this third strategy made it possible to bring the development of the independent parliamentary automatization into balance again. The Member Budget Information System (MBIS), which permanently enables a thorough analysis of the budget (and can also visualize exceedings and depletions) has given the American Congress - according to Frantzich - a considerably stronger position of power (see for comparable conclusions Ryan 1976 and Worthly 1984).

Other investigations give a mixed picture, however. Kraemer and King mention an investigation into informatization in a large number of states, from which it turns out that the increase of possibilities to check the executive is usually restricted only to some fields of policy and never becomes better on all points. Fear of incompatible databases keep many parliaments from developing their own information systems: apparently they are afraid that they will still lose the '*data-wars*' with the bureaucracy - which slow down the decision making processes - in the end. Moreover they often have great confidence in the information that is delivered by the bureaucracy, which hinders the development of their own information systems. Another interesting outcome of this investigation - contrary to Frantzich's findings, which we mentioned earlier - is that when they invested in their own parliamentary information systems it rarely becomes visible in major changes of policy (Kraemer and King 1987: 96).

When Congress or other representative organs succeed in adequately using informatization for better control ('oversight') over the executive, then this does not necessarily mean that parliament will win the battle with the executive. The complexity of the political arena in which the executive and the legislature make war makes it difficult to draw unambiguous conclusions about the influence of informatization on their mutual balance of power. (An example of the impact of ICTs on the position of local representatives is given in chapter eight of this volume).

### 9.3. The Internal Dimension of Parliamentary Informatization: the Democratization of Parliaments

Greater transparency, which always seems to involve the application of automatized information systems, puts an end to the traditionally strong position of - usually elder - members who had important positions in parliamentary committees in the American Congress. The (in)formal pecking order was both cause and effect of the poor accessibility and spread of important information before the arrival of these information systems. The elder members had a good appreciation of the situation, and for a long time led the resistance against further parliamentary automatization. In the end the politically successful work of younger members using ICTs made further resistance impossible (Frantzich 1982, OTA 1987).

Sometimes computer innovations were effectively blocked, as the staff of the informatization bureau of the American Congress discovered when they wanted to automatize the scheduling of committee meetings (Committee Information and Scheduling System). By doing so they would, however, take an important strategic weapon from the committee chairmen, namely their capacity to plan meetings at the most suitable times or places (in order to avoid publicity or, on the contrary, to seek it, or to make that certain persons would or would not be present at the meeting, etc.). The chairmen of the committees strongly resisted the automatization plan and managed to prevent it from being carried out (Frantzich 1982: 147 and Abramson, Arterton and Orren 1988).

The democratization of parliament which was the result of digitalizing information networks has also caused an emancipation of the individual representative. New members can be settled in more quickly, because the accessibility of computer networks turned out to be larger than the previously used 'Old Boys' networks. Formerly only the chairmen of the committees were able to give the correct information about the progress of legislation projects. Now it appears fully automatically on the screen of every member who has asked the computer system (Bill Status System) to keep him or her posted about critical decision points of legislation projects in certain fields of policy. For this type of information the dependence on information from party specialists and chairmen of committees belongs for the

greater part to the past. It seems reasonable to expect that the traditional structure of
the parliamentary information network, which is characterized by, among others,
hierarchy and solid anchorage in committees and procedures (see Van Schendelen
1975: 108), will be put under pressure by informatization. The parliamentary lion's
den seems to have become more transparent.

More transparency is also enhanced by computerbased voting systems. For parties
and members analyses of the voting behavior of certain groups of members which
have been made by the system contain very important politically-strategic information, but are also important externally. First of all in election campaigns, where (the
large and systematic amount of) information about representatives and senators is
important political ammunition. But the executive also gains by it. At the time of the
Carter-administration the White House was able to gain access to the system, because
the Vice President of the United States is presiding officer of the presidium of the
Senate. Especially post-vote analyses and progress information turned out to be
interesting. The White House based very effective lobbying-strategies on it. After-
wards more detailed rules led to more restrictive agreements about the access of the
White House to the datafiles of the Senate (Hager 1987, Kevenhörster 1984).

## 9.4.   Electronic Politics

According to a number of authors the increasing possibilities to provide and reveal
the consequences of parliamentary decision making for different parts of the electorate will result in a fierce battle (Frantzich 1982 a and b, Kevenhörster 1984, Nathan
1987, Kraemer et al. 1987). The political battle can increasingly be waged on the basis
of a keen insight into who will be the winners and who will be the losers of a
certain policy proposal. In connection with what has already been mentioned above
about the transparent electorate and political computing, it is to be expected that
particularly (the consequences of) *allocations* will be more highlighted in the political
debate (Nathan 1987).

Consequences of decisions, even if they display themselves in other fields of
policy, can be easier revealed by the opponents of these decisions. Frantzich expects
that, due to this, reaching a consensus - certainly in cases in which one fights at
daggers drawn - will become more difficult. When the luxury of 'not knowing' no
longer exists, political decision making will become more difficult and compromises
will sometimes not be able to persist. Fragile compromises and coalitions of mixed
expectations thrive in low-information settings (Frantzich 1982).

Not only winners and losers can be shown more clearly, but also the *presuppositions* of the models emerge more clearly. Frantzich elaborately sketches how
President Reagan's proposals for the reform of taxes got bogged down in an unexpectedly heated debate in Congress, when the opposition - which calculated the
consequences of the proposals by way of its own calculation models - could ascribe
many of the expected effects of policy to the *supply side* propositions which lay at the

bottom of the calculation models of *reaganomics* (Frantzich 1982, see also Dutton 1982, Kraemer *et al.* 1987).

## 10. Concluding remarks

The preceding paragraphs make clear that the Orwellian and Athenian scenarios initially held a dominant position in the debate regarding the relations between democracy and information society. It was, among other things, this dominance - with all its ideological symbolism - that obstructed more empirical research. As it will become clear in the following chapters of this book, this situation seems to have changed.

First of all, more and more studies see the light in which the relation between democracy and ICTs is no longer studied from a primarily normative, but from an empirical point of view. This development has been strongly stimulated by the fact that more and more concrete applications of ICTs are actually developed in a context of democratic decision making. The number of cases studied has increased enormously in the past years, a number of projects could even be followed for a few years (Arterton, 1987). Especially the advent of interactive communication-capacities has further enhanced ICTs' aptitude for supporting various democratic routines and activities. New projects, that make use of the newest technical applications are being developed at such a high speed that it is practically impossible for research to keep pace.

Furthermore, many scholars have shown the complex ways in which both goals and outcomes of these projects are related with existing paradigms and interests that dominate the arenas in which they are developed (e.g. Guthrie and Dutton 1991). Both the earlier scenarios (Orwell and Athens) heavily relied on rather deterministic conceptions of the relation between technological artefacts and socio-political consequences. Each of the positions was - to a large extent - projecting its view on the dominant characteristics of ICTs on the political system. Some were emphasizing surveillance and control, some others were emphazising transparency and interactive communication.

Although the debate about the 'nature of ICTs' is still going on (Winner 1993 and also the chapter Pratchett contributed to this book), most scholars would tend to confirm that ICTs are, in fact, highly ambiguous technologies and that informatization is a highly complex process in which the technology itself is shaped by and shaping the social conditions in which it is introduced (Guthrie and Dutton 1991, Frissen 1992, Van de Donk and Frissen 1994). What characteristics of ICTs will be of importance in a certain context will, thus, also be determined by some characteristics of that context itself. ICTs simultaneously bring about surveillance and transparency, control and interactive communication. Electronic voting systems enlarge possibilities to vote at convenient places (at home, abroad) but it also means that the votes are registered. In an electronic Athens, the Orwellian potentialities of ICT are present, too.

# CHAPTER 3

# Informatization and Views of Democracy

Arthur R. EDWARDS

*Erasmus University Rotterdam, PO Box 1738, 3000 DR Rotterdam,*
*The Netherlands*

**Abstract.** In this chapter the significance of ICTs for democracy is explored in a deductive way by identifying the communication and information implications of three views of democracy: (a) the populistic view, (b) the liberal view and (c) the republican view. The analysis is focused on the relationship between the electorate and their representatives and between the representative assembly and the government. From the perspective of these three views some applications of ICTs in Dutch municipalities, which are directed at strengthening the position of citizens and supporting the work of councillors, are reviewed. On the basis of a framework of different views of democracy, the 'design philosophy' of ICTs applications in politics can be identified and different strategies for embedding ICTs in political processes can be indicated.

## 1. Introduction

The use of information and communications technologies (ICTs) in politics can be of great influence on the functioning of democracy. How far this influence may extend is not as yet clear. In political practice, especially at the local level, we find a variety of applications of ICTs.

In existing literature the significance of ICTs for democracy is predominantly analyzed in a more or less inductive way. In this chapter, a deductive line of reasoning is followed by exploring the significance of ICTs for democracy from the perspectives of three different views or conceptions of democracy, (a) the populistic view, (b) the liberal view and (c) the republican view. These views are rooted in the history of political philosophy and in the development of democratic institutions in Western societies. The aim of this chapter is to identify the information and communication aspects of different views of democracy. A number of opportunities for applying ICTs can then be discerned and, more importantly, alternative strategies for embedding ICTs in political processes can be indicated. For the purpose of empirical research, the assumptions underlying existing applications can be defined and related to specific conceptions of democracy. Also, the development of applications of ICTs in political systems can be analyzed on the basis of the institutional features of the political system in question.

Communication and information aspects of ICTs will be explored in the context of two relationships which are fundamental to democratic structures:
- the relationship between the electorate and their representatives;
- the relationship between the representative assembly and the government.

The relationship between citizens and government will be left aside, although it has important informational aspects and could also be related to the three views (Bekkers and Van Duivenboden, this volume).

I look at democracy as a mode of decision-making in political systems. It can be characterized as a set of procedural rules for the performance of volitional and informational acts. A volitional act is aimed at influencing a state of affairs or at directing actors' behavior. An informational act is directed at gathering or giving information. In a democracy both volitional acts and informational acts play an essential role in the relations between voters, representatives and members of government. Of course, the gathering of information is generally aimed at supporting volitional acts. Volitional acts entail a certain information load. But informational acts may have a normative significance of their own. Also, it is typical of a democracy that there exist procedural rules for eliciting volitional acts of the voters and their representatives. For example, the act of voting at elections can be seen as a volitional act directed at designating representatives, choosing a government or influencing policy. The performance of this act entails a certain information load. Elections can be elicited by procedural rules governing the change of the government. When elected representatives decide to submit a policy issue or proposal to an opinion poll, this can be taken to be an informational act, which can then influence future volitional acts of these representatives vis-à-vis the government. But holding opinion polls as a mode of information gathering can be seen as a device with an intrinsic value in a democracy, in the same way as consulting interest groups.

In the following paragraph our classification into three views (or models) of democracy will be developed. In subsequent paragraphs, each model will be considered more closely. After a general characterization, we examine the two relationships mentioned above. Each paragraph will be completed with a paragraph in which the applications of ICTs characteristic for the view concerned will be briefly indicated. After these four theoretical paragraphs an empirical paragraph is included. We will look at some existing applications of ICTs in politics and try to characterize them on the basis of the three views of democracy.

Informatization takes place in the context of a complex society. All three conceptions have played their role in the development of democratic institutions as we have inherited them and we should take a fresh look at their potential as strategies for democratization in the future. Therefore, we will close this chapter with some observations on the viability of those conceptions, taken separately and in combination, as strategies for democratization.

## 2. Views of Democracy

In the literature on democracy, distinctions are made between different traditions, conceptions or models of democracy. Upon closer consideration these distinctions often appear to be conceptually cognate, for example those between an 'individualistic' and a 'collectivistic' conception (Rejai 1967: 24) and between a 'liberal' and a 'populistic' view (Riker 1982). Held (1987: 4) distinguishes nine models of democracy but he also indicates that they can be grouped into two broad types, liberal or representative democracy and direct or participatory democracy. The terms being used refer in some instances to a specific perspective, as in the distinction between individualistic and collectivistic conceptions. In other instances, attention is drawn to the origin of democratic traditions ('anglo-american' versus 'continental'; (Sabine 1952) or their position in political philosophy ('liberal' vs. 'populistic'). The aim of this chapter is to investigate the informational and communicative aspects of different views of democracy. This suggests an analytical perspective. But it is equally important to seek contact with traditions in political thought, since they have shaped the democratic institutions in Western societies. These traditions provide arguments for the discussion of the pros and cons of different applications of ICTs in politics. For our purposes, the distinction between individualistic and collectivistic views constitutes an appropriate first categorization.

As a tradition in political philosophy, the liberal or individualistic view has its roots in the work of Locke and Montesquieu, amongst others. At stake is the balance between maintaining the state as an arrangement guaranteeing the functioning of civil society, on the one hand, and protecting individual freedom against encroachments by the state, on the other. The core of this tradition can be designated in terms of the articulation and aggregation of individual preferences, competition for positions of governmental power and 'checks and balances'. Taking the 'market' as the paradigm of democratic politics in this conception, we have a perspective of view for identifying informational and communicative aspects.

The collectivistic tradition has been connected in general to the French Revolution and to thinkers like Rousseau and Condorcet. The central values in this tradition are popular sovereignty and political equality. When we take a closer look at the way this tradition is elaborated in the literature, a further distinction seems appropriate. A case in point is the role attributed to communication in public meetings according to the views of Rousseau. These views are treated differently in the literature. For example, Habermas (1992) distinguishes a liberal and a republican conception of democracy. The central value within the republican conception is, according to Habermas, popular sovereignty and he places Rousseau in this tradition. In Habermas' own theoretical framework, the republican conception is elaborated in communicative terms. According to Habermas, the paradigm of democratic politics in this tradition is 'conversation'. From this point of view Habermas criticizes Rousseau, a republican thinker to be sure, but still caught in a subject-centered 'philosophy of consciousness' (Habermas 1992: 133-134).

Grofman and Feld (1988) propose a formalization of Rousseau's concept of the general will on the basis of the voting theory of Condorcet. This theory is based on Rousseau's notion that the members of a political community who have to pass their judgement on the question of whether a law being proposed is in accordance with the general will, should do so by majority voting (Rousseau IV-2). Condorcet attempted to prove that the probability that majorities will pass correct judgements is higher than for individuals. Grofman and Feld emphasize the condition of 'voter independence' in Condorcet's theory and they connect this condition with a passage in 'Du contrat social' where communication between citizens attending the general assembly is ruled out (Rousseau II-3). They conclude from this that Rousseau is oriented towards deliberation 'as one taking place within individuals rather than in terms of a group debate. Each voter is polled about his independently reached choice, without any group debate' (Grofman and Feld 1988: 569). In a response Estlund and Waldron (1989) state that this conclusion does no justice to Rousseau's views. What Rousseau did rule out were strategic talks between citizens but not a public discussion in which rational arguments are exchanged.

Against the backdrop of this dispute Miller (1993) distinguishes 'deliberative' and 'epistemic' democracy. Epistemic democracy is directed at finding (objectively) correct solutions for societal problems. Democracy provides the best procedure for finding these solutions, namely majority voting. Deliberative democracy is directed at finding solutions which are acceptable to all participants concerned, after an open and unconstrained debate has taken place. Miller (1993: 76) makes the observation that 'Rousseau's view is ambiguous as between deliberative and epistemic conceptions of democracy'. Here we do not need to take sides in this dispute. For our purposes, Miller's distinction is clearly of importance. Frissen (1989: 97-98, 259) argues that informatization can lead to a development in which legitimacy is seen increasingly as dependent on the scientific quality of information processing in the political system.

So, the first dimension of our categorization is the distinction between collectivistic and individualistic conceptions of democracy. It concerns the political culture of societies, the orientation of democratic processes and the motivation attributed to the citizens, viz. the welfare of the community (the 'common good') or the welfare of the individual.

The distinction between epistemic and deliberative conceptions was developed as a secondary dimension within the collectivistic category but it can be used within the individualistic category as well. On the one hand we can characterize the liberal view as epistemic, following Habermas' conceptual strategy in which strategic rationality is conceived of as essentially cognitive. In that case, we assume that actors behave as self-interested, calculating individuals. Anderson (1993) however argues that another style of liberal thinking can be discerned ('liberal rationalism') in which it is assumed that actors restrain their egoism in respect of the rights of others. He proposes that 'an adequate policy science of democracy (..) might best be founded by weaving together the schemes of political thought represented by liberal rationalism and practical reason', a model of democracy designated as 'liberal deliberative' by Dryzek and Torgerson (1993: 134). Here, I shall develop the 'republican view' within the collectivistic conception, following Habermas' theory of communicative action, and then extend it in the direction of the individualistic conception.

To sum up, the following three views of democracy will be distinguished (in the order of presentation):
(1) the populistic view (collectivistic/epistemic);
(2) the liberal view (individualistic/epistemic);
(3) the republican view (collectivistic, individualistic/deliberative).

The following three paragraphs begin with a general characterization. Firstly, we will indicate the function of politics and the nature of the political process according to the view concerned. Subsequently, we will expound the underlying values and the basic orientation towards structures of democracy (especially in terms of direct versus indirect polarity).

## 3. The Populistic View

### 3.1. General Characterization

In the populistic tradition, politics is the process by which the members of a social community arrive at a collective judgement about the common good. The political process aggregates individual judgements about solutions for societal problems. This view of democracy is based on the principles of popular sovereignty and political equality. These principles provide the normative foundation of majority voting (Dahl 1956: 36-38). Majority voting provides the best procedure for finding correct solutions. The outcome of majority voting is indicative of the general will.

In this tradition, direct democracy constitutes the ideal against which the quality of representative democracy should be judged. The touchstone for the quality of representative democracy is the opportunity it offers for laying down the will of the people in the policies of the government. According to Rousseau, all citizens should attend public assemblies in which the general will is articulated. In a famous passage in 'Du contrat social' he rejects the idea of representation (Rousseau III-15). But he clearly saw the conditions that must be fulfilled in order that direct democracy could function well. Firstly, he pointed out that direct democracy is only feasible in small communities. In addition to this, he drew attention to social and economic conditions, such as simplicity of manners, equality of status and wealth and the absence of luxury.

The relations between voters, representatives, government and bureaucracy are hierarchical, as shown in the figure below (Thomassen 1991: 26).

| voters | ---> | representatives | ---> | government | ---> | bureaucracy |

## 3.2. *The Relationship between Voters and Representatives*

From the populistic point of view, a representative democracy should be character-ized by identity between voters and representatives. Only then will there be a guarantee that the representatives will perform the same volitional acts as the people would have done if they had the opportunity to decide themselves. This identity can be achieved in two ways. One possibility is to tie the actions of the representatives down to the will of the represented ('mandate model', Pitkin 1967: 144-167; or 'delegate model', Thomassen 1991: 172-176). The second is to let the legislature be a faithful mirror image of the population. This is called 'descriptive representation' by Pitkin (1967: 84-85) or 'mimetic representation' by Ankersmit (1990: 272-279). The idea of description or reflection can refer to (a) demographic variables, (b) opinions and (c) interests (Van Schendelen 1975: 6-7). In a representative multiparty-system political parties represent different ideological positions in terms of opinions and interests. Descriptive representation presupposes that the respective parliamentary groups consistently act in accordance with their declared ideological positions.

The delegate model has almost no adherents anymore (Thomassen 1991, ibidem). The descriptive theory of representation still exerts some influence and is institution-ally visible in some European democracies which have a system of proportional representation.

In the populistic tradition, high expectations are held about the information level of the population. As Zolo (1992: 70) observes, following Schumpeter, 'the idea of the existence of a 'common good' as an object of popular will (...) presupposes that every normal adult citizen is able to see without difficulty what is good for himself and others'. The following passage in 'Du contrat social' is salient:

> 'From the deliberations of a people properly informed, and provided its mem-bers do not have any communication among themselves, the great number of small differences will always produce a general will and the decision will always be good' (Rousseau II-3).

In Condorcet's calculations this expectation recurs in his assumption that the compe-tence of the individual citizen, expressed in the chance that (having to choose between two alternatives) he will choose the correct one, is higher than 0.5. In a strict epistemic interpretation of the populistic tradition, the citizen ideally possesses all the information which he needs to judge whether a policy measure is a correct solution for a problem. Using concepts of the policy sciences: the citizen should be able to judge the correctness of the descriptive, causal and normative assumptions underlying a policy measure. This information load applies not only to direct democracy but also to the delegate model of representative democracy. In addition, in the delegate model the voters should have all information needed to judge the performance of the representatives.

In the descriptive model of representation the information load for the voters is less burdensome. One can assume that since the legislature is a faithful mirror image of the population, its judgements will run parallel to those of the voters. In that case, the information load for judging policy proposals will rest upon the shoulders of the representatives.

In the delegate model, the representatives must keep themselves well informed of the opinions of their voters, not only as to the content of these opinions but also as to the proportions in which they are held.

### 3.3. *The Relationship between Representatives and Government*

As was indicated above, in the populistic view the touchstone for the quality of representative democracy is the opportunity which it offers for laying down the will of the people in the policies of the government. The relationship between representatives and government is pivotal here. In principle, this relationship is hierarchical. It means that the power position of the incumbent parties, which make up the majority in government, prevails but in particular it means that the main function of the volitional acts of representatives belonging to the incumbent parties vis-à-vis the government is to ensure that the activities of the government are in accordance with the policy plans of the majority party or with the plans agreed to by the parties in the coalition, or - at least in cases not covered by these plans - with the current popular will.

The information load for the representatives is heavy. They should be able to follow the 'work in progress' in government, not only (the output of) the process of formulating policies but also their implementation. As for the parties in opposition, they at least can take advantage of information that may expose inconsistencies between intended policies and outcomes.

### 3.4. *Informatization*

ICTs make it possible to overcome the physical barriers to direct democracy. Referendum democracy can fulfil Rousseau's idea of general assemblies. In the context of representative democracy, ICTs can fulfil three important functions.

Firstly, information systems can relieve the information load for citizens which is assumed by the delegate and descriptive models of representation, and where direct democracy (referenda) fills the gaps of indirect democracy. If all information produced by policy institutes, and all policy information produced by governmental agencies themselves was made available to the public in digital form, the information load for citizens, which is assumed by direct democracy and the delegate model of representative democracy, would be relieved. Tracking systems, enabling citizens to monitor proceedings in parliament and the voting records of individual represen- tatives and parliamentary groups, would provide for greater transparency of the performance of representatives, in line with the delegate and descriptive models of representation (Van de Donk and Tops, this volume).

Secondly, regular polls and referenda can contribute to the identity between voters and representatives, at least as an informational device (polls) but also as a mode for expressing the popular will to which the representatives can be more or less tied down (referenda). Van de Donk and Tops (this volume) discuss the few experimental projects carried out so far with electronic plebiscites. They also go into opinion polls as a form of populistic democracy. The influence of these polls on the behavior of politicians may have increased. But they point as well to another side of the matter: 'The electronic plebiscites do not only enhance citizens' control over decision- makers, but also the decision-makers' control over citizens; it is the (political bureaucratic) elites that decide on the questions, determine the information channels and decide what happens to the results' (page 17).

Thirdly, information systems can support the members of representative assem- blies in monitoring the formulation and implementation of policies. Tracking systems could enable the representatives to follow the planning and programming activities of agencies, as well as their operations, and to relate this information to agreed policy plans (see Taylor, Bardzki and Wilson this volume).

## 4. The Liberal View

### 4.1. General Characterization

In the liberal view, the function of democratic politics is the aggregation of individu- al preferences into collective choices 'in order to program the state in the interest of society' (Habermas 1992: 326). Society is conceived of as a constellation of relations between individuals structured by the market and not - as in the populistic tradition - as a collective unity with an identity of its own. The political process is characterized by competition for positions of governmental power. The competition between alternative teams of political leaders provides an indirect mechanism for producing policy programs more or less in accordance with the wishes of the people (Miller 1983: 134). Moreover, the possibility to vote the incumbent leadership out of office prevents serious infringements upon the freedom of the citizens (Riker 1982: 9).

This view of democracy is based upon the principle of individual freedom. In the liberal view, democracy is shaped by a representative, multi-party system. Even if direct democracy were feasible, representative democracy would be given preference because it provides a 'division of labor' in which the relationships between voters, representatives, government and bureaucracy are characterized by a balance of power ('checks and balances') and not by hierarchy as in the populistic tradition.

The paradigm of the liberal view is the market. In order to explore the informational and communicative aspects of liberal democracy I take Downs' economic theory of democracy (Downs 1957) as point of departure.

## 4.2. *The Relationship between Voters and Representatives*

In Downs' economic model the voters are seen as utility maximizers:

> 'This axiom implies that each citizen casts his vote for the party he believes will provide him with more benefits than any other' (Downs 1957: 36).

The candidates of political parties are characterized as teams of people competing for positions of governmental power in order to attain personal benefits such as income, prestige and power (Downs 1957: 28).

In the basic model of the 'logic of voting' the citizen casts his vote on the basis of a comparison of the performance of the incumbent parties with the hypothetical performance of the opposition parties (or on the basis of expectations of the performance of these parties in the coming period). It is not very plausible that the voters possess all the information necessary for such a decision or are prepared to bear the costs of obtaining it. By voting on the basis of ideological positions taken by the political parties, voters are relieved from this information load. An ideology is a means of saving on information costs (Downs 1957: 36-50, 98-100).

Political parties will be guided by the majority principle as one of the key rules of the game in the competition for power. In the basic model of the 'logic of governmental decisionmaking' the incumbents submit every policy proposal to a hypothetical poll and choose the alternative preferred by the majority of the voters (Downs 1957: 51-60).

As we can infer from the two basic models outlined here, the information load for voters and representatives is, in principle, heavy. It seems that the populistic and liberal views show a common feature in the supposition that voters and representatives can meet the information load required for the performance of the volitional acts, as assumed in the respective views. However, Downs draws attention to another side of the matter. He points out that beyond certain limits the disposition of information by voters and representatives can harm the functioning of politics. If political parties have full information about the preferences of the voters, and voters have full information about the effects of alternative policy measures, Arrow problems (Arrow: 1963) will loom up, and the political system will collapse because there are no opportunities for political parties to follow a majority strategy:

> 'Perhaps we can conclude from this that democracy cannot function in a certain world unless consensus among voters is almost complete on all issues. In the real

world, uncertainty masks the dilemmas which society would face if it had to confront its diversity squarely; hence democracy is possible. This reasoning demonstrates how fundamental uncertainty is to political life in all large societies' (Downs 1957: 62).

In modern democracies, different actors and institutions specialize in providing information to citizens, government and political parties. Representatives relieve political parties of the need to know the utility function of every individual citizen. Downs characterizes representatives as 'specialists in discovering, transmitting, and analyzing popular opinion'. He concludes: 'uncertainty thus helps convert democracy into representative government' (Downs 1957: 89).

In standard descriptions of the liberal model of democracy, representation is mostly conceived of as an autonomous, creative activity of forming judgements. Pitkin (1967: 165) gives the following formulation which fits into the liberal view fairly well: '...the representative must act independently in his constituents' interest and yet not normally conflict with their wishes...'. The information load for representatives is still fairly high in this view. Representatives must keep themselves informed of the wishes of their voters, at least in order to assess the room they have to distance themselves from these wishes.

We have used Downs' model of democracy to illustrate the relationship between voters and representatives within the liberal conception, because it pays so much attention to the role of information. Some comments must be made. The main claim of the model is that competition forces political parties to adopt policies which are more or less in accordance with voters' wishes. One could say that this indirect mechanism fits the populistic conception as well. Of course, the motivation attributed to the voters differs strongly between the two conceptions. A relevant critique - or perhaps one should say, a more realistic extension - of the model is directed at the assumptions concerning the behavior of voters and political parties. As Miller (1983: 146-147) remarks, the model presupposes that voters' preferences are independent of the behavior of the parties. This assumption is unrealistic. Schumpeter (1943) argued, quite convincingly, that voters' preferences are to a great extent 'manufactured' by outside influences, such as 'political marketing'. Political marketing also suggests other tactics. Not only can preferences be manufactured, but majorities as well. By segmenting the voters market in more homogeneous sections, specific interests can be appealed to and Arrow problems can be avoided. This also means that political parties can afford to rely less on ideologies to meet voters' information costs. The information to be provided by political parties can be attuned to the characteristics of subgroups of voters (Van de Donk and Tops this volume).

## 4.3. *The Relationship between Representatives and Government*

In the liberal view the relationship between the representative assembly and the government is characterized by a certain balance of power. In presidential systems, the ideal type of this case, president and parliament each derive their power from their own electoral mandate. This means that assembly and government take more independent positions vis-à-vis each other. So, the assembly has more political scope for controlling the activities of the government, for example against encroachments on individual freedom in the course of the implementation of policy.

The information needs of representatives resulting from this process can be less specified than in the populistic view, but they are extensive and, in principle, infinite.

## 4.4. *Informatization*

Information can be seen as a condition influencing the play of power. The market paradigm and the notion of checks and balances suggest a 'balance of information' between voters and political parties. The provision of information to citizens, which enables them to judge the performance of the incumbent and the opposition parties, forms one side of this balance. 'Political marketing' forms the other side of it. ICTs (tracking systems of voting records of parliamentary groups, 'computer-based vote-targeting') can support these developments. Other applications of ICTs fit within the liberal model as well. Opinion-polls, for example, can have a signalling function for the representatives. Forms of plebiscitarian democracy as opinion polls and referenda should not be linked exclusively to populistic democracy. 'Corrective referenda', in which the citizens are asked to pass their judgement on new legislation can function as an institutional checks within liberal democracy.

ICTs are of great importance in maintaining the balance of power between parliament and public administration. Information systems can fulfil an essential role in the exercise of the oversight function by the representatives.

## 5. The Republican View

### 5.1. *General Characterization*

In the republican conception of democracy, the function of politics can be defined in the same way as in the populistic conception: to arrive at a collective judgement about the common good. Specifically republican is its view on the nature of the political process, viz. mutual deliberation and open debate about alternative conceptions of the common good. Each participant in the debate tries to convince the other participant(s) by putting forward arguments which could be acceptable to the other(s). Every participant is willing to change his/her point of view in the light of arguments put forward by other participants. Political discussion functions as a collective learning process. The normative notions which underpin the deliberative procedure are equal access to public communication and thematic openness (no constraints on the themes to be discussed).

The republican tradition can be related to the ideal of an associative direct democracy. De Haan (1993) refers to the Italian city-states during the Renaissance and their notion of citizenship stressing qualities as virtue and eloquence. In modern political philosophy John Dewey is one of the advocates of the idea of democracy as a 'way of life' involving the spread of 'plural, partial and experimental methods' such as debates (MacPherson 1977: 73-76).

Habermas' (1981) conception of practical discourse can be seen as a reconstruction of the republican model within the collectivistic tradition of democracy. He stresses the argumentative nature of the search for the common good. Of course, there is a tension between the reality of pluralistic and individualistic societies and the regulative ideal of rationally motivated consensus. This tension could be reduced by 'weakening' the communicative presuppositions which are attributed to the participants in political discourse, as in McCarthy's suggestion that rationally motivated agreement may involve elements of compromise and accommodation (McCarthy 1991: 195-199) or by adapting the presuppositions about the motivation of individuals in the direction of the individualistic tradition. In the introductory paragraph, I referred to 'liberal rationalism' (Anderson 1993) in which the pursuit of private interests is restrained by the mutual recognition of legitimate rights. Rational discussion about the legitimacy of certain rights might play an important role in the settlement of conflicts of interests. In this way we can extend the republican, deliberative view of democracy into the individualistic tradition. This possibility is indicated, in fact, by Arterton (1987: 63-68) who characterizes the dialogue projects of ICTs as 'pluralistic' as opposed to 'populistic'.

In modern societies the republican ideal applies in the first instance to the process of public opinion building:

> 'At the heart of the institutionalization of the deliberative procedure is the existence of arenas in which citizens can propose issues for the political agenda and participate in debate about those issues' (Cohen, 1989: 31).

The arenas mentioned by Cohen constitute the 'political public sphere' as conceptualized by Habermas (1985: 417-418). It has its foundations in a civil society, understood as an institutional domain in which diverse voluntary organizations and informal groups are active.

However, the idea that democracy comes down to 'government by discussion' (Lindsay 1951) also applies to representative government and parliamentary politics. In the republican view, the legitimacy of parliamentary decision making is seen to be dependent on the extent to which the political discussions in parliament take notice of public debates in society and draw from insights which proved robust in these debates.

## 5.2. *The Relationship between Voters and Representatives*

Although the republican view does not apply primarily to the domain of representative democracy, it is possible to indicate how it would conceive of the relationship between voters and representatives. On the one hand it would adopt the liberal notion of representation as a more or less autonomous activity. If representatives had to act as delegates, there would be no room for mutual learning. On the other hand, a republican view of representation would seek contact with the descriptive theory of representation:

> '... if our concern is that a country's assembly should be the forum for every opinion that the country contains, it is natural and reasonable to suggest that the assembly should be composed of descriptive representatives drawn from every opinion-holding group' (Griffiths and Wollheim 1960; see Pitkin 1967: 83).

The number of representatives from each opinion-holding group would be less relevant; so there is no need to apply proportional representation very strictly (Pitkin 1967 ibidem).

The expectations about the information level of citizens can be indicated only in general terms. Citizens are active participants or attentive spectators of public discussions in society and of political discussions in representative institutions. We can add to this that, in comparison with the populist model, the participants in discussions, as seen in the deliberative model, are not bound to find correct solutions but acceptable ones. The 'normative horizon' legitimately sets limits to the information one has to dispose of. However, participants should be able to relate themselves to the perspectives taken by other participants.

Representatives must keep themselves well informed of the state of public opinion, particularly the points of view of participants taking positions which are close to their own ideological position.

## 5.3. *The Relationship between Representatives and Government*

'Government by discussion' characterizes the interaction between representative assembly and government. The structural conditions described in the liberal model appear to fit better into this way of functioning than the hierarchy assumed in the populist model.

## 5.4. *Informatization*

The republican point of view focuses on the vitality of civil society as a field of actors engaging in public debate. The communicative resources of civil society can be increased by applications of ICTs which support active citizenship and two-way communication between citizens and between citizens, politicians and administrators. The 'dialogue projects', which are discussed for example by Arterton (1987), are typical republican applications of ICTs. In this volume Schalken and Tops describe Digital City in Amsterdam, an example of Free-net systems which are now increasing very rapidly, especially in Northern America. Encouraging public debates is one of the central objectives of Digital City; it offers a variety of platforms for discussions about different issues of common interest in the city.

Of course, ICTs can provide for the necessary information for citizens engaging in public debates in the same way as in the populistic model of democracy (see section 3.4.).

ICT-applications which support the work of representatives should enable them to keep up to date with public discussions.


## 6. Empirical Observations

In the introductory paragraph, some options for empirical research were mentioned, one of those being the identification of the assumptions underlying existing applications of ICTs in politics. Arterton (1987: 65) stressed the importance of research into 'design choices' embodied in ICTs. In this paragraph some applications of ICTs in Dutch municipalities will be reviewed. I will try to characterize them in terms of the three views outlined above. My analysis is based on material from research by Depla, Van de Donk, Schalken and Tops (in: Zuurmond *et al.* 1994). I will look at two sorts of applications, firstly some applications which are directed at strengthening the position of citizens and secondly the use of ICTs which supports the work of representatives.

## 6.1. *Citizens*

In several Dutch municipalities experiments are being carried out into different methods of consulting citizens. We will look at three of them.

In the city of Rotterdam so-called Radio Referenda are held. In these programs an issue is discussed between a proponent and an opponent. The listeners cannot participate in the discussion. After the discussion the listeners may give their reaction by telephone with a simple 'for' or 'against' statement. These referenda have no bearing on actual political decision making in the city.

In the city of Delft a panel of citizens is periodically asked by local government to give its opinions about city issues and local autority output, for example the safety in the city and the services of the local police. The participants in the panel receive a closed questionnaire, which is analyzed quantitatively. This panel consultation was introduced after a reform of municipality in the direction of a market-oriented service organization.

In the city of Amsterdam, so-called City Conversations are broadcast by the local television, in which a panel of individual citizens, representatives of interest groups and local politicians and administrators discuss a political problem. The viewers can react by telephone or interactive TV devices, and these reactions are introduced into the discussion.

A characterization of these methods would require a thorough enquiry into their design philosophy and into the institutional setting in which they actually function. On the face of it, Radio Referenda could be characterized as a populistic arrangement in which the local population - in a virtual Rousseauean assembly - is asked for a collective judgement about issues concerning the common good. The discussion preceding the 'vote' adds a republican element. It could be seen as a model of a public discussion in which the listeners are attentive spectators. The citizens panel in Delft can be interpreted as a liberal arrangement. As Habermas (1992: 402) suggests, in a liberal Schumpeterian model of democracy the normative expectations of citizens of the political system will shift from the input side to the output side. If citizens can exert only indirect influence on political decision making about policies, they will develop more interest in the actual performance of the system. It seems that in the underlying philosophy of the citizens panels the citizen is conceived of as party to a market transaction, a consumer whose private needs are supplied.

City Conversations in Amsterdam are distinctly republican. They stimulate discussions in the local public sphere about issues of common interest.

## 6.2. *Representatives*

In many Dutch municipalities, information systems are introduced to support the work of councillors. They can be categorized in three types.

In the city of Tilburg, for example, the system can be typified as a documentation and library system. It is primarily directed at the unlocking of official documents which have been dealt with or decided on in the city council. By using this system it has become rather easy for councillors to reconstruct the administrative history of a policy issue.

In The Hague a more extensive management and administrative information system has been developed, accessible to both councillors (including the aldermen) and civil servants. The system contains not only official documents but also financial information and statistical data. The system has been developed to support decision-making processes, including the monitoring of the municipal services.

A third type, a communication or interaction system, can be found in Voorburg, a small city in the vicinity of The Hague. This system functions primarily as an internal communication facility between the councillors (see also Frøkjær, Korsbæk Færch this volume).

The information systems developed so far are still in their infancy and it is very difficult therefore to characterize them in terms of views of democracy. The documentation and management systems of Tilburg and The Hague can certainly fulfil liberal functions of democratic control but also the populistic function of monitoring 'work in progress' by which the popular will is turned into concrete policy output. Communication systems could of course develop into a republican facility if they allowed communication with external actors. But the documentation systems, for example, could fulfil a republican function as well, if they could record the opinions of social movements, interest groups and other opinion building actors in (local) civil society.

## 7. Conclusion

By analyzing the information and communication aspects of different views of democracy I have tried to show what ICTs could mean for the development of democratic arrangements. On the basis of a framework of different views of democracy, the assumptions underlying existing and intended applications of ICTs in politics can be identified and subjected to a critical debate.

Moreover, the framework suggests alternative strategies for embedding ICTs in political processes. By following a certain strategy ad hoc applications of ICTs aimed at enhancing democracy can be avoided. This does not mean that the choice of a guideline for democratization has to be limited to one of the views. In the historical development of Western democracies the three traditions were always intertwined. Also for future democratization we can look for combinations of viewpoints derived from the three views.

If we follow this line, the viability of the views in terms of their assumptions about the motivation and information level of citizens and about the socio-political conditions in modern society have to be taken into account. In this respect our theoretical discussion of more or less 'classical' conceptions of democracy was of course very limited. Zolo (1992) makes matchwood out of what he calls the classical (populistic) and neoclassical (liberal) conceptions of democracy. Habermas' communication theory gets the same treatment, although Zolo's critical analysis of the working of the political system and of political communication in Western societies corresponds to a considerable extent to Habermas' account. Zolo's own position is that the sole promise that democracy should (and can) keep is that social complexity has to be protected against the dominance of one of the societal subsystems. In my view, this position comes close to a plea for updating the classical liberal notion of 'checks and balances' and judging from some prescriptive suggestions at the end of Zolo's book, a new combination of the liberal and republican views might be promising.

Although it is outside the scope of our analysis, there is an additional argument in favor of considering all three views as strategies for democratization, which concerns the variety of domains in which democratization can be sought. Bobbio (1987:55-57) emphasizes that an important indicator of democratic progress is the number of contexts outside the domain of classical democratic theory where democratic procedures, such as voting, are functioning. He particularly refers to state bureaucracy and private enterprise as 'two great blocks of descending and hierarchical power' for assessing the prospects for a democratic transformation of complex societies. This being true, it is obvious that democratization in the economy means something very different from democratization of institutions in civil society (Cohen and Arato 1990). Different conceptions of democracy can be followed for democratization in different domains.

# CHAPTER 4

# Channeling Democratic Influence Through Bureaucracies

*A Review of Democracy Theory*[1]

Ignace Th.M. SNELLEN

*Erasmus University Rotterdam, PO Box 1738, 3000 DR Rotterdam, The Netherlands*

**Abstract.** A 'cultural lag' exists between the use of modern information and communications technologies (ICTs) for direct democratic as well as, informational and volitional, representative democratic arrangements and traditional democracy theory. The use of ICTs for the purposes of direct democraty, such as opinion polls and instant referenda, tends to impair the coherence and consistency of democratic policies and to erode the basis of legitimacy of representative democratic arrangements.

As traditional democracy theory insists on channeling of democratic influence through institutionalized representative bodies, the erosion of the legitimacy of existing democratic arrangements will probably continue.

In the mean time the development of ICTs is providing opportunities to channel informational and volitional democratic influence through the bureaucracy. Such channeling erodes the basis of existing institutionalized politics.

As long as this channeling of democratic influence through bureaucracies is not accepted, bureaucrats have an excuse to look only at the technical aspects of applying ICTs and to negate the democratic aspects of those applications. It will be the task of democratic political theory to refuse to allow management of ICTs in Public Administration such an easy alibi, and to draw their attention to the democratic opportunities and consequences of developments of ICTs in public administration and political systems.

## 1. Introduction

Literally democracy means: 'a population ($\delta\epsilon\mu o\sigma$) that governs ($\kappa\rho\alpha\tau\epsilon\iota\nu$) itself'. In a democracy a collectivity, or the members of a collectivity, are supposed to determine which problems are defined as collective problems, and in which way these problems should be approached and solved.

---

[1]  I am grateful to Arthur Edwards for his helpful comments on a former draft of this chapter.

The three traditional manifestations of democracy are:

* *representative democracy*, through which members of a representative assembly act as delegates of (groups within) the collectivity. Important questions are:
  (1) whether these members represent separate groups: their 'constituencies' and their partisan interests, or the population as a whole: the 'electorate' and its general interest.
  (2) Whether the members are mandated by their constituency, or whether they are supposed to follow their own understanding of the general interest. (Burke's answer was clear: My voters didn't choose me because I would represent their opinions (and their interests) closely, but because of my expert insight into the general interest.)
  (3) Whether representatives are responsible only to their constituency or also (or primarily) to their political party. (As Burke was mainly responsible to his parliamentary patrons, Pitkin: 282-283).
* *direct democracy* or so-called participation, which means that all citizens have an opportunity to participate in the collective decision making process and are enabled, as much as possible, to arrange their own life and to choose their own life styles, according their own preferences. Direct democracy implies also that democratic decisions are taken at the lowest possible level of society. Devolution and decentralization are conditions for improving opportunities for direct democracy and participation.
* *democratic constitutional freedoms*, through which a democratic basis is created for representation and participation, and which restrict governmental interference to those sectors where this intervention is required for the protection of basic interests and personal development.

## 2. Informational and Volitional Relationships in a Democracy

*Constitutional freedoms*, like freedom of opinion, freedom of association guarantee (inter alia) that the collectivity which is represented by the state, does not interfere with those domains which are deemed to be private. These freedoms also guarantee that the 'volitional' and the 'informational' relationships between the collectivity and the governing bodies of the state remain 'open'. It means, that the population is able to convey its preferences, and information to government, freely and untrammelled.

Information and preferences can be channeled to the governing bodies in a *direct democratic* way, where governing bodies and the collectivity are assumed to be one and the same, or in a *representative democratic* way, where the governing body is chosen from the electorate, or is composed separately and is balanced by representatives chosen from the population.

Representative democracy is generally considered to be a 'second best' solution, because distortion or misrepresentation of preferences are likely to occur. As Robert Dahl says: representative democracy is 'a sorry substitute for the real thing'. Representative democracy is deemed to be necessitated by the impossibility of realizing direct democracy. In direct democratic arrangements, preferences, and information about problematic situations, come to the fore without any intermediation. It is assumed, that every person's opinion is heard and that there is no danger of distortion or misrepresentation. Thus real self-government of the population is approached more closely by direct democratic arrangements than by representative democratic arrangements.

However, representative democracy is a 'necessary evil', because:

* massification of democracies makes *real deliberation*, in which everybody's opinion is heard - as would be the case in direct democratic arrangements - *impossible*;
* the complexity of policy, caused by its interdependencies with policies in other sectors of society, leads to *intermittent and iterative decision cycles*, which are *hardly feasible* in direct democratic mass meetings;
* the intervention of the welfare state in diverse but increasingly interconnected sectors of society is still growing. An actively *participating citizen* would have *no time left* for other activities, such as his occupation and leisure;
* the growing diversity of interests together with the plurality of the population make it difficult to understand the preferences and opinions of the electorate as such and its diverse constituencies. A *'general interest'* would be almost *impossible to establish*.

## 3. ICTs and Democratic Developments

However, developments in information and communications technologies (ICTs) have strengthened the wish to expand direct democratic arrangements at the expense of representative democratic arrangements. Many futurologists and forecasters as well as utopianists, predict that in the future people or their households will be hooked into computer networks and will express their preferences, on a daily basis, in instant opinion polls or instant referenda. As a side-effect of this, 'electoral mandate' and 'recall' are gaining in importance to correct the flaws in representative democratic arrangements discussed above. (Developments in the U.S.A., and especially California are good examples of these trends.)

Other writers contend that replacing representative democratic arrangements by direct democratic arrangements such as opinion polls and referenda, would impair the coherence and consistency of democratic policies. They argue that the future of direct democracy is bleak, because of the following reasons.

* Direct democracy would lead to a *single issue* approach. Successive majorities on single issues would introduce incompatible policies within and between sectors. Integrative policies would be missing.

* The basic *rules of a democracy*: 1. the majority decides; 2. the minority obeys the majority decisions; 3. the majority shows consideration for (deeply felt preferences of) the minority, would be *endangered*. Direct democratic mechanisms are not adapted to communicate the relative intensity or the passion with which they are held, which the basic rules of democracy require to be taken into account.
* The absence of deliberation, which characterizes many proposals for direct democratic arrangements tends to strengthen an *instrumental view of the state* and its apparatus. In every instance, where a decision has to be taken, a preliminary question that has to be answered is, whether it befits the state or the collectivity to concern itself with the problem. Direct democratic opinion formation impedes separate attention to this preliminary question.
* The way in which questions are posed in direct democratic arrangements such as referenda or opinion polls is always subject to debate. Most political problems cannot be answered with a simple 'yes' or 'no'. Apart from that, short term reactions expressed through instant referenda or opinion polls *obliterate the long term perspective*, in which many political problems have to be seen.

On all these grounds it can be argued that developments in information and communications technologies (ICTs) will have only a marginal effect on the development of democracy. Although opponents of direct democracy are mistaken in contending that intermediary opinion formation by political parties, through the media and through other political and social forums will necessarily be made impossible, the ad hoc character of direct democratic mechanisms such as referenda and opinion polls, makes a bright future for their application improbable.

On the other hand it can be noticed that there is a tendency to stress the individualistic participatory aspects of ICT developments and their possibilities for democracy and to shift deliberation aspects to the background. It may be too strong a statement to say that in this way the role of politics will be eliminated, but the symbolic and interest articulation functions of indvidual politicians, political parties and people's representative bodies, are at least of decreasing importance. Diminishing participation at elections is generally seen to be an indication of the weakening legitimacy of democratic representative arrangements.

Thus, *findings* with respect to democratic developments and the influence of ICTs are: The legitimacy of representative democracies, and arrangements, such as parliaments, houses of congress, regional or local councils, political parties, and so on, is weaker than the legitimacy of direct democratic arrangements such as referenda, citizen participation, obligatory consultation, recall, and so on.

The development of ICTs enhances the possibilities and the attraction of *direct* democratic arrangements and contribute to a certain erosion of legitimacy of *representative* democratic arrangements. However, representative democratic arrangements remain 'a necessary evil' because of the dominant characteristics of the context of modern political decision making and because of the negative effects of direct democracy in that context.

Democratic theory does has not yet taken into account the opportunities (and threats), which are contained in the development of information and communications technologies for the functioning of democratic arrangements. The legitimacy of these arrangements must be rethought and their normative and empirical foundations reformulated.

## 4. Knowledge Gaps, ICTs and Democracy Theory: Back to Burke

Democratic theory must adapt to the impact of ICTs on parliaments, political parties and politicians and find a new balance between direct and representative democratic mechanisms. The basic assumptions of democratic theory in relation to the workings of democratic representation are less convincing than before. When ICT developments make the relationship of opinions and preferences of political constituencies to positions taken by political representatives more and more transparent, the mismatches between the two become more apparent. As indicated above, the basis of legitimacy of representative democratic arrangements is becoming eroded by such mismatches.

Edmund Burke's ideas with respect to representation, discussed by Hanna F. Pitkin, are revelant in this respect. People's representatives, according to Burke, could state that their constituencies didn't choose them to represent their opinions, but to represent their interests, and that they were not chosen to act as instructed ambassadors for those interests, but because of their personal insight in those interests. The representative, as an expert, may even pretend to have a better insight in the interests of his/her constituency than the members of that constituency themselves. This gap, which I call 'knowledge gap 1', legitimates, according to existing democracy theory, that representatives in parliamentary bodies vote without mandate or consultation.

Besides, members of a constituency have only partial insight into the deliberations in parliament and into the considerations on which political decisions and trade-offs are based. This knowledge gap, which I call 'knowledge gap 2', legitimates, according to Burke, that a representative does not represent the opinions of the electorate, but their (basic) interests, as seen by the representative him/herself.

However, when a representative appears to contradict consistently the interests as perceived by the people he/she represents, incompetence or corruption has to be involved. Such a 'quasi knowledge gap', according to Burke, only occurs in marginal cases. In all other instances the insights of the representative in the interest of his/her constituency and in the general interest must prevail.

Under the influence of ICT developments the legitimation provided by those knowledge gaps ceases to exist. Information systems, such as Geographic Information Systems (GIS), leave no doubt about the interests of regions, different categories of the population, and the specific constituencies of individual people's representatives.[2] (Proposals to install mixed representative systems, in which the electorate has two votes, one on a categorical basis and one on a regional basis, may be considered to be an attempt to fill this legitimacy gap!) The legitimation provided by knowledge gap 1 looses its meaning, as publicly available databases permit an accurate picture of different groups in the population. Knowledge gap 2 looses its legitimizing value also, because the activities of parliaments and other representative bodies become more visible. Tracking systems enable insiders and outsiders to monitor parliamentary processes as well as the voting records of individual representatives. As van de Donk and Tops (see this Volume p. 30) remark: 'The parliamentary lion's den seems to have become more transparent'.

The erosion of the legitimacy of representative democratic arrangements which is caused by ICT developments, will probably not be compensated by growing opportunities for direct democratic participation which are also created by the development of ICTs. The low turn-outs in elections make it clear that the channeling of democratic influence through popular representative bodies is failing more and more, and that direct democratic arrangements do not adequately compensate. The reasons for this are discussed above.

## 5. Some Empirical Evidence at the Municipal Level

In his dissertation Depla (1995) describes several initiatives undertaken by Dutch municipalities to improve and modernize democratic practices at the local level of public administration. These initiatives are comparable to initiatives in many American states and Western-European countries. In many instances of 'democratic renovation', described by Depla, one of the main objectives appears to be to improve living conditions and housing.

Depla makes a distinction between initiatives 1) which enhance the controling power of city management, 2) which strengthen the position of the city council or 3) which increase opportunities for citizens and their organizations to participate in the making of those policies which affect their living conditions.

The outcome of his research is, that most of the time initiatives to improve the democratic power of local councils, or of citizens and their organizations result in a tighter grip by the local bureaucrats on the policy process. With respect to ICT applications for improving local democracies, he notes particularly a tendency to marginalize politics and politicians in the policy making process. Whereas bureaucrats make use of management reports and statistics to monitor policy processes, the opportunities for individual politicians and city councils to intervene in the policy process decrease. The more ICT applications are used within local bureaucracies to

---

[2]     Interestingly enough, Edmund Burke developed his idea in a system of regional representation, in which interests of regions more than of categories of the population, were paramount.

monitor policies and to improve their effectiviness, the more political bodies are kept at a distance. The same is true for those initiatives which involve citizens in 'co-production' of improvements of their housing or living conditions. The more bureaucrats succeed in involving citizens in improving their own situation, the less political intervention appears to be necessary or appropriate. So, where local initiatives to mobilize citizens enter the stage, the importance of local political institutions is marginalized. Depla concludes: 'The organs of the institutionalized political system are no longer considered as the only institutions which are important for the authoritative allocation of values; the central role of politics is increasingly relativized.'

## 6. Bureaucracies' Democratic Role

The analysis of Depla makes it clear that attempts to renovate local democracies with the help of information and communications technologies may restaure the primacy of institutionalized politics as such and at the same time relativize the central role of formal political organs of local democracy (Depla 1995: 95).

His analysis also points in the direction that city bureaucrats probably will play a major role in reviving the primacy of institutionalized politics, without re-invigorating the existing political organs.

My contention is, that this role of bureaucrats has to be accepted in practice as well as in theory, to further democratic developments in information societies. Democratic arrangements will have to be adapted, and extended, to encompass the representative democratic role bureaucrats are increasingly playing (or having to play).

The conclusion must be that democracy theory is in need of revision, and maybe of extension to other arrangements than traditional representative bodies and direct participation. An additional route for the channeling of democratic influence - via bureaucracies - has been found in practice and has to be ratified by democracy theory. As bureaucrats have a share in the democratic policymaking acitivities in which people's representatives participate, a channelling of democratic influence through bureaucracies seems to be a viable approach.

According to normative democratic theory, bureaucracies are supposed to be subservient to their political masters, the people's representatives. Realist democratic theory (Bobbio, Zolo a.o.) recognizes that bureaucracies are of paramount importance in policy development and legislation. Nevertheless, democratic theory restricts its tenets to the volitional and informational channels between electorates, political parties and parliamentary factions and coalitions.

In view of the role of bureaucracies in policy development it seems to me to be of growing importance to investigate opportunities for enhancing democracy by using ICT facilities to channel influence on policy making through bureaucracies. (As indicated in Fig. 1)

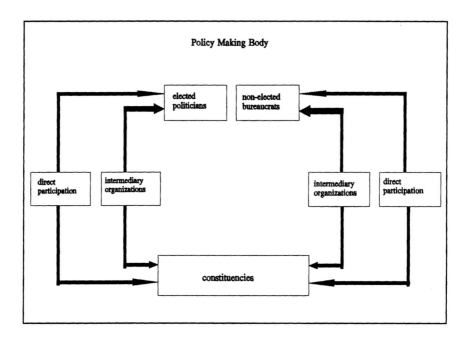

Fig. 1:    Democratic channels of Influence on Policy Making

Bureaucracies could be developed into democratic representative bureaucracies. The existing literature on 'representative bureaucracies' only takes into account, whether bureaucracies mirror the population in their composition (ethnic minorities, gender, regional backgrounds, etc.). Normative democratic theory practically excludes discussion about representative bureaucracies in a democratic sense.

However, ICT applications which are used by bureaucracies to improve relationships with their 'constituencies' in their policy sector enhance opportunities for bureaucracies to act as democratic representatives. And the professional background of most bureaucrats deepens their democratic relationship with those 'constituencies'.

It will be a challenge for democratic theory to expand its scope to policy making by elected politicians and non-elected bureaucrats alike.


## 7. ICT Applications as Democratic Instruments

Examples of ICT applications which strengthten the democratic role of bureaucracies are:

* Geographic Information Systems (GIS), which visualize the areas where some problems or clusters of problems are located;

* Relational data bases, which have the same kind of function (as GIS) for categories of the population;
* Tracking and Monitoring Systems which indicate the quality of public services provided to different sectors of the population.

By means of such information systems, bureaucracies become essential *informational* channels for democratic policy making. They are the appropriate bodies to fill the knowledge gaps mentioned above. The stronger the informational relationships of bureaucracies become with (parts of) the population, the more the function of representative democratic bodies is eroded and the more urgent it is to look for compensatory democratic arrangements within and around bureaucracies.

*Volitional* channels could also be created via bureaucracies. Bureaucracies increasingly make use of marketing-like ICT devices to measure the quality of public services and the needs and desires of their clientele. The will of the people is established directly by bureaucracies and can be imported directly into the policy making process. However, when local bureaucracies behave like this, the municipal councils which are supposed to monitor and control bureaucracies, may begin to feel mariginalized.

## 8. Adaptation of Democracy Theory

To create acceptance for the channeling of democratic influences through bureaucracies democracy theory must be adapted in different ways.

*First of all*, the theory will have to be formulated to allow bureaucracies to behave as democratic machines, in the same way as political parties interest groups and representative bodies play their democratic role.

As to the behavior of political parties, the so-called Responsible Party Model specifies the following requirements (Berelson *et al.* 1954, Campbell *et al.* 1960):

* political parties must present voters with real choice options, which differentiate the parties from each other;
* political parties must be sufficiently cohesive to rely upon the loyalty of their representatives in parliament, and to guarantee that party manifestos will be put into practice.

The analogous requirements for the functioning of democratically responsive bureaucracies would be:

* preferences for certain (conflicting) policy options from the perspectives of different policy sectors must be clarified and made public.

* bureaucracies must be transparent about the way in which they will develop policies. The implications of different policy alternatives must be made explicit and available for public debate;

A basic condition for realizing the representative democratic function of bureaucracies is to make public administration as open as possible. Without openness it would be highly problable, that the channeling of *volitional* and *informational* influences will be dominated by bureaucratic and other interests, and this would be almost impossible to control.

*Secondly* the relationship between popular representative bodies and bureaucracies would have to be redefined by democracy theory.

There are different possibilities:

* representative bodies, like parliaments, could restrict themselves to meta-steering or procedural steering of the activities within bureaucracies;
* bureaucracies could be obliged to establish the preferences of (sectors and categories of) the population and to take these into account in a controlled responsive and responsible manner;
* it would be possible to oblige bureaucracies to permit themselves to be monitored by popular representative bodies in a systematic way, and to develop forms of self-evaluation, reviews, annual reports etc. which would support the functioning of representative bodies.

## 9. Final Remarks

It will be a matter of 'political ergonomics' (Winner 1987) to invent and design arrangements for the 'democratic bureaucracy' through which ICT applications could assist in creating opportunities for the democratic participation of the population. Democracy theory must create room for such arrangements

As long as democracy theory recognizes only the legitimacy of elected politicians as channels for expressing the popular will, bureaucrats will be allowed to restrict their thinking exclusively to the technical aspects of ICTs, as Pratchett rightly indicates (in this volume).

It will be a task for democratic political theory, not to allow those managers in public administration, who are responsible for ICT applications such an easy alibi and to draw their attention to the democratic opportunities and consequences of modern developments in public administration and political systems.

CHAPTER 5

# Laying Down the Infrastructure
# for Innovations in Teledemocracy:
# The Case of Scotland

John A. TAYLOR, Barbara BARDZKI and Caroline WILSON

*Glasgow Caledonian University, Cowcaddens Road, Glasgow G4 0BA, United Kingdom*

**Abstract.** Local governments can actively stimulate forms of democracy through the deployment of telecommunications-based systems and services which are designed to enhance the relationship of the citizen to state. Representative, pluralist and direct forms of democracy are all susceptible to electronic forms of mediation. In looking for examples of teledemocracy in Scottish local governments research findings suggest that such instances as are occurring may well have been contingent upon profound shifts in the telecommunications environment, such as competition and/or infrastructural improvements, together with the raised awareness amongst potential user groups which accompany these shifts. Because enhancements in the telecommunications infrastructure are unevenly distributed some Scottish local governments will be innovators in teledemocracy whilst others will lag behind.

## 1. Introduction

This chapter provides an opportunity for reporting on early research findings from a project on the theme of teledemocracy in Scotland. The work is focusing upon applications of electronic media in those aspects of the democratic sphere where local governments have opportunities to innovate. The work therefore sets out not only to comment upon instances of teledemocracy at the local level in Scotland, but also to cast light upon the processes of innovation (and those which sustain inertia) in Scottish local governments through which these instances do or do not occur. As such the authors are not engaged at this stage in evaluation of the nature of initiatives using the seemingly inevitable Utopian-dystopian continuum (Dutton 1992), but, rather, in identifying their existence and beginning to raise questions about why innovations around the theme of teledemocracy are occurring in Scotland and, indeed, why they are not.

The research has, to this point, focused upon Scotland's largest local governments, that is its Regions, of which there are nine, its three all-purpose Island governments (Orkney, Shetland and the Western Isles) and its four largest District authorities (Glasgow, Edinburgh, Aberdeen and Dundee).

The current politico-administrative context in the UK is making this work all the more pertinent, giving rise as it is to two main sets of concerns about democratic activity in local government. Scottish Local Government is currently the subject of a thorough-going review and reorganization by central government, with a core emphasis upon shifting the system from one dominated by a two-tier model to a consistent, country-wide, all-purpose, single tier set of arrangements. Whilst the precise delineation of these reforms is not yet entirely finalized, including the membership of the new local governments, the first point of concern emerging from this context of reform is over questions of democratic representation. Under proposals announced by the Secretary of State for Scotland in April 1994 the number of locally elected council members was to decline from 1611 to 1042, a reduction of 35% (Jones 1994). The extent of this reduction in public representatives has since been lessened, with a more recent announcement (Scott 1994) suggesting that there will be 1161 councillors after reorganization, a revised reduction therefore of 29%. Scottish political opinion on this reduction in numbers varies. The Secretary of State for Scotland, a member of the Conservative government, sees it as necessary if the right balance is to be struck between local representation and business efficiency. The Scottish National Party has stridently declared it as signalling the death of local democracy and the loss of local control, and the other main political parties in Scotland are similarly disquieted about the likely impact of the reforms on democratic relationships.

The second concern emerging from the current politico-administrative context in the UK focuses upon the growth of 'extra-governmental organizations' at local level (Charter 88 Trust 1994). In the education sector, for example, many organizations which were hitherto internal to the government structure and thereby subject to the conventions of public scrutiny and appointment have been externalized and become relatively detached from forms of local accountability and control. This concern is voiced across contemporary government reform movements in the UK and is especially pertinent at local level given the fundamental reform which is occurring there also.

Thus, in short, not only is the number of local functions which are subject to the conventions of public accountability being diminished as organizational fragmentations occur, but so too is the numerical strength of local representation being reduced.

One question which arises in this context is whether the *quality* of local public representation and other forms of democratic activity can be improved, thereby acting as a counterweight to what are at least face-value arguments which see democracy in decline. (See also the contributions of Bellamy cs and Pratchett in this volume). The remainder of this chapter in effect seeks to address this question by looking specifically at new technology applications in the local democratic context. Putting it at its most heroic, and using the title of a recent lecture on this subject, the question arises 'can technology save democracy?' (Dutton *et al.* 1994).

## 2. Teledemocracy

The term 'teledemocracy' can be interpreted in a variety of ways though each of them incorporates the use (usually in tandem) of computers and telecommunications in the relationships of governmental and political party organizations with individuals and groups in society. At its broadest, the term is used to denote changing relationships within the polity as governments use telematics applications in delivering services to public service customers and in furthering their obligations to citizens. Thus, on this definition, teledemocracy can be taken as including the delivery of electronic services rather than as being solely concerned with the management and development of citizenship. On this *inclusive* view of teledemocracy the delivery of service wholly or in part through electronic means is seen as a form of teledemocracy because it 'holds the potential for changing the way the public interacts with candidates, officials, and public agencies....' (Dutton 1992). Research on teledemocracy through this very broad interpretation of the term would thus of necessity include both mapping and assessing all those relationships between local governments and their citizens which are electronically mediated, whether those relationships are primarily between producer and consumer or between state and citizen.

A second, narrower and more *exclusive* view of the nature of teledemocracy is used in this chapter, however. On this narrower interpretation of teledemocracy there is a core point of focus which differentiates it from the first - a focus on *information flows within the processes which link the state to the citizen qua citizen*. So, for example, some of the arguments to be found in the recent work of the Office of Technology Assessment in the USA conform to this narrower view of teledemocracy where a key point is that 'assuring equitable access' (to information) 'is important to reduce, not widen, the substantial gap between the information 'haves' and 'have-nots' (OTA 1993a). That corpus of work has thus taken on the case for the building of an 'electronic superhighway' which would offer enhanced community access networks, including better access for the citizen to the agents and agencies of government (OTA 1993b).

Thus far our concern has been to undertake research within this somewhat narrower interpretation of teledemocracy. We have therefore sought to look at the extent to which local governments have, within their own jurisdictional boundaries, been promoting citizenship values through the use of new technologies and we have investigated this by reference to three kinds of developments. Firstly, we have looked at the degree to which local governments in Scotland have been seeking to provide locally elected representatives with enhanced information resources. This 'majoritarian representative' form of democracy remains the most evident form there is in the polity and we have been concerned to investigate the extent to which it is becoming *informatized*. The case has been made (Westcott 1993) that local representatives should be supported via ICTs in a variety of ways, including improved communications facilities, better access to committee papers, access to policy relevant information such as expenditure statements and enhanced office support. The strongest example which we have found in the UK which serves as an exemplar here, is in the city of Swansea in South Wales. There, local councillors have provided themselves with a comprehensive facility for communications and access to information. Thirty of the local councillors have a P.C. and modem in their homes (there are also communal facilities in the members rooms at City Hall) and are able to use email, arrange their diary, search all committee minutes, enter the housing repair schedule, and examine the general ledger and the capital monitoring systems. The email system is used both for communication between councillors and between councillors and officials from senior to middle rank.

Secondly, we have looked at the extent of electronically enhanced pluralist democracy in and around local governments in Scotland. Have local governments in Scotland been making available opportunities for enhanced communications amongst and within citizen groups? Here the strongest example in the UK of which we are aware is that of the Manchester HOST network. This network has been developed in the city since 1991, employing a minicomputer to manage access over the Public Switched Telephone Network (PSTN) to low-cost communications and information systems such as email (short and long distance), wordprocessing, bulletin boards etc. The project began with a concern for stimulating local economic development and, more specifically, giving small and medium sized businesses access to information resources at an affordable cost. The project very quickly has become one concerned too with the development of community, and the creation of urban equivalents of Electronic Village Halls (EVH) has supported this development. Thus the HOST has become a social as well as economic project and, through the EVHs, is making access to services possible for both geographically defined communities and physically scattered communities of interest. There is evidence that women's groups, ethnic minorities, and disabled groups, for example, are using the facilities in order to strengthen their ability to communicate within their groups and thus become more effective in shaping local public policy towards them (Gibbs and Leach 1992).

Thirdly, we have sought to identify forms of electronically stimulated direct democracy as they are occurring or being planned in Scotland. Whilst a number of well-known examples of this subset of teledemocracy exist in European countries and in the USA (Dutton 1992, Dutton *et al.* 1994, Van de Donk and Tops 1992), we have found no instance within the UK of this kind of electronically stimulated democracy which we would consider exemplary, though it is clear that some local governments in Britain are beginning to think about developments of this type (Graham 1992).

The following paragraph of this chapter sets out available evidence on teledemocracy innovations in the UK. In the first place we set out data which we have substantially reworked which derives from the annual survey of the Society of IT Managers in local government (SOCITM). In the second place we set out evidence from our own survey of selected Scottish local governments. This latter survey has been directed wholly at an examination of innovations around the theme of teledemocracy which are in line with those models of teledemocracy discussed earlier in this chapter.

## 3. Teledemocracy in the UK - Evidence from the IT Professionals

Each year SOCITM undertakes a nationwide survey of the use of information technology by local government called 'I.T. Trends in Local Government'. The survey aims to provide broad-ranging information on trends and current issues in information technology (IT) and information systems (IS) in local governments and is regarded as being both reliable and extensive. Response rates to the survey have increased steadily from its first year in 1987 (26%) to the most recent in 1993 (48%).

Despite the compendious nature of the SOCITM surveys there is little to be found in them which bears directly upon the issues at the heart of this chapter. Their orientation is towards the gathering of information on internal IT operations (eg costs, staffing, strategy development, service-specific applications) and they have had little to say about IT applications which involve the development of external relationships, especially relationships to citizens.

From these reports we have gleaned three sets of information of broad relevance to this chapter. First, there is general data which confirms that trends in IT in Scotland are running about level with those in the rest of the UK. For example, whilst local government spending on IT as a whole across the UK has risen from £500 million in 1987 to £1100 million in 1993, Scottish local governments spend more per 1000 per head of population than English authorities, other than London local governments, with whom they are directly comparable.

The same general trends are to be found in IT strategy development. The majority of local governments now have IS/IT strategies. 77% have a strategy document and 16% have one in preparation. In Scotland 75% of local governments have an IS/IT strategy and 21% are in the process of producing one. Therefore, in these general respects Scottish local governments appear to be in line with their counterparts in the rest of the UK.

On issues more specific to this chapter, SOCITM data was of interest in only two areas. In the first of these - support for elected members - the evidence suggests that very few local governments are seeking to stimulate the role of elected representatives through the provision of information resources. For the UK as a whole the predominant use by councillors of computers is for word processing, with only 17% of local governments offering some email facilities and 6% providing access to email at home.

Broadly the same picture is revealed in Scotland. Of the 21 respondent authorities, 4 gave councillors home access to office automation, and 1 to email from home. 3 gave no support at all in council offices and 9 gave councillors access to committee minutes and to other basic functions. No authorities were providing Videotex services to councillors.

The second area in which SOCITM data was of specific relevance to this chapter came in the 1992 survey question about 'external electronic services' for electronic data interchange (EDI). 17% of local governments replied positively to this question although the authors of the survey report felt that many more authorities were piloting schemes and that future developments would depend on the provision of more enhanced telecommunications infrastructures.

The survey has also addressed specific questions about the availability of Public Access Terminals (PATs) with managers being asked if their authorities had installed or were planning to install them. However, no questions were asked about the location of the terminals, what sort of information could be accessed over them or whether they were interactive. In 1992, 67% of responding authorities had no plans for PATs, 14% planned to install them and 19% had them in place. From the 1993 survey 15% were planning to install PATs though in this year only 17% of respondents had PATs. Again for Scotland the figures are broadly commensurate. For 1992, 46% of Scottish local governments had no plans for PATs, 39% were planning to install them and 15% had them already (response - 26 authorities). In 1993, 57% had no plans for PATs, 25% had them planned and, by now, 21% had them installed (response - 28 authorities). Table 1 captures this data in summary form.

Table 1: Public Acces Terminals in UK Local Government

|  | UK | | Scotland | |
| --- | --- | --- | --- | --- |
|  | 1992 | 1993 | 1992 | 1993 |
| Installed | 19% | 17% | 15% | 21% |
| Planned | 14% | 15% | 39% | 25% |
| Not planned | 67% | 68% | 46% | 57% |

In addition to this data the surveys show that the number of authorities using Viewdata is increasing. In 1990, the average number of Viewdata frames being used by UK local governments was 1,000 but by 1993 this number had risen to 2,600. The survey asks no questions about the nature of the information being provided nor about who is using the facility.

In summary, the annual SOCITM surveys provide information of immediate concern to IT managers such as software, equipment, expenditure and the use of I.T. in specific service areas such as social services and housing. The surveys also highlight the main concerns of local government employees in particular years such as local government reorganization and Compulsory Competitive Tendering. Concern for members' and public access to and exchange of information are not high priorities for in this survey. Where there is relevant data from this survey it reveals that little is happening in the UK as a whole, or in Scotland in particular, which can be related to the definition of teledemocracy outlined earlier.

## 4. Teledemocracy - Evidence from Scotland

Table 2 provides a summary of our findings to date from our survey of selected Scottish local governments.

We have sought to show in this table five sets of information, each of which is designed to cast light upon local government's take-up and use (current and planned) of telematics, particularly in the context of teledemocratic development. The columns are organized around local government types, with the three island (all-purpose) local governments first, the eight respondent regions next, and then the four main city districts. The first column of table 2 summarizes each local government's adoption of advanced telecommunications. Each of these authorities employs professional computing and telecommunications staff and it is not surprising therefore to find that many of them have moved strongly towards the adoption of digital communications. Many have some fibre optics in their networks, and some of the more remote authorities are using satellite communications in selected instances. Many of them are adopting ISDN alternatives so as to augment the scope and quality of their private networks. The second column of table 2 reveals instances of electronic support for councillors. Here the overall picture is patchy and, at the level of the individual authority, none of them has developed support as strongly and coherently as our exemplary local government, Swansea. Lothian Region and the cities of Glasgow and Aberdeen would appear to have gone furthest in their development of support for councillors. Each of these authorities is providing councillors with access to computerized information and, in the cases of the cities, there is the provision of a telematics facility for home-based working - FAX (Aberdeen) and Email (Glasgow).

The third column of table 2 sets out what, if anything, these local governments are providing by way of network support for local communities and interests. Here too none of the authorities has developed an equivalent of the exemplary authority (Manchester) to which we referred earlier. Three of the city governments have introduced non-interactive 'public access terminals'; two authorities - Strathclyde Region and the Western Isles - have developed 'telecentres' which offer telematics services in some of the smaller and more remote towns; and, most interestingly, the Highlands Region and the Shetland Isles are involved in a European RACE program sponsored project - Lambda - which is developing multi-media terminals for use in a number of service contexts, including remote interviewing for social services claimants and the delivery of text and images from the Scottish Museum Service primarily for use in schools.

Table 2: Summary of findings to date from survey of selected Scottish governments.

| Authority | Use of advanced Systems/Telecomms | Councillor Support | Community Support | Direct Democracy | Futures |
|---|---|---|---|---|---|
| Western Isles | Some ISDN Occasional use of satellite Videoconferencing | From office only Stand alone PCs at home | 'Outreach centres' or one stop shops | None | Homeworking Satellite Teleconferencing |
| Shetland | Some ISDN & fibre Microwave telephony | Access to minutes from dept. Stand alone PCs at home | Wide info pro-vision project education/ tourism/social services | None | Expansion of community support program |
| Orkney | 1 digital private circuit | None | None | None | None |
| Lothian | Some fibre in private circuits | Some email Access to Man Info. Sys. | Use of email to link schools to universities | None | ISDN Cable networks |
| Fife | Some fibre Extensive digital private circuit | Stand alone PCs; Access to Viewdata from members lounge | Free FAX in public offices for contact with officials and councilors | None | email for councillors Viewdata |
| Tayside | Some fibre | email in office | None | None | None |
| Grampian | Digital private circuit Some fibre & ISDN | Access from members room only to W.P. | None | None | None |
| Highland | ISDN Extensive digital private circuit | Access to man info from members' room | Wide info pro-vision project education/ tourism/social services | None | Increase in community support Pilot email from home for members |

| Authority | Use Of Advanced Systems/Telecomms | Councillor Support | Community Support | Direct Democracy | Futures |
|---|---|---|---|---|---|
| **Central** | Some digital in private network some optic fibre | None | None | None | Enhancing private networks |
| **Strathclyde** | 90% digital private circuit Some ISDN Some fibre | Viewdata provision in members' room | Some telecottaging in islands | None | ISDN Discussion with Cable & Scottish Power |
| **Dumfries & Galloway** | None | Video-confe-rencing at local elections ie for members access | None | None | ISDN Video-conf. Digital network |
| **Edinburgh** | Unknown | Unknown | P.A.T.s | Unknown | Unknown |
| **Glasgow** | ISDN Some fibre in private circuits | email, some from home. Access to minutes, meetings, schedules | P.A.T.s | None | One-stop shops |
| **Aberdeen** | 80% digital 10% fibre ISDN | Party rooms have PCs/ printers. FAX at home. Notebooks. | P.A.T.s | None | More ISDN More P.A.T.s |
| **Dundee** | Some fibre in private circuits | Access to info. through department al systems | None | None | P.A.T.s ISDN Cable for phones |

There are no instances of direct democracy applications coming forward from our sample of local governments, though a couple (Strathclyde Region and Edinburgh District) are reportedly beginning to look at the opportunities which are arising around developments in the cable TV industry.

Most of the local authorities which we have surveyed have strong plans for telematics developments. Column five of table 2 shows that few of these plans appear to be offering strong developments around teledemocracy. Exceptions to this general statement are Fife and Highland Regions which are signalling the development of projects to provide local councillors with email facilities; and the Western Isles, the Shetland Isles and the Highland Region are involved with the Lambda project which will continue to develop both in its 'spread' and in the number of services which it provides.


## 5. Explaining Teledemocracy Development in Scotland

The data which we have brought forward in this chapter, both that from the UK-wide SOCITM survey and that from our own work in Scotland, suggest that instances of teledemocracy, as defined earlier, in UK local government are few and far between. We touched earlier on an exemplary instance of teledemocratic support for local councillors (Swansea) and on an exemplary instance of teledemocratic support for community groups and action (Manchester). We know too that there are other instances of a similar type in some other UK local governments, and that some are beginning to look at ICT applications in support of more direct forms of democracy (Graham 1992). These instances, however, are exceptions to the norm.

One simple hypothesis which we would put forward in seeking to explain this dearth of teledemocratic activity in UK local government in general, and in Scottish local government in particular, concerns the presence or absence of champions of change in local government.

The literature on innovation processes surrounding the adoption and application of new ICTs has tended to stress the role of individuals and small groups in promoting and sustaining change in organizations (Ginzburg 1981, Leonard-Barton 1988). Such championing of change and innovation could derive from many points in local government, the most obvious of which is the ICT professionals. Yet, on the evidence of the annual surveys undertaken by and for these professionals, there is little to suggest that teledemocratic activity is viewed as having significance for them as a set of professionals. The view might be taken that the organizational characteristics of UK local government - its procedures and cultures for example - act to inhibit or even to squeeze out attempts at innovation brought forward by zealous professionals, but the evidence of the SOCITM survey suggests that innovation around teledemocracy, or around more adventurous forms of electronic service delivery, is not being considered by them in any sustained way.

A second and more complex hypothesis which we wish to test in seeking to explain this slow development of teledemocratic innovation in Scottish local governments, links the issue of championing to wider questions about the development of communications infrastructures in local government areas. In previous research (Taylor 1994, Taylor, Williams and McLeod 1993a, Taylor, Williams and McLeod 1993b) we have shown that the presence of competition in telecommunications provision raises awareness amongst potential user groups of the possibilities for innovative applications. This then becomes a second element in the hypothesis: the championing of innovations may be related in many instances to factors beyond the immediate organization, in this instance competition in telecommunications provision.

This hypothesis must to be further complicated however. The development of competition is not the only significant external factor in UK telecommunications. We want also to include in our hypothesis that innovations may be more likely to occur where telecommunications infrastructures are enhanced *regardless of the presence of competition* so long as knowledge of that enhancement is widely disseminated. One of the clear implications emerging from the current debates in the USA and the UK about national information infrastructures or 'information superhighways' is that universal provision of enhanced telecommunications infrastructures, including broadband, can be an important source of business and public service innovations (HMSO 1993, OTA 1993a, Raab this volume). A core debate therefore within the superhighways concept concerns questions about how to achieve *universal* broadband infrastructures within public policy regimes characterized by plural and geographically uneven provision.

To summarize therefore our hypothesis is that change champions are more likely both to emerge and be successful in the field of teledemocracy where the visibility of telecommunications has been increased either through the presence of competition or through the trumpeted enhancement of the telecommunications infrastructure.

In the paragraph which follows we begin to examine this hypothesis by looking at the main public telecommunications infrastructure developments in Scotland during the period within which telecommunications policy in the UK has become increasingly liberalized. Implicit in this examination is the view that the quality of the public switched network (rather than private networks) is of crucial significance to teledemocratic innovations because, by definition, teledemocracy has universal requirements which private circuits could not reasonably be expected to satisfy.

## 6. Telecommunications Infrastructure Developments in Scotland

There are four inter-related aspects to the development of the hard-wire, including cable, public telecommunications infrastructure in Scotland. These are:

*   the laying down of infrastructures by the UK's main PTOs, British Telecom (now BT) and Mercury Communications Ltd (MCL).
*   an initiative from BT and the Highlands and Islands Development Board from 1989 designed to bring an Integrated Services Digital Network (ISDN) to the north of mainland Scotland and to the main northern and western islands. This development is known as the Highlands & Islands Initiative (HII).
*   the plans of other licensed network operators to trade in Scotland, notably the electricity supply companies.
*   wiring for cable TV in specific places in Scotland.

### 6.1.    *The Main PTOs in Scotland*

Under the conditions of its license BT is required to provide universal service for telephony throughout the UK. Its network in Scotland is consequentially extensive though this network and the switches which support it are highly variable in their degree of modernization (Taylor *et al.* 1993a). BT's trunk network is now exclusively comprised of optic fibre though outside its trunk network the company's policy is to retain and renew with copper cable where this is deemed to be commercially appropriate. MCL, BT's main network competitor has also developed a fibre network linking the main cities of Britain, including those in Scotland. Beyond its own trunk network MCL has relied heavily on its interconnection agreements with BT for delivering services into premises in all except its main city center business. MCL business strategy has been to target the city centers to 'skim the cream' of telecommunications business in these places and it has not largely unwilling to engage in infrastructure development in Scotland beyond these city areas and its trunk network. Business opportunities beyond the main city centers have been 'cherry picked' using specific solutions such as microwave. Previous research in Scotland has shown that where there is a clear and visible competitive presence then awareness amongst users of the potential of telecommunications rises (Taylor and McLeod 1993a). What is also clear for Scotland however is that this competition, with all its potential for awareness raising, is only to be found in the main city center areas. For the most part therefore BT has remained just as it was in its publically owned days, *the* telecommunications provider in Scotland.

### 6.2.    *The ISDN Initiative in the North of Scotland*

The HII marked a small-scale reversal in UK telecommunications policy, though the government made it clear at the time of the initiative that it was not to be replicated elsewhere. The proposal for the development of a modern ISDN infrastructure for the north of Scotland came jointly from BT and the Development Board and it was funded by these two organizations. The policy shift embodied in this change was that the HII represented attention to the supply side of telecommunications without strong reference to demand. Both before the initiative began in 1989 and since, UK network infrastructures have been developed along business lines in response to demand.

BT has now installed 65 digital switches in the HII area and has upgraded the network as necessary to support ISDN standards. The HIDB (now Highlands and Islands Enterprise - HIE) has both economic and community development objectives in its remit and in consequence the network was signalled from the outset as providing both business opportunities (encouraging inward investment, providing access to data services etc) and community development opportunities in the provision of advanced services at local call rates across this large, sparsely populated region (Taylor and Williams 1990). The HII has been a much vaunted initiative and, as we shall argue below, appears to be of progressively increasing importance for public service organizations in the area.

## 6.3.  *The Emergence of Other Network Service Providers*

In the first two years of the 1990s the UK government set out the parameters of its policy intentions for telecommunications in the second decade of regulated competition (Department of Trade and Industry 1990, 1991, Competition and Choice 1990). The essence of the new policy stance was to move on from the duopoly provision which had emerged in the 1980s (BT & MCL) towards the development of more thoroughgoing competition. As a consequence of this policy change a number of other network service providers have come forward and are beginning to offer services. British Rail, British Waterways, (National Networks - a subsidiary of the British Post Office), and the Electricity Supply Industry have all signalled their intention to trade in telecommunications and indeed in some instances they are beginning to offer services.

In Scotland the main additional PTOs emerging are Scotland's two electricity supply companies - Scottish Hydro and Scottish Power. The former will offer services in the north of Scotland and the latter in the highly-populated central belt and the south. Each of these companies is linked to the new UK-wide electricity industry telecommunications arm, Energis, and will therefore be able to offer service throughout the UK over the industry's own network. Both of the Scottish companies boast of a number of features in their operations which will allow them to offer high quality telecommunications services to all kinds of customers. Both have installed fibre-optic networks, for example, and, in the case of Scottish Hydro, have a successful track record of supplementing this with micro-wave provision to the more remote parts of Scotland. Equally these companies argue that their universal access to premises via electricity supply lines, as well as the way-leaves and ducting which accompanies that, gives them the potential very quickly to become major competitors to BT and MCL. As yet, however, their telecommunications operations are only beginning.

## 6.4.  Cable Operators

The UK experience of cable television has been characterized by slow growth in the 1980s followed by a strong surge of investment and user uptake in the 1990s. The number of cable franchises awarded by the UK Cable Authority currently stands at 130, though many of these have lain dormant for many years. The number of active franchises currently stands at 65 (Independent Television Commission News Releases 1994). Figure 1 reveals something of this picture, looking at the growth in active franchises since 1991.

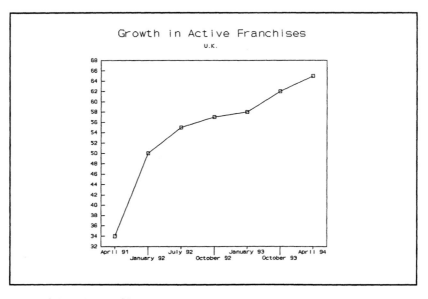

Fig. 1: Growth in Active Franchises

Figure 1 shows clearly the explosion of interest in cable in the UK from the early 1990's. Legislation and regulatory decisions at that time changed the business environment for cable companies in three fundamental and interlinked ways giving rise to this surge of interest shown in figure 1. Firstly, the restriction on non-European companies controlling cable franchises was removed under The Broadcasting Act of 1990 with the consequence that US companies have become very active in the UK. Secondly, from 1991 cable companies have been permitted to enter the telephone market to provide services in the 'Local loop', a decision which has fundamentally changed the economics of cable provision in the UK. Thirdly, the existing PTOs have been excluded from the provision of entertainment services over their networks, thus protecting and promoting investment in cable.

These changes applied to the UK as a whole including Scotland where the number of active cable franchises is currently 6 from a total of 14 franchises awarded throughout the country. In Scotland, the active franchises are to be found in the largest conurbations figure 2 provides evidence on franchises held (both active and inactive) and opens up comparisons between the member countries of Great Britain.

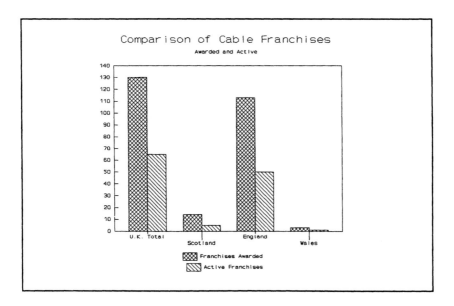

Fig. 2: Comparison of Cable Franchises

In summary, two conclusions should be drawn from this brief survey of Scottish telecommunications. First, at the present time BT remains the de facto monopolist in most of the country, though MCL offers competition in the largest cities. Competition in telecommunications between the two main PTOs varies considerably by place therefore. Secondly, the HII was a unique intervention which has raised the quality of the telecommunications environment in the north of Scotland. It is an instance of a high profile supply-side improvement in the local telecommunications infrastructure rather than a business response to perceived demand as might typically be the case in a regime of 'competition and choice'. Thirdly, further competition is beginning to emerge in particular through cable company provided telephony and through the electricity companies. It is too early yet to have a strong sense of where this competitive threat to the existing PTOs will occur, either geographically or in non-geographically defined consumer markets. Our previous evidence suggests however that with this increased competition will come enhanced consumer awareness, though clearly we would expect this effect to be strongest if competition occurs in places where it has not been present previously. Fourthly, it is not yet clear what the overall quality of the telecommunications infrastructure in Scotland will be. Again this is in part a point about geographical provision, though it is also about bandwidth. Thus it remains uncertain whether the new burst of telecommunications activity in the UK is leading to the laying down of infrastructures which will bear the advanced, interactive and multimedia services upon which some forms of electronic service delivery and some forms of teledemocracy will depend (House of Commons Report 1993/4).


## 7. Telecommunications Infrastructure and Innovations in Teledemocracy

During the course of this chapter we have set out argument and evidence which bear upon our central hypothesis that innovation processes in the field of teledemocracy in local governments are contingent upon circumstances pertaining to telecommunications infrastructural developments rather than simply upon internal organizational characteristics such as the presence of groups and individuals willing and able to champion them. In order to test this hypothesis, albeit in a preliminary way, we now wish to place the evidence which we have brought forward in table 2 alongside the evidence of infrastructural developments in Scottish telecommunications which was brought forward in the immediately preceding paragraph of this chapter. Once this juxtaposition is undertaken then three points of significance emerge. First, whilst, as we have indicated, none of these Scottish authorities is strongly developing applications in and around the theme of teledemocracy, three of them - Highland Region, the Western Isles and the Shetland Isles are involved in Scotland's largest public service systems project - the Lambda project - which is designed in part to offer up information and communications support for Island and other remote communities.

Additionally, these authorities have gone further down the path of information support for councillors than most of the other authorities in our sample. These particular authorities lie at the heart of the HII which we discussed above and it would seem therefore that their telematics activities provide *prima facie* support for our hypothesis. However if we take this one step further, then we have to ask why Orkney (also within the HII area) is comparatively inactive in the teledemocratic field. What this may well demonstrate, in further support of our hypothesis, is that enhanced telecommunications infrastructures are a necessary though not a sufficient condition for innovations to occur and that organizational factors such as championing must also be taken into account. Thus, in Orkney, it is only in 1994 that computing and telecommunications specialists have been recruited on to the Council payroll. Until 1994 technical support in ICTs was provided, at a distance, by Highland Regional Council. It should not therefore be viewed as surprising that ICT related innovations, including those surrounding teledemocracy, have not been occurring in this particular Council. Whilst the much heralded enhanced infrastructure is clearly present the aware local champions have not been in place until very recently.

The second point of significance which arises from the juxtaposition of evidence from table 2 and that concerning telecommunications infrastructure development is that two city governments - Aberdeen, Glasgow - together with Lothian Region and, to an extent, Fife Region and Dundee, are relatively advanced in teledemocratic terms particularly in the support which they are offering councillors. None of these authorities has an interest in the HII but each of them includes areas where telecommunications competition is strong. MCL is active in each of these areas and there are active cable franchises here also. Again therefore this data appears broadly and in a *prima facie* sense to validate our hypothesis.

The third point of significance which emerges from this data lies in an examination of those authorities which are neither in the HII area of Scotland, nor in an area where there is a competitive presence in telecommunications. Dumfries and Galloway and Central Region fall perfectly into this category, neither of them having been the subject of telecommunications developments of the sort with which we have been concerned in this chapter. Both of these Regions exhibit a distinct lack of activity in and around advanced telematics in general and teledemocracy in particular.

## 8. Conclusions

Innovations around the theme of teledemocracy are arguably of considerable significance in an era in which some aspects of traditional democratic practice are giving way to new governance structures and procedures infused with business efficiency values. Teledemocracy may indeed be seen, at least in part, as providing ways of rescuing democracy and ensuring its lasting effectiveness. The evidence emerging from UK local governments as a whole is that innovations in teledemocracy are occurring only patchily and unsystematically. One possible reason for this weakness which we have raised is the apparent lack of interest in this topic displayed by the IT professionals in local government. A second possible reason is a more general lack of awareness of the potential for developments brought about by UK telecommunications policy which is causing uneven distribution in telecommunications infrastructure enhancements and uneven distribution of telecommunications competition. Where competition is present, and where infrastructure enhancements are made, then awareness of the potential importance of telecommunications rises and, as our Scottish data shows, innovations appear to occur more frequently.

# CHAPTER 6

# Community Information Systems: Strengthening Local Democracy?

Christine BELLAMY and Ivan HORROCKS
with
Jeff WEBB
*The Nottingham Trent University, Burton Street, Nottingham NG1 4BU, UK*

**Abstract.** This chapter reports on ongoing research by the authors into one dimension of informatization in local government - electronic exchange of information with the public (EIP). After a general introduction to the research program, and brief review of the political context in which EIP is being developed in English local government, the chapter reports on the preliminary findings from the first stage of the research. The focus is on one specific type of EIP project - community information systems (CIS). Finally, the implications for, and of, the development of EIP projects are discussed.

## 1. Introduction

The research on which this chapter is based is part of a program investigating the innovative use of EIP (the exchange of information with the public) to support new forms of service delivery, including the development of community information systems (CIS), in English local government.

The research is concerned with the factors which are promoting, inhibiting and shaping EIP projects, and thus determining the ways EIP is mediating relationships between citizens, bureaucrats and other local political actors. The context is the widespread perception that local government in England requires a new *raison d'être*, and that its future rests on positioning local authorities within new, stronger forms of local politics.

Our program sits within a debate which, in continental Europe and in North America, has focused on the potential for political and community development in (what have variously been called) 'public information utilities', 'citizen information systems' or 'community information systems'. These terms refer to wide access networks which are capable of carrying wide ranging, loosely edited, public information; providing interactive communications (both between citizens and between political leaders and other political actors): and offering customers facilities to undertake a wide range of transactions with public services.

The argument that such networks may have important political implications rests on a number of grounds, reflecting different levels of analysis. Thus, for those who see power in terms of the distribution and exchange of political *resources,* electronic networks may change the significance and distribution of information as a crucial political resource. For example, Doctor sees access to information as a key factor in processes of political 'empowerment' (Doctor 1992). And for those with an interest in the interplay of constitutional forms and political behavior, interactive electronic networks may become an important mediator of the roles and strategies adopted by political actors. Thus van de Donk and Tops (1992) have reviewed the literature which has discussed the impact of new communications techniques on different forms of democracy: representative democracy (for example, email communication between electors and their representatives); 'direct' democracy (for example, electronic plebiscites), and 'active' or 'strong' democracy (for example, communitarian initiatives such as interactive electronic town meetings). For those who focus on the power relationships which structure a political system, new ICT applications have the potential radically to change the flows of information which shape relations between citizens and the state. Thus Arterton (1987) concluded 'They [new technologies] can be used to facilitate the means by which citizens communicate with each other and with their chosen leaders.' Hence a new 'politics of information' would be capable of altering the constitutive relationships of the polity (Bellamy and Taylor 1994).

More fundamentally still, the information carried on new ICTs may embody meanings and symbols which shape perceptions of political systems (Mulgan 1991). Informatization may therefore have profound implications for the 'mobilization of bias' which is manifest in the power relations which underpin the polity. This facet of informatization is perhaps one of the more important in relation to democracy, because of the close connection between democratic rhetoric and the process of legitimation in modern polities. One of the most significant questions, therefore, in discussing the relationship of information technology to local democracy, is the role of new technologies, and the new forms and flows of information which they support, in the definition and redefinition of local politics.

In this chapter we begin to address some of these issues. The structure of the chapter is as follows. Firstly, we provide a brief description of our research. Secondly, we explain briefly the political context in which EIP is being developed in English local government. This paragraph is particularly important because we believe that empirical findings can only be interpreted by reference to the specific context of a country's political culture and institutions. Thus, our major criticism of the existing literature is that discussion of the potential impact of CIS and teledemocracy has been largely abstracted from analysis of the motive forces which shape EIP in specific contexts. Thirdly, we report on the initial findings of our investigations, concentrating on a specific type of EIP - the community information system (CIS). And, finally, we use our findings to speculate on the implications of EIP for the future of local politics in England.

## 2. The Research Program

The initial stage of our research consisted of an extensive review of the international literature on EIP and related applications. This review provided us with historical data on the emergence of electronic EIP, especially the development of community information systems (CIS), and on the development of academic study of this field in both the USA and continental Europe. Together with a preliminary survey of project reports on EIP initiatives in English local government, the publications of practitioner networks, telephone conversations with project managers, and previous survey data, this literature informed our early writing, and provided a basis for our analytical framework.

The major output from this stage was a typology of EIP applications which was developed in response to two problems in mapping the field (Bellamy, Horrocks and Webb 1995). The first problem is that there is a wide range of functionally-specific applications, and the second is that there is an inconsistent and imprecise terminology. We have differentiated applications by reference to two criteria: function, and the degree of 'informatization'. In this way we have arrived at a number of clusters of projects which each form a distinctive 'type' of application (see Fig. 1 below).

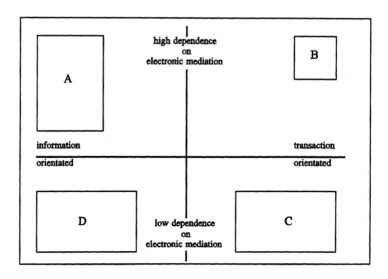

Fig. 1: Exchanging Information with the Public: Mapping the Field

The blocks represent the clustering of types of EIP project. The technologically dependant projects (for example, CIS) fall in blocks A and B. In reality clustering is not as clearly defined. This is particularly true with D and C, where projects actually migrate from one to the other.

(Note: although not indicated on the diagram the axes are continuums)

Key:  A  =  community information systems.
      B  =  electronic one stops shops (eg. expert systems).
      C  =  one stop shops.
      D  =  first stop shops.

We are using this typology to explore the interaction of technological investment and development, on the one hand, and the development of information-dependent services, on the other. In contrast to most of the literature which has concentrated on the *impact* and *utilization* of EIP, our analysis concentrates on the organizational and political *shaping* of EIP. Drawing on Guthrie and Dutton's insight on CIS, that

> '...one can view [its] adoption and design ... as a process comparable to legislating public policy on citizen participation.' (Guthrie and Dutton 1992).

we are focusing primarily on the supply-side politics of technological development and information management.

The second stage of the research is in-depth case study investigation of a limited number of one specific type of EIP ie. community information systems. By April 1994 we had selected six local authorities to participate in a year-long study of the development and operation of CIS. Of the six, five are county councils and one is a metropolitan district council. All our cases are established projects but each one is experiencing ongoing development, though in different ways. Three projects are initiatives of public library departments, one is an initiative of a chief executive's department but is being developed and operated by a library department, and two are initiatives of, and are being developed and operated by, chief executives departments. The collection of data relating to the history of these projects has now been completed, together with an initial round of interviews with key personnel. An extensive round of interviews with a wider range of stakeholders will then be undertaken, and the operation and development of the projects will be tracked.

## 3. The Political Context of EIP

It is frequently said that local government in England consists of a set of locally administered services, rather than the holistic government of a local community. Unlike most continental countries, local authorities in England have no general legal competence to act in the interests of their localities, but operate under discrete series of statutes in relation to each locally-provided service. Similarly, administrative codes, regulations and advice are issued by the central government minister concerned with each policy sector, not by a single Ministry of the Interior. Hence, a local authority can be seen as a set of segmented services, each the responsibility of a different department, each answerable to a different committee of elected representatives, each operating under a different set of laws and regulations, and each relating to a different central government ministry. Despite attempts from the 1970s onwards to strengthen the 'corporate', management of authorities each service remains the domain of a discrete professional group of bureaucrats.

Local government in England performs social investment functions (providing local infrastructure development to support local property and business) and social consumption functions (providing personal and welfare services to individuals). By the 1960s, local authority expenditure was rising at a significantly faster rate than that of central government, reflecting the growing importance of social consumption functions within the welfare state. This growth also produced, of course, a sustained increase in the size of local bureaucracies. For these reasons, local government has been at the center of the so-called 'fiscal crisis of the state' caused by the mismatch of rising expectations and chronically low economic growth (Cochrane 1993). Local government has also been a major employer of members of the 'new' professions - for example, teachers, town planners, social workers, housing managers (Laffin and Young 1990). Thus the 'vertical' policy communities which have formed around different policy sectors connect professional bureaucrats between local and central tiers of government (Rhodes 1986), and it is alleged that these policy communities insulate local services from 'horizontal', local or 'community' influence (Dunleavy 1980). Likewise, professional know-how has formed an effective source of authority in competition with that of the elected representative. Thus, although local authorities have been more active than ever before, it has been argued that their local roots and political autonomy have been progressively weakened (Chandler 1991).

Potentially the most significant counter to professional power has been the expansion of party politics. City councils have been organized on party political lines since the nineteenth century, but by the 1970s, party politics spread to almost all councils (Gyford, Leach and Game 1989). However, party organization has probably not strengthened control by local electors. In many councils, senior politicians form a 'joint elite' with senior professional officers, so that party organization supports rather than counters bureaucratic power (Young and Mills 1983). Secondly, voting behavior at local elections has followed national trends rather than local events. Thirdly, judged as a system of representative government, local government apparently has a large democratic deficit. At around 40%, turnout at local government elections is high by comparison (for example) with the USA, but it is significantly lower than in British parliamentary elections and in most other EU countries (Rallings, Temple and Thrasher 1994). An official report published in 1986 found that less than a third of electors could name their representative (Widdicombe 1986) and Lynn has found that less than one third knew which political party controlled their district council (Lynn 1992). Elected councillors are unrepresentative of the electors in general - being overwhelmingly male, middle aged, and better educated (Rallings, Temple and Thrasher 1994) - and, more worryingly, there is an increasing turnover of councillors and increasing difficulty in recruiting them. Fewer people are willing to stand for election, and even fewer are prepared to serve more than one term. Thus Game and Leach have concluded that local government is approaching a 'precipice' where the tradition of voluntary service will no longer be sustained (Game and Leach 1993). The problems may be reinforced by the complex structure of English local government: thus recent studies have shown that less than a half of the electorate can identify their county council (Widdicombe 1986) and many are confused about the responsibilities of each tier of local government (Morris and Brigham 1993).

The conclusion to be drawn from this analysis is that local authorities have been sheltered from local electoral control. Moreover, neither the discourse nor the practice of local government has been oriented to interests beyond the party activists, the local status systems and the producer, supplier and professional interests. Thus one important feature of local politics has been its 'dual' structure. A network of powerful, competent, 'insider' groups with rich political resources has existed alongside a much less tightly structured set of transient, less competent 'outsider' groups, who have failed to acquire or deploy the political resources that give access to systematic political power.

## 4. EIP Initiatives in Contemporary Local Government

In line with this analysis, EIP projects in contemporary local government can be evaluated as part of the response to two major problems:

> *i/ perceptions within public administration of a widespread loss of confidence in representative government and traditional processes of public accountability which are associated with growing disillusionment with the monolithic, bureaucratic, producer-dominated local state.*

One major consequence of this perception is the 'new public management' (NPM). NPM is the label applied to a set of broad changes in the environment of government (Hood 1991), but, in the UK, one of the most obvious factors has been the ideological influence of the 'New Right' (Farnham and Horton 1993). Thus a recurrent theme in 'new public management' doctrines has been the claim that big bureaucracies inevitably become insulated from electoral influence. Hence, the introduction of contractual relationships, quasi markets, competition and consumerism have all been identified as important instruments for increasing the efficiency and quality of public services. In consequence, local authorities have been compelled by law to contract-out many of their services. The management of many local services, notably education, economic development and industrial training, has been removed from local government, or has been devolved to bodies which are directly controlled by consumers or stakeholders. Hence, though local government departments have become smaller, and the scope of party politics reduced, the organization of local services has been made even more complex. In consequence, both producer and consumer interests in local services have become more segmented.

In the 1980s, the threat posed by NPM to local authorities provoked an alternative response to NPM: the 'public service orientation' (PSO) (Stewart and Clarke 1987). The PSO can be seen as an attempt to strengthen the role and legitimacy of local government by mobilizing popular support for local authorities. However, the proponents of the PSO acknowledged the long term democratic deficit in local government. Hence they attempted to show how local authorities might develop their support in local communities, and thus strengthen local democracy. Thus the PSO had three objectives: increasing efficiency; enhancing responsiveness to *individual customers* who use public services; and, most importantly, rebuilding local government as the *political* organ of the local *community* (Rhodes 1987).

In the 1990s, some of the ideas associated with the PSO have converged with ideas being generated by NPM, as the consumerist tendency within NPM came to the fore under the Major government. In consequence, there has been a growing interest within local authorities in ways in which they become more responsive to their customers: for example many local authorities have decentralized management of services to local communities (Burns, Hambleton and Hoggett 1994). Likewise, the contemporary fashion for one stop services reflects two contemporary preoccupations of local authorities. Firstly, one stop services express a greater orientation to customers, by treating them holistically. Secondly, one stop shops allow local authorities to present a united corporate face to customers, and thus raise the profile of the local authority. Thus, one question posed by our research is the extent to which internal information flows are capable of being reconfigured to support these new kinds of customer interface.

Together with the development of quasi-market relations, the 'new public consumerism' in British public administration has led to the extensive publication of service quality information. For example, hospitals and schools are now compelled to produce 'league tables' which rank services according to a range of performance indicators.

### ii/ the review of the structure and boundaries of local government in England and Wales.

In 1991, central government announced a major Review of the structure of local government, with the aim of creating 'unitary' authorities. The government believed that the existing two tier system of local government in the 'shires' (whereby local government services are divided between a county council and smaller district councils) confuses the electorate and inhibits public accountability. The present two tier structure is the result of a traditional belief that the size of local authorities is a trade-off between democracy and responsiveness (which imply *small*) authorities, and efficiency and technical effectiveness (which imply *large* local authorities) (Redcliffe-Maud 1969). The conventional answer to the democratic deficit in local government - reflected in the original guidance notes for the review - has been to reduce the size of local authorities and to rationalize the structure of local government (Leach 1994). This would imply the abolition of county councils. However, by 1993 the Local Government Commission, the body which is conducting the Review, had stated that the IT revolution had made size an increasingly irrelevant factor in the current review (Local Government Commission 1993).

This statement prompted many English county councils to seek to demonstrate:

i/    that they are actively promoting a public service orientation and are strongly attached to their local communities
ii/   that new information and communications technologies are capable of being exploited in such a way that will invigorate local authorities' relationships with the public.

The result has been that an increasing number of local authorities - particularly county councils - claim to be developing electronic CIS. In practice, the vigor with which CIS are being developed varies considerably.

## 5. Preliminary Research Findings

In the majority of the cases of which we are aware, CIS projects have been developed, and are operated by, local authority public library departments. However, as we have seen, there are three exceptions in our own set of cases which reflect the growing corporate interest of local authorities in CIS.

### 5.1. Motivation

There are three overlapping and conflicting motives for developing CIS. Firstly (chronologically) the development of CIS reflected professional paradigms of service development and quality. For example, many librarians have been moving away from their traditional image as 'bookminder' and are becoming 'information specialists'. This shift has led them to adopt a broader view of a 'good' library service whereby quality is no longer simply measured by the number of books on the shelves but also by the volume and quality of information resources which a public library can provide. Thus, many local authorities have renamed their public library departments 'library and information services' - although this change of orientation has often brought them into conflict with other local authority departments which also provide information.

Secondly, CIS have also been promoted to enhance efficiency in operating library or information services. Local authorities are under chronic financial pressure, and promote the use of ICTs to save staff. For example, new library management systems permit more efficient management of library stock, and some CIS projects amount to no more than the computerization of information already held in public libraries.

Thirdly, and most recently, there is growing corporate pressure for developing CIS, because CIS have been widely identified as an innovative use of new technology to 'get close' to the public. All the county councils in our sample have made, or anticipate making, submissions to the Commission which is conducting the Review, citing their commitment to innovative EIP. In many cases, this commitment supports a policy of decentralization to areas or neighborhoods. One of the most ambitious is Gloucestershire County Council's proposal to develop a network of thirty electronic town halls, located around the county.

### 5.2. Ownership and Shaping

All the initiatives of which we are aware are officer - not politician - led. The importance of committed project champions cannot be overstated, and a feature of all projects in our sample is the existence of one or two people who have taken personal ownership of the project (see also Taylor *et al.* in this volume). However, the most developed projects are those which have also gained top-down support either within the host department or at a corporate level.

We know of no case where a CIS project has emerged from a corporate IT strategy. However, one of our cases is being developed and promoted by a central computing department although it was only one of the actors involved in originating the project. Indeed, what is noticeable is the insulation of CIS projects from central computing capabilities in local authorities which continue to be oriented to mainframe computing to perform 'horizontal' administrative functions (especially finance). For example, CIS are generally run either as a module attached to a library service mainframe system, or on a PC network, and have typically evolved from videotext systems. Both typically use dial-in lines to connect remote public terminals to centrally maintained databases. We have also noticed that many project champions are prepared to undertake modifications to PC programs, to customize standard commercial packages in order to construct a CIS. For example, a widespread complaint about the commercial databases which are available to run public information services is the absence of a facility to organize fields by geographical area, which undermines a major rationale for developing CIS, especially in large county councils. In contrast to the growing technical skills of project champions, it is consistently reported that central computing staff have little awareness of 'vertical' community or service oriented applications of ICTs. If this finding is borne out in further interviews, it may be of considerable importance for the future professional shaping of CIS and EIP in general.

## 5.3. Funding

Almost all CIS projects are significantly under resourced, largely because local authorities have very small uncommitted expenditure available as a proportion of their total budget. Very little finance is available to invest in new technology for innovative, service delivery purposes, and even less is available for the staff time required to develop and customize systems. Consequently, the choice of packages to run CIS has often been determined by the need to find a bolt-on for existing systems, and this problem has restricted the functionality of systems.

The problems of developing (as opposed to initiating) CIS reflect the fact that public information systems form a marginal service in local authorities. Other than the provisions of the 1985 (Access to Information) Act (which requires most council papers to be made available to the public) local authorities have a limited legal duty to provide information, and none to provide information services. Thus CIS take second place in the competition for resources behind statutory services. Secondly, although many public library services see value in CIS as part of a wider information function, CIS does not fall within service delivery paradigms of most local authority professions. Thus, there are major problems is securing cross departmental support for CIS.

These problems have led to the consideration of commercial sponsorship, or partnerships with business interests. It is no accident that the most developed project in our set has an agreement with a commercial sponsor to carry advertising in return for the provision of additional terminals. The new terminals are being placed in shopping malls and other well-used public places, whereas most CIS terminals are located in council offices or libraries. However, respondents from other projects report a reluctance to enter into commercial sponsorship or advertising because they fear loss of control. In addition, many projects do not yet have a sufficient number of outlets to attract commercial involvement, and this issue has been recently clouded by the commercial failure of a company which had successfully tempted the champions of a number of projects into partnership.

## 5.4. *Information Supply and Management*

Local authority CIS typically carry a range of information about local government services, and a growing range of information about community organizations and services, for example, information about local colleges, services for the disabled or medical self-help groups. Some systems also carry information provided by central government. For example, the Social Security Benefits Agency provides monthly packs of information about welfare benefits and local offices specifically for use in public IS. And the Central Office of Information (COI) provides packages with other central government information. Increasingly, too, local authority CIS projects are receiving approaches from other statutory local agencies, especially community health authorities which are now compelled to provide information for consumers of their services. And, as we saw above, there are active questions about whether, and to what extent, public CIS should carry commercial or quasi-commercial information. Indeed, there is a problem in defining commercial information. For example, should CIS carry tourist information provided by local hotels?

There are a number of important issues tied up in the range and sourcing of information carried by CIS. These issues are made much more salient by the increasing fragmentation of local public services, and by the threat to local authorities by the Local Government Review. For example, there is a tension between the professional aspirations of information specialists - to provide comprehensive information to the public - and the promotion of County Councils' corporate identity. For example, we can cite a case where a county council CIS has been prohibited from carrying information about district councils within the county, without the payment of a fee.

As well as advantages for the quality of service provided to the community, there are also advantages of scale and scope for public authorities in collaborating in providing CIS. Thus, the sharing of hardware, telephone lines, mainframe computing time and information processing know-how, could all permit the provision of a more comprehensive, more widely-available service, at lower cost to each provider. However, in practice, the realization of these advantages is inhibited by a number of problems. The first problem is that, although the COI and a few other large agencies produce purpose-built information for public IS, most information is generated by the operational requirements of the agencies which produce it. Thus it is not held in a form which is suitable for public use, and it is also held in a widely distributed range of (incompatible) computer systems and clerical files. At present, therefore, electronic importation of information into CIS is not occurring on a significant scale, and most information is transferred by means of paper and manual inputting, or on disk. This process involves significant financial costs and it also means that most CIS is restricted to carrying relatively stable datasets. For example, we know of a CIS which carried lists of job vacancies provided by the local Job Centre, but withdrew the service when it found that the lists could not be updated quickly enough. This appears to be a problem which applies to a good deal of the information on CIS.

A second set of problems concern the specification and editing of information carried on CIS. Most public service information must be substantially edited to be suitable for public exposure on a CIS. There are two sets of issues here. The first is, simply, who pays for the editing? This problem is being exacerbated by the current program of externalizing local government functions and by the shift within local authorities to devolved budgets and internal cost centers. More information is seen to be 'commercially sensitive', and, even where departments or agencies are willing to share it, it is acquiring a price. The second, more politically difficult, issue arises because of the diversity of professional discourses from which information is sourced. Library and information specialists are asserting their professional expertise in the design of public IS, including the screen design, and the terminology, synonyms and symbols which are used to order and present information. Thus they are cutting across the idioms of other professions, in ways that challenge their power to control their own discourses. For example, we have found an example of a social services department which withdrew information from a CIS, because it failed to prevent the CIS displaying information for a disadvantaged group in 'politically incorrect' language. In this case, the librarian in charge of the CIS insisted on organizing information under a field-name she judged to be in general use.

Despite these difficulties there are a number of factors which are creating pressures on authorities of many kinds to expand the informational range of CIS. Firstly, we have already noted that 'the new public consumerism' associated with NPM is forcing many public services - including hospitals, schools, and colleges - to make information public, and there are obvious advantages in collaboration with other agencies. Secondly, there are bottom-up pressures from members of the public and, therefore, from street level staff. Indeed, a problem for CIS is that, although public service information is owned by specific service providing agencies, clients have holistic information requirements. Hence, we suggest that in order to secure high volumes of usage, and therefore widespread public acceptance, CIS projects will be forced to increase the range of information carried. Thus they will be forced to extend the range of agencies from which it is sourced.

In practice, the range of CIS will probably be determined by a series of inter-departmental or inter-agency alliances which will be negotiated by project champions. The external sourcing of information for CIS meets, indeed, many of the classic conditions for a long term partnership to be formed between suppliers and operational managers. That is, CIS projects need customized information, supplied reliably and consistently. Furthermore, because economical information transfer would be promoted by compatible computing systems, there is also a degree of asset specificity (Williamson 1975). Two political implications follow from this analysis. Firstly, the range and content of CIS will be determined by the patterns of local partnerships which are formed in each locality. Thus CIS will be shaped by the propensity of agencies to enter into, and maintain, such partnerships. Secondly, the technical and organizational capacity to assemble, collate and format community information, and to make it available for CIS in appropriate form, is not likely to be distributed widely within the community. Thus, the costs and risks to a local authority of developing and maintaining CIS will be reduced, the fewer suppliers it uses. Indeed, we have found a pattern whereby CIS projects are forming partnerships with 'umbrella' community organizations rather than dealing direct with a large number of small community groups. Hence, we postulate that information processing capabilities may be crucial to the emergence of a new role for intermediary bodies.

## 5.5. Distribution, Access, Function and Usage of CIS

In county councils with large geographical jurisdictions and a high proportion of rural areas, CIS are being used to provide a county council presence in villages and townships where there has hitherto been a sparse coverage. In this sense, CIS are producing a 'Heineken effect', reaching parts of counties that other services do not easily reach. However, to save costs, terminals are often placed in public buildings, especially small branch libraries. Hence, access to systems may be restricted to the traditional customers of the host service.

It would be interesting to compare the usage of terminals in public libraries with those in shopping malls, but most projects do not analyze usage terminal by terminal, or by socio-economic category of user. One reason is that most commercial packages are adapted from business information systems or library management systems, which do not offer this facility. However, the very sparse information which does exist suggests that the propensity to use electronic CIS is particularly high amongst young males, who are perceived to be hard to reach by more traditional methods.

Interviews with project champions indicate that they are attempting to extend the coverage of terminals, and to target specific types of client group. There is consistent interest in placing CIS into schools and colleges. This would permit the provision of customized information services for a receptive age-group, and would encourage 'political education' by promoting awareness of local government among the young. Project managers report high interest from teachers, but the financial costs to schools of open access dial-in systems are often prohibitive. Hence, a major imperative for many projects is to develop off-line versions of CIS which could be run from disks.

As we said above, there is some awareness that CIS might eventually form the core of one stop shops for council services (as proposed in Gloucestershire) or to support community based services or neighborhood forums (as [supposedly] in Bradford). Amongst the councils who have identified the potential for 'reengineering' information flows on a corporate basis is Oxfordshire County Council. The salience of cross departmental information flows to support the OXCIS system (which is one of the most advanced examples of local authority CIS) has stimulated fundamental questions about the nature and coordination of information management within the authority. A recent report has therefore highlighted ways in which information flowing to elected members could be improved, as well as ways in which the better use of information could support more uniform, higher quality services throughout the county.

We have, as yet, no systematic information about the awareness and use of CIS by elected representatives, although some councils make equipment available to councillors, either communally or privately. We have also identified a few politicians who have promoted CIS in committee. CIS usually carry political information (council agendas, dates of meetings, details of councillors etc.) but the evidence is that this information is seldom used. This lack of interest is frequently taken as justification for not developing 'teledemocratic' facilities but our firm impression, thus far, is that teledemocracy is not on an active agenda. Nevertheless, county councils are beginning to collaborate with parish councils in the provision of CIS. We interpret this interest to be generated in part by the need to mobilize parish councils in defence of the present structure of local government. In the same way, interest in the interactive use of CIS is sporadic. The historical genesis of CIS in library services has placed an emphasis on the one-way *dissemination* of centrally edited information, conceived of as a public resource.

## 6. Discussion

The widespread interest in developing CIS has spawned a number of projects. This chapter has been concerned with the motivation for, and inhibitors of, CIS projects within the political context of English local government. In effect, therefore, it has focused on the way in which the informational requirements of projects interplay with the dominant features of local politics and government. In this last paragraph, we speculate about the implications for, and of, the development of EIP, basing our discussion on the example of CIS.

First we consider how far EIP might strengthen local electoral control, and reduce the 'democratic deficit' of local government. In establishing and implementing the Review of local government structure, the Government and the Local Government Commission have both worked on the assumption that effective representative government requires electors to be informed about, and to identify with, their elected local authority. Hence, many local authorities are submitting evidence from social surveys to testify to the knowledge and preferences of local people. County councils have therefore adopted CIS as a short term device to raise their profile, especially in more remote parts of their counties. To a large extent, this objective has determined the presentation and nature of information carried on CIS, with prominence being given to enhancing the image of the provider. It is also determining some of the target client groups or locations at which CIS is being aimed. In other words, CIS can be seen as an attempt to use electronically mediated information to shape cognitions of, and to legitimize, existing governmental structures.

While central government has emphasized the need to rationalize local government, the New Public Management has, at the same time, increased the complexity of local governance structures. We saw above that the political need to achieve high acceptance and usage of CIS (by widening the range of public service information) may conflict with the requirement to raise the profile of county councils (at the expense of other authorities). Our conclusion is however that CIS do not respect administrative boundaries. We suggested above that as CIS develop, there will be a strengthening of street level pressure to include a wider range of public service and community information. Thus we suggest that if CIS were to become widely available and widely used, their overall effect might be to challenge administrative fragmentation. Indeed, CIS might create a stronger sense of a holistic community as a counter to the disaggregating effects of NPM, and in this way they might support more communitarian conceptions of local politics.

However, this analysis points up the political significance of the *construction* of CIS. Our thesis is that the structuration of fields within the databases on which CIS are based reflects, and shapes, perceptions of the important client interests served by local authorities. Thus, we saw above that a common feature of local government CIS is the redefinition of fields by geographical area, thus permitting the customization of information for specific neighborhoods or villages. Similarly, CIS databases have been reconstructed to target specific client groups. The simple point is that, along with contemporary EIP initiatives to develop one stop shops (or other projects) aimed at specific client groups or neighborhoods, CIS may have two major political implications. The first is that the way EIP is constructed is not distributionally neutral: such initiatives structure access to public services. Secondly, and perhaps more significantly, they shape, confirm or challenge the perceptions of political actors of the cleavages around which politics is structured within a community. Thus, in a more profound way they also structure political agendas.

For these reasons, the control of EIP applications is likely to be politically important. Thus one important question is whether EIP will strengthen or weaken the professional domination of local government (see also Snellen this volume). The answer, we think, is that its effects will be ambiguous. On the one hand, the development of information-rich public services, like CIS, one stop shops or neighborhood offices, will challenge professional domains. This is because all these types of project depend upon the sharing of information horizontally *between* services. Hence they challenge the vertical segmentation of public services. Furthermore, we saw above that CIS challenges not only the ownership of information, but the control of the discourse on which its specification is based. Thus, EIP goes to the heart of the identity and ideology of professional groups. This is a major reason, indeed, why true one stop shops and inclusive CIS are politically difficult to construct (Bellamy and Taylor 1994).

On the other hand, the development of EIP may stimulate the emergence of new, powerful, public service professions - ones with horizontal rather than vertical remits. Thus, many studies of electronic service delivery have emphasized the power of computing specialists with technical skills - in collaboration with commercial suppliers - to shape applications and the services on which they depend. In contrast, our research has identified the potential power of *information* specialists to shape EIP. This power rests on a number of factors. Firstly, their professional experience combines with the high level language used in many commercial applications to permit them to take hands-on control of systems. Secondly, although central computing departments still frequently advise on procurement procedures in local authorities, the new emphasis on devolved management, and the contracting out of many computing departments has given computer users - including CIS project managers - greater freedom to develop their own systems. Thirdly, public access to information services has given information specialists the basis for mediating between information providers and the public, in the nominal interests of the end users of information.

Just as Pratchett has demonstrated the power of policy communities in influencing the shape of local authority computing systems (Pratchett 1994), so, in the course of our research, we have become aware of an emergent policy community in the field of local authority information systems. This policy community comprises project managers, commercial suppliers and representatives of national 'peak' organizations, such as the Local Government Management Board. The policy community operates through two networks. Firstly, small user groups have formed around each of the major commercial applications which are available in this field, with the objective of shaping their development. Secondly, there is a national group (*The Society of Public Information Networks - SPIN*) with membership from a wide range of projects, consultants, suppliers and academics. *SPIN* seeks to provide a forum for discussion, exchange of information and to some degree act as a coordinating and liaison body within the policy community. For both these reasons new CIS projects are likely to be significantly influenced by projects already in the field. Hence, we see the development of producer domination of the politics of EIP.

The last issue we discuss is whether EIP will modify the dual structure of interest groups in local politics. In particular, will it reduce the influence of large umbrella or intermediary groups? Whereas many academics have argued that the application of ICTs will weaken political intermediaries (see van de Donk and Tops, chapter two), our analysis of the politics of information *supply* produces a more ambiguous view. Thus we place emphasis on the capacity of organizations to acquire, process and communicate information. In the context of EIP we see the distribution of such capacity to be an important political resource: hence, intermediary organizations are likely to be well placed, for two main reasons. Firstly, and most obviously, they are likely to have the financial, technical and human resources to develop a relatively sophisticated information capability. Secondly, in the case of CIS they may be well positioned to mediate in the politics of information supply by being able to provide a bridge between the professional sensibilities of information suppliers and the requirements of CIS project managers. For these reasons we believe that the extensive development of EIP which requires externally sourced, or relatively highly processed information, would be likely to lead to the reconstruction rather than the dissolution of dual political structures. By the same analysis, the professionalization of citizen-oriented information management may extend the CIS policy community into the larger voluntary organizations, as well as providing the basis for coordination between the statutory public service agencies.

## 7. Conclusion

The overall conclusion of this chapter is that EIP may have important consequences for local politics. Thus EIP may undermine the present vertical segmentation of local politics, and may therefore go someway towards supporting a new holistic identity for local communities. Nevertheless, we do not see EIP as promoting greater local democracy. We have argued in this chapter that though the producer-dominated, *functionally oriented* politics of local government may well be under challenge, the development of new kinds of information-dependent services may cause it to be reconfigured rather than dissolved. In particular, we may be witnessing the emergence of new kinds of professional influence, based on authority to mediate the management of information. Indeed, our analysis suggest that it is access to information management capabilities that may in future distinguish insider and outsider interests in the emerging information polity, and will be an important factor in the alliances and political networks which will control and shape local politics.

# CHAPTER 7

# Informatization of Public Administration as an Instrument of Change to a More Democratic Society

Mirko VINTAR

*University of Ljubljana, School of Public Administration,*
*Kardeljeva ploščad 5, 61000 Ljubljana, Slovena*

**Abstract.** Especially in countries in transition democratization of the society is normally considered to be a question of establishing a coherent system of democratic institutions, starting with freely elected representative bodies at all levels of the state. However, our experience is that this may not be enough. Especially at the local level, other activities and instruments may be as or even more important. That is, in municipalities, the guarantee of equal opportunities and treatment of citizens by local authorities, may be an equally important dimension of democracy. This means that the relationship between the citizens and local authorities could be the best indicator in everyday life of democratization.
In this chapter we analyze the opportunities offered by new information and communications technologies (ICTs), and computer supported cooperative work systems in particular, to bridge the gap between the citizens and public services in local authorities in Slovenia.

## 1. Introduction

How and to what extent informatization can in future lead to changes in democratic procedures and decision making processes is a wide-open question. There is no doubt that in the information societies, which are emerging in most developed countries of Western Europe (Bangemann 1994), where there is a well established democratic tradition, systems of governance will have to be adjusted to new social and technological conditions.

In the broadest sense informatization of public administration implies better flow of information and better access to information for those involved in communications both in public administration and generally in society, including both the various public authorities and agencies.

It is our strong belief, that the relationship between the citizens, on one hand, and the quality and accessibility of public services, on the other hand, is one of the practical ways in which democracy is put to practical test. Besides, this is also the point in the political system where information and communications technologies can be used most effectively to improve the present situation.

When we analyse the role of ICTs on the quality of public services, we can utilize a long list of possible improvements and benefits which are already more or less known (Polomski 1993, Reinermann 1992). These benefits include:

* the acceleration of administrative work,
* better access to information,
* reduction of costs,
* professional improvement of administrative work,
* improved reliability of administrative work,
* transparency,
* closeness to the citizen,
* rationalization,
* systematization,
* standardization,

a.s.o.

However, for the purposes of our discussion, there are two issues on this list, on which we should focus in the first place. These are:

* improved access to information, and
* closeness to the citizens.

Taking the first point (i.e. better access to relevant information for citizens and those who play more active roles in political life) ICTs have been used in the past more or less as a 'one way street'. That is, it has been used i.e. to collect information about citizens and their property mainly for the purpose of taxation, for other similar administrative tasks and for different statistical and planning purposes. An average citizen did not benefit much in return.

In contrast, the main emphasis in future informatization will need to be on the second issue. That is, it will be on bringing all public services closer to their users and this way it will close or even eliminate the gap between citizens and public officials.

By 'closeness to the citizens' we understand the establishment of a 'user friendly' administrative system which can provide citizens with:

* better access to public servants and their help when it is needed,
* a more active role in solving administrative problems,
* a more active role in decision making processes,
* better control of public servants and their work, a.s.o.

In the next paragraphs of this chapter we will analyse the changes in the process of informatization in public adminsitration which will be necessary in the future to improve the present situation in the ways we have discussed.

## 2. Informatization as an Instrument of Change

For many years, the use of ICTs in public administration has been percieved mainly as the automation of routine tasks and procedures. This approach has resulted in the creation of more or less isolated technological islands, while the organizational context has been virtually unchanged.

We can say therefore that in the past the use of ICTs was mainly technology driven rather than content driven: the real needs of administrative processes were not in question. On the contrary, the question which was normally asked was what technology should be used to automate administration. That is, the usual supposition was that all automation brings positive results.

Only very recently has the term informatization acquired wider meaning, and it now implies organizational and even social change, as well as technological innovation.

By 'informatization', a term originally coined by Nora and Minc (1978), we normally understand a proces including five elements (Frissen 1989):

1. The introduction of information technology to shape or take care of information retrieval by means of automated information systems.
2. The rearrangement of information flows and information relationships to facilitate the management information process.
3. The adjustment or change of the organizational structure into which information technology is introduced.
4. The development of information policies as a differentiated area of decision-making within the organization.
5. The introduction of specific expertise in the field of information technology through functionaries or consultants with tasks in this field.

We believe that all this five elements of this definition of informatization can be applied to the area we are addressing in our chapter. The introduction of new ICTs offers a good opportunity to radically change working procedures and reengineer processes. But this is possible only if we understand informatization to include the dimensions which are summarized above.

## 3.  A Case Study of Document Management Systems Used by Governmental Agencies at Local and State Level in Slovenia

Implementation of ICTs in public administration started in Slovenia quite early, in the late 1960s when some very big computer centers were built and automation of two larger administrative areas, for example tax collection, and registration of real estate began.

Today with an average of one PC for every four employees in governmental agencies, it is possible to say that informatization in public administration in Slovenia is well under way. The so called second generation of tools and solutions is about to emerge, and will replace almost everything to which we were used in the past. In introducing this new generation, the main battle to be fought will be between paper documents and paper based administrative procedures and so-called electronic documents, for which a new administrative paradigm still needs to be conceived and implemented in practice.

The management of documents and records within administrative processes at local and state level plays a very important role in efforts to improve efficiency and reduce costs in public administration.

The majority of records, which flow through information systems in public administration today, are now (different kinds of) applications, official letters, contracts and other documents by means of which citizens try to solve their private or business problems under the law.

Hence this is the main communication channel and sorce of conflict between citizens and the administration, where the closeness of public services to the citizens can be tested every day. In order to illustrate the complexity and the various dimensions of this important problem we will give the results of a survey carried out in Slovenia at the local administrative level:

* Authorities in public administration have to handle over five million administrative files (or about twenty million documents) every year (Slovenia is a relatively small country with only about two million inhabitants). And this only at the local level.
* ten-fifteen percent of the labor force in public administration is directly employed in clerical jobs which are involved in classifying, registering and conveying paper documents and maintaining records, files and archives.
* About twenty-thirty percent of all office working time is spent handling, writing and searching for written documents.
* The transportation of administrative files in paper form is the most time-consuming activity within the processing cycle of a file, and this accounts for up to ninety percent of all the time spent processing a file.

A great deal of the communications among different parties in public organizations and with citizens is still based on clerical forms and papers, even though new communications technologies, like electronic mail, telefax, telex, an so on are well under way. Systematic management of written documents is an important instrument of efficient management and control in all public services. PC-based filing systems were introduced at the end of the eighties in most governmental agencies in Slovenia, in the context of the organizational system shown in figure 1.

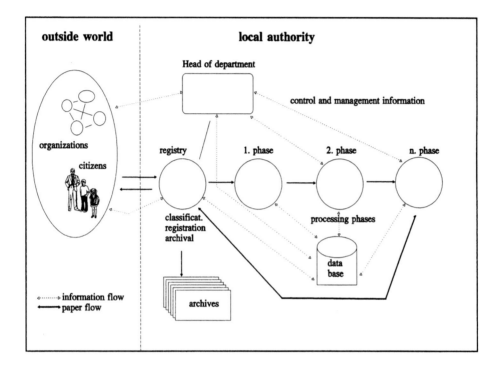

Fig. 1: The organizational model based on the first generation of the computer based filing systems

By means of a special survey we tried to assses the results of this process, and its influence on the quality of public services. We can summarize our findings in the following points :

* The common opinion of the users was that the flow of information inside agencies has been improved considerably, and this has contributed to the improvement of efficiency and has increased productivity.
* Searching of files and documents has improved considerably.
* Heads of organizational units and departments have much better insight into the state of files and important administrative cases.

Nevertheless many problems in the past have remained virtually unchanged. For example :

* no great changes happened, although the system provided a platform for a new, better organizational way of processing administrative files,
* the throughput of organizational units did not change noticeably,
* response times and overall quality of service for citizens did not improve noticeably.

We can conclude therefore that from the point of view of the average citizen who must too often wait in front of the different counters and doors of officials, informatization has not, thus far, brought much comfort. Nor has it removed the traditional gap between citizens and public servants.

## 4.   Implementation of New ICT Solutions as an Instrument of Change

The common platform on which a great number of administrative procedures will be executed in the near future will be a kind of a computer supported cooperative work system (CSCWS). This is an acronym for a set of software solutions which provide a computer supported platform (groupware) for groups or teams working on common tasks or problems. There is a very versatile family of approaches, solutions, packages, document management systems, tools, which roughly fit together but often have hardly anything in common.

We will discuss CSCWS by looking at an area which is very important for every day practice in public administration. That is, we will analyze the opportunities of implementing groupware systems and technologies for processing administrative files, which represents a major aspect of work in governmental offices at the state and municipal level. Our analysis is based on our own experience, which was gained through introducing these type of solutions in government agencies in Slovenia.

There are at least two concepts which must be analyzed in more detail:

* workgroup computing/management and
* workflow computing/management.

Both concepts have been only roughly defined, and different authors understand those terms to mean different things (Pickering 1994, Boelscher 1994). Both concepts have been connected for some years with a special sort of software product, for which the generic name 'groupware' has become very popular. In order to take our own analysis further, we must first try to define what we understand by both of those terms.

Workgroup computing is a concept around which a family of software solutions, tools and packages has been developed, trying to support the work of groups on the following activities:

* time management,
* workflow management,
* group decision making,
* teleconferencing,
* brain-storming,

a.s.o.

As can be seen, workflow management is a much narrower concept which can be (but is not necessarily) a part of the workgroup management solution. Workflow management solutions can be treated as a development of Email systems. We can define the following types of workflow management systems (Moukhtarzadeh 1993):

* document flow systems,
* process automation,
* job automation.

We can also make a further distinction between these two concepts. By workgroup computing, we mean computer support for a group of people working on a set of activities which are mainly unstructured, and where each member of the group must be given as much freedom as possible, to contribute creatively to the work and results of the group (Reinermann 1992). On the other hand, the concept 'workflow management' is focused on a set of structured activities related to the processing, and movement (and monitoring of this movement) of objects where these objects can be of different types (Boelscher 1993).

These solutions can be used to support processes, where:

* many administrative or professional workers are working on the same procedure or task,
* the procedures or tasks are similarly well structured and repetitive,
* the competition of the procedure consists of many steps and activities,
* processes are work-intensive,
* processes are important for the organization and its functioning.

As we can see, both concepts we have analyzed lead directly to the idea of computer supported cooperative work systems (CSCWS) which promise many advantages compared to the majority of existing office automation solutions, that is:

* With new ICTs, inter-organizational information systems are becoming reality. We need to redefine organizational structures, responsibilities, and boundaries to make progress in the direction of inter-organizational IS.
* The strict sequential processing of administrative files, which was necessary in the past because of the physical nature of paper based files, will need to be redefined.
* There will need to be less Taylorism and a less strict division of labor.
* Most of the centralized functions of registry offices will need to be decentralized.

All of these changes will bring about many other changes especially in relation to the main subject of our present discussion. That is, with inter-organizational information systems citizens will be able to secure much more direct access to the public services than before. We will be able to establish a new paradigm for the organization of public information systems which is shown in figure 2, with, for example, a much better flow of information, better control, and more transparency of procedures. The traditional walls between the citizens and public servants and public authorities could be virtually eliminated.

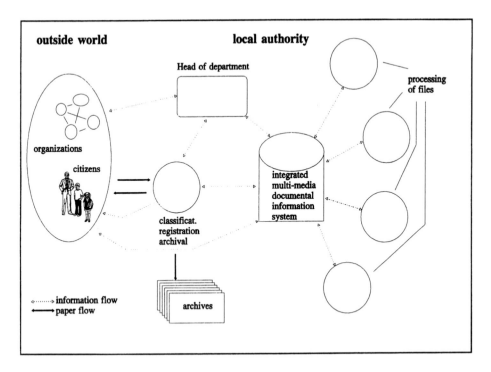

Fig. 2: The organizational model based on the use of CSCWS

## 5. Towards a new Organizational Paradigm in Public Administration

Nearly all administrative procedures, organizational solutions, instructions and standards, in use today, which govern the behavior of governmental agencies, originate from the 1960s or 1970s, and are based on the assumption that all the information necessary to carry out a procedure will be stored on paper documents. Hence paper documents are still the main medium of communication between the citizens and public servants.

With the first flood of mainframe based computers and even with later on PC based solutions, this situation did not much change.

We believe that implementation of CSCWS can bring many changes, and should be based on:

* reengineering administrative processes and
* replacement of paper documents with 'electronic' documents.

It can be easily seen that nearly all office technologies known today should be integrated, to secure an efficient platform for implementing CSCWS in public administration. In addition, the following questions are pertinent to the use of CSCWS in public administration, and should be raised and analyzed, if we are to avoid past mistakes arising from the prevalence of technology-driven solutions.

These questions are about:

* the goals of modernizing and automating public administration, in terms of the further development of administrative practice,
* the necessary characteristics of CSCWS in the light of the goals, which are thus defined,
* document management and the replacement of paper documents by electronic documents,
* reengineering administrative procedures,
* possible drawbacks of the use of CSCWS in public administration.

We can expect an acceleration of administrative work processes to arise from the implementation of CSCWS. This expectation is based mainly on the assumption that CSCWS will replace the majority of paper documents by electronic documents. As a consequence, the time taken to process and transport, which represents up to 90% of all the time necessary to deal with a typical administrative file, will be shortened or even eliminated.

The improvement of professional administrative practice is certainly a high priority among the improvements to be anticipated from the implementation of new technologies. There are many ways in which CSCWS can influence how administrative work is carried out. Using CSCWS every activity of public servants will be much more traceable, visible and controllable, a fact which can contribute to the overall improvement of administrative and professional work.

## 6.   Reengineering Administrative Procedures

From our definition of the term 'informatization', it will be evident that simply understanding how new technology works offers no guarantee that it will be successfully implemented. When we talk about integrated solutions, such as CSCWS, it is very important to analyze organizational issues along with technical issues. These issues include: analyzing flows of data and documents, formal and informal communication paths, and problems of social acceptance.

The classical organizational model in public administration has been based on the assumption that the paper document is the basic communication medium. Administrative files start their life cycle where they are registered and then proceed from stage to stage being physically transported from one public servant to another. The first generation of computer based office tools and solutions, did not lead to much progress in the organizational sense. Administrative procedures remained virtually the same.

With the next generation of ITs, of which CSCWS are a good example, we will need to reengineer nearly all existing administrative processes, and redefine organizational structures, responsibilities and boundaries to make progress in the direction of inter-organizational IS.

Strict sequential processing of administrative files, which was necessary in the past because of the physical nature of paper-based files, can now be abandoned and avoided. The organizational structures and hierarchies can become flatter with fewer organizational levels and a less strict division of labor.

All these changes will bring about many other changes, including the nature of and the skills which are necessary, personnel structure, a.s.o.

## 7. Conclusions

We have tried to present our own experiences of implementing ICTs in public administration in Slovenia, focussing on a new generation of computer solutions based on CSCWS. The implementation of new ICTs is rapidly on the way, but organizationally, legally and even psychologically the majority of public organizations are unprepared for this step.

The most important characteristic of CSCWS is a capacity to improve communication between workers, departments, agencies and the outside world, including the citizens who are the main customers of public services. The flexibility of electronic documents proved to be very beneficial, especially in more complex administrative cases. Public servants will be better informed and able to react more promptly and professionally.

All these changes can improve the quality of public services and bring them closer to users, and this is an important attribute of democratic society.

# CHAPTER 8

# Computer based Tools for Cooperative Work among Politicians and Officials in Danish Local Government

Erik FRØKJÆR

*Datalogisk Institut Københavns Universitet*
*Universitetsparken 1 DK-2100 København Ø*

Helge KORSBÆK

*Christiansvej 29 DK-2920 Charlottenlund*

Halldór FÆRCH

*Kommunedata I/S*
*Lautrupparken 40 DK-2750 Ballerup*

**Abstract.** A council system - an experimental CSCW (Computer Supported Cooperative Work) system with the objective of supporting the daily work of politicians - was introduced and applied by town councillors and a section of the administration in Ravnsborg, a small Danish municipality, during a two-year period from 1992-94. The town council participated in a project which aimed at a simpler municipal administrative structure than the one laid down in the legislation for local government, by omitting out the permanent committees under the town council. The computer based system has supported the effectiveness of the implementation of political decisions by strengthening the exchange of information and the coordination between the politicians and the officials. The essential problems raised by the system relate to a possible deterioration of human contacts, and to unintented changes in the functioning of parts of the organization.
A brief presentation of the content and form of local government in Denmark is included to aid understanding of the political administrative context of the experiment.

## 1. Introduction

An experimental system with the objective of supporting the daily work of politicians in relation to the officials and to other politicians was introduced and applied by town councillors and a section of the administration in a small Danish municipality, Ravnsborg, during a two-year period from January 1992 to February 1994. The system, which is an example of a rather new, interesting type of computer based tool, called

CSCW (Computer Supported Cooperative Work) systems (Baecker 1993, Grudin 1991, Rodden 1991) or groupware (Coleman 1993, Ellis, Gibbs and Rein 1991), is currently under implementation on a more permanent basis. So far, few examples of a successful organizational implementation of this type of system have been reported.

The town council decided to participate in a project which aimed at simplifying the municipal administrative structure compared to the one laid down in the local government legislation, by leaving out the permanent committees of the town council. As part of the project, Kommunedata, the nation wide software company servicing the Danish municipalities, developed a CSCW system that gave the members of the town council electronic access to the agendas of the council meetings including the supplementary written information. Further, a news service, an overview of municipal key-figures, and, not least important, an electronic mail-system (Email) with facilities to support 'discussions' between members of the council were made available by the system. During the two-year experimental period the CSCW system was used only by the council members and the officials of the council secretariat. Following a decision of the council in May 1994 to continue to use the CSCW system, the system will be extended to cover the rest of the municipal administration.

To give the reader an understanding of the political administrative context of the experiment in the municipality of Ravnsborg, a concise presentation of the content and form of local government in Denmark is included as paragraph 2.


## 2. The Position of Local Government in Denmark

Public administration in Denmark is divided between the state, 14 counties and 275 municipalities including Copenhagen and Frederiksberg, the two units which together constitute the central part of the Capital and which have a dual status being responsible for county tasks as well as municipal tasks.

Each county and each municipality has its own politically elected government. According to article no. 82 of the constitution 'the right of counties and municipalities to manage their own affairs independently under the supervision of the state shall be laid down by statute'. This formula was introduced in the first free constitution in 1849. It implies: (1) the existence of a number of municipalities which have certain tasks which are managed with a degree of independence; (2) the existence of supervision by the state; and (3) the municipal tasks and the degree of independence for the municipalities in their management is for parliament to decide, not for the government or a minister. A further implication is that municipalities and counties respectively are formally put on the same footing in relation to the state.

The distribution of tasks between the state, the counties, and the municipalities has over the years been characterized by an increasing decentralization, especially after the latest municipal reform which became effective after 1970. According to the present distribution of tasks, public services that are frequently used by the citizens are provided by the municipalities, e.g. primary schools, kindergartens, different kinds of day-care institutions and a variety of professional services. The main tasks of the counties on the other hand, are the maintenance and construction of highways - other than motorways - hospitals, secondary schools, and residential social institutions. The remaining public tasks are taken care of by the state, i.e. police, courts, defence, universities, research institutions, the main public museums, and a number of non-privatized enterprises, e.g. the post and railway services and state forestry.

As a result of this distribution of tasks the state is directly responsible for activities that take about 39 percent of public expenditure, whereas the municipal share is 41 percent, and that of the counties nearly 11 percent. The remaining 9 percent is left to different social funds, primarily funds for unemployment benefits. Total public expenditure amounts to about 520 billion DKR or 60 percent of the gross national product at market prices (Statistisk Tiårsoversigt 1993).

Turning to public employment, one finds the same pattern. Out of a total labor force of 2.9 million persons (Statistisk Tiårsoversigt 1993) about 27 percent were employed in the public service sector. In 1991, 193,000 persons were employed by the state, 152,000 persons by the counties, and 447,000 persons by the municipalities (Statistisk Årbog 1994).

The number of counties and, especially, the number of the municipalities was drastically reduced in the municipal reform of 1970 in an effort to create larger municipalities that were less dependent on the state-subsidies for the management of their current affairs. The differences in size are still considerable. Out of 275 municipalities, including the two metropolitan municipalities, 137 had less than 10,000 inhabitants, 123 had 10-50,000 inhabitants, and only 15 municipalities had more than 50,000 inhabitants. The differences between the 14 counties are relatively smaller. Only one county had less than 200,000 inhabitants, seven counties had 200-300,000 inhabitants, four counties had 300-500,000 inhabitants, and two counties had more than 500,000 inhabitants. (Befolkningen i Kommunerne 1994).

In 1990 county income taxes corresponded to nearly 2/3 of the counties' expenditure while nearly 21 percent was met by general grants from the state. Each of the other income sources were marginal. For the municipalities the share of local income taxes corresponds to 40 percent of the total expenditure, about 10 percent was covered by general grants and as much as 1/3 by reimbursements from the state (Kommunale Finanser 1991). The equalization mechanism is briefly described in section 2.5.

## 2.1. The Government of Municipalities

The rules governing municipal government can be found in the law of May 1968, with later amendments. The law is the same for counties and municipalities. According to this law, each newly elected local council will adopt a local by-law specifying the rules to be valid for each individual county or municipality for the coming election period, i.e. a period of 4 years. The by-laws must be sent to the Minister of the Interior and to the relevant supervisory board (for their information) and it should be made public in the municipality or county. The council elects from its members a chairman, the mayor, who prepares, summons, and presides over the meetings of the council and sets up agendas for the meetings. He is also the day-to-day leader of the municipal administration. He is the link between the members of the council and the administration, and must in this capacity ensure that the decisions of the council are executed. The mayor is authorized, in case of emergency, to make decisions on behalf of the council (Basse and Jørgensen 1993).

## 2.2. The Traditional Model of Municipal Government by Committees

According to the law, the council must set up an economic committee and one or more permanent committees. The mayor is born chairman of the economic committee which is responsible for the economy of the municipality, for the coordination of the municipal plans, and for the administration. The economic committee must be consulted on all economic and administrative motions before they are adopted by the municipal council. The principal task is to prepare the proposal for the budget on the basis of contributions from other committees. A municipality has normally three more standing committees: a social committee, a committee for building and physical planning, and a committee for education and culture. Other committees may be set up if necessary, e.g. a harbor committee. The counties normally have the same standing committees, but the social committee also covers health matters except hospitals, which have their own committee.

The committee structure must be laid down in the by-law together with a specification of the fields of responsibility. In the traditional model of municipal administration, the municipal council has the superior responsibility and competence. Any member of the council can demand to have access to information sent out to the members of any committee, even if he is not himself a member of that particular committee. Other characteristics of the model and the law of the municipal government are regulations to protect political minorities and to secure openness, e.g. to lay down that council meetings are open, and further, that the official record of decisions from the council meetings must be made public.

To this may be added that, as part of the public service, the municipal administrations are subject to the legislation concerning open government, and also to the recent law of public administration, which basically is a formalization of 'good' administrative practices, e.g. that decisions concerning citizens or enterprises should be accompanied by an explanation of their motives, that notice should be given when it is clear that the consideration of a case might take a long time, that the administration must respect plaintiff's right of contradiction, and guide information on complaints procedures where relevant. One may finally note that the Ombudsman, who covers the state administration, may have his competence extended into the municipal field in consequence of an investigation published in 1994.

## 2.3. Deviances from the Traditional Model of Municipal Government

In Copenhagen and three other large municipalities the council, which is the superior governing body in the municipality, elects a bench of magistrates, consisting of a mayor and a number of aldermen. Each member of the magistracy is the day-to-day political leader of one or more departments of the administration. The magistracy attends to the matters that in the traditional model belong to the economic committee. Also the magistrate municipalities have standing committees, but since the day-to-day leadership rests with the mayor and the aldermen, the committees play a less prominent role. With the magistrate model being applicable only in the largest municipalities, the traditional model for many years was the one used in all the other municipalities.

According to a recent report from the Ministry of the Interior, there has been a tendency since the mid 1980's to simplify the committee structure in order to concentrate the consideration of tasks, or to accentuate the responsibility of individual council members for the totality of the municipal affairs by cross cutting solutions, rather than dealing with the cases from more restricted perspectives in the specialized committees (Betænkning 1994). The effort to reduce the use of politicians' time for details of individual cases also seem to have been a motive. Thus the regulations embedded in the traditional model have gradually been eased.

The most comprehensive step in this development was the introduction (in 1985) of the so-called free municipalities for a probationary period of 4 years, which was prolonged until 1993. In the free municipalities the existing rules for municipal tasks were replaced by special rules that were valid only in those municipalities. The Danish project was inspired by a more limited Swedish project. At the end of the probationary period in 1993, 30 municipalities and 6 counties had been approved as free municipalities. The opportunities presented by the law were used for experiments, notably within the following fields: schools and libraries, environment and physical planning, rationalization of the municipal administration, improved service to the citizens, and the transfer of competence from the state to municipalities or counties, or from the local councils to committees and institutions (Løgstrup 1990).

Inspired by the free municipalities project a number of amendments were introduced to the law of municipal government. The following two should be emphasized: (1) The possibility of an intermediate form between the traditional model and the magistrate model, in which the chairmen of the various committees are also members of the economic committee. (2) The possibility of a committee-less municipality governed directly by the council and the mayor without an economic committee or any other standing committees. The intermediate form is expected to be adopted by some larger municipalities, whereas the committee-less form is expected to appeal to the smaller municipalities. Finally, the new law has a section that permits the Minister of the Interior to exempt ad hoc. This power can be used to allow further experiments with local government.

In September 1994 there was only one municipality, Ravnsborg, that utilized the opportunity to govern without any standing committees.

### 2.4. The Nature of the Municipal and County Tasks

In relation to the mandate of a municipal or county council the tasks can be split into three groups:

* tasks that must be performed according to the law;
* tasks that may be performed according to the law; and
* tasks that the municipality/county is at liberty to perform, although the tasks are not mentioned in the law.

The first two groups of tasks do not normally give occasion to much doubt as to principles. For the third group this is different. The traditional thinking is that a municipality covers a certain geographical area and serves its population who pays for these services through taxes, excises, or direct purchases. The municipality must therefore not engage in activities that do not serve the common good of its population. Consequently it is not allowed, for example, to support or benefit an individual or an enterprise at the cost of other individuals or enterprises. Further, a municipal production plant must be economically self-sufficient, because a surplus is ultimately a kind of taxation, which requires special legislation to be legal; conversely a deficit is ultimately a subsidy from taxpayers to the buyers of the enterprises' products. Practice has gradually been built up around such reasoning. The basic philosophy has however been modified in recent years. Two laws from 1992 have opened up municipal participation in regional development programs, including co-financing of European Union programs, and participation in systems export and participation in private companies that are ready to buy municipal know-how.

### 2.5. Economic Equalization

Prior to the municipal reform of 1970 the economic relations between central government and the different local authorities were characterized by a large number of different grants and reimbursements for a variety of purposes. One of the main goals of the municipal reform was to create larger units for local government which would therefore be more able to finance local services without assistance from central government. But although the number of municipalities was heavily reduced, from 1391 to 290, in consequence, the differences between them were still too large to finance services of the same quality across the entire country. Therefore some kind of equalization arrangement was necessary (Betænkning 1968).

The existing system of state reimbursements had proved to have some unfortunate effects, from a general economic point of view. Thus, very high rates of reimbursements of municipal expenditures could lead to an expansion of local activities beyond the interest of the society. Socially undesirable effects were also generated in cases where closely linked local services were reimbursed by the state at very different rates, e.g. much higher rates for disablement pensions than for rehabilitation. So a secondary aim of the reform was to create a reimbursement system, that would not encourage uneconomic behavior by local authorities and would not distort their goal-setting. Finally, central government should not profit financially from the reform although an increasing number of tasks should be taken over by local authorities (Ministry of the Interior 1993, Betænkning 1993).

To meet these different aims a new system was introduced which had three components:

* equalization among the municipalities (or counties) of the expenditure needs;
* equalization among the municipalities (or counties) of their taxation base; and
* state grants to local authorities as a compensation for specific tasks being taken over by the municipalities (or counties).

In order to equalize expenditure needs a system of measures was introduced, whereby needs are calculated on the basis of so-called objective criteria, which are assumed to reflect the circumstances that give rise to the expenditure needs of municipalities (Ministry of the Interior 1993). For example, the criterion for day institutions and health visitors is the number of children under six years old; or for road expenses: kilometers of road at a certain date. It is important that a criterion cannot easily be influenced by the municipality. The criterion should be easy to recognize. This means that it should figure in the official statistics for all municipalities. Finally, there should of course be a recognized causality between a criterion and one or more municipal expenditures. In the system there are some so-called social criteria, that cannot be related to particular expenditures. They were introduced in order to take into account special social conditions.

The equalization of the taxation base is being pursued in a similar schematic way as the equalization of expenditure need. The starting point is a calculation of the taxation base for each municipality. In both cases special arrangements are made for the Copenhagen area.

In addition to these equalization procedures special grant arrangements of minor importance have been introduced for certain expenditures, for instance for refugees and immigrants, AIDS patients, and ferry services to islands.

## 2.6. Economic Coordination

In consequence of the considerable weight of the local authorities in the national economy it has been necessary to find a practical way to integrate their activities into the country's economic policy. The tradition which has been established aims to establish a contract between the Government which is represented by a ministerial committee and representatives from the municipal organizations, plus the two metropolitan municipalities. According to this practice certain goals are established for the municipalities together and the counties together, i.e. the goals shall not be fulfilled by each individual municipality or county.

The agreements are of course entered into the implied condition that serious disagreement could lead to discussions in the Parliament, and, eventually, legislation. Until 1980, goals were formulated in terms of degrees of self-financing of local investment. Since then goals have been formulated in terms of maximum totals for expenditures and taxes. These agreements have been supplemented by special agreements to strengthen effort in specific areas of political interest.

## 2.7. The State Supervision of the Local Governments

The state ensures that municipal and the county councils observe existing laws and acts, and takes measures where other complaints procedures are not specified. Furthermore, the state attempts to influence the municipal economy in accordance with general economic policy. (Ministry of the Interior 1993). The Ministry of the Interior is the highest authority for supervision of the municipalities and counties. The supervision of the counties lies with the ministry, whereas the direct supervision of the municipalities is handled by supervisory boards, which are set up in each county with a state county governor as chairman and four members elected by the county council among its members. The minister can lay down guidelines for the practice of supervision, but may not interfere in individual cases, unless they are brought before him by a member of the supervisory board.

The supervisory board can annul a decision of a local council if it finds that the decision is inconsistent with the law, or if the decision has no legal basis. Individual members of the local council may also be subjected to penalties until the illegal situation has ceased; and the supervisory board can hold the members of a local government council personally liable for losses inflicted upon the municipality or county as the result of illegal decisions.

## 3. The Municipality of Ravnsborg

Measured by its population the municipality of Ravnsborg is among the smallest in Denmark, with 6,200 inhabitants ranking it 230 out of 275. But its geographic size of 200 sq. km makes it among the largest. Of the 6,200 inhabitants 1,100 live on two islands, each about 12 sq. km, and about 2,000 live in 8-9 villages.

The town hall, which houses the municipal council and the administration, is situated in one of the villages. There is a branch office on one of the islands, Fejø, and a service center in the western part of the municipality, which from east to west measures 20 km (Mostrup 1994).

Ravnsborg municipality runs 5 institutions for elderly people, 5 schools of which 2 are located on the islands, and supports 5 institutions for children. However, in some areas Ravnsborg has to rely on cooperation agreements with larger neighboring municipalities for the provision of public services, e.g. libraries and laboratories for the inspection of food.

In 1994 the taxation rate in Ravnsborg was the highest among the county's 24 municipalities. The total municipal expenditures of Ravnsborg, as well as its expenditure om administration, were in 1992 higher than 22 of the 24 municipalities in the county when calculated per inhabitant. At the beginning of 1993 the municipality employed 470 persons, with about 60 persons in the administration of the town hall and its branch offices (Kommunalstatistisk Årbog 1992).

Of the 15 members of the municipal council, the Social Democrats had 7 members including the mayor, the Liberals 4 members, and four other parties one member each.

### 3.1. The Ravnsborg Experiment: Committee-less Municipality and Computer Support for Council Work

In January 1992, in collaboration with the Ministry of the Interior and the National Association of Local Authorities (Kommunernes Landsforening) the municipality of Ravnsborgset up a project to evaluate municipal government based on the model of the committee-less municipality (see section 2.3.). In Ravnsborg the basic model was modified by the use of small preparatory ad hoc committees. These committees were typically composed of two council members, two officials, and two citizens directly affected by the matter in hand.

Ravnsborg Municipality participated in the project to achieve the following main objectives (Folketingstidende 1992-93):

* Broader political influence, because the individual member of the council will achieve influence at the political level when all political cases are treated by the entire municipal council.
* Improved opportunities for recruiting local politicians, because the work of a member of the council will be less time-consuming, with fewer meetings.
* More openness and better service to citizens, because both citizens and the press will be able to follow the negotiations and decisions in the council meetings. Further, the treatment of individual cases will be faster.
* Easier to maintain an overall awareness and corporate responsibility for the affairs of the municipality, since the members of the council would concentrate on the main goals and overall guidelines if individual cases are delegated to the administration.

In view of the profound changes in the format of meetings and of communications imposed by the experiment, the Municipality of Ravnsborg decided in cooperation with Kommunedata to construct a CSCW system to support the daily work of the politicians and the officials in the council secretariat, see section 3.3.

### 3.2. *The Council Members' Work - Without the CSCW System*

According to a study by Færch (1994) each council member in Ravnsborg spends from 150 to 200 hours per year on council work and participates in 20 to 30 meetings a year. These figures rank as low when compared to other council members in the country. The large municipalities in Denmark, with 60% of all council members in the country, hold 55 to 235 meetings a year, while the smaller municipalities, with the remaining 40% of all council members, hold 25 to 144 meetings a year.

The time of council members for political work is spent in the following way:

* Meetings of the municipal council: 45%.
* Party group meetings: 22%.
* Other meetings (external boards, specific issues, with citizens): 33%.

The time for meetings of the municipal council is spent as follows:

* Preparation for council meetings: 30%
* Participation in council meetings: 55%
* Follow-up from council meetings: 15%

Each member of the council receives much information in writing as part of their work, namely from 2,000 to 2,500 pages per year. 90% of this is mailed from the town hall. Further, each member requests supplementary information on specific issues. 50% of this latter information comes from the town hall while 20% comes from other members of the council. Some members of the council find it hard at times to obtain supplementary information. Nearly all members of the council file most of their mail. They find that they use much of their time retrieving information from their own files. On the average, a council member inquires at the town hall once a week, either by telephone (53%), by personal appearance (36%), or by mail or telefax (11%). The time of the day when members do their the political work varies greatly and depends upon whether their professional work is at home or outside. The most common working period for council members is in the evening between 6 pm and midnight.

### 3.3. *The Council System - a CSCW System for Politicians and Officials*

Technically the system in Ravnsborg is based on a local area network placed in the town hall with 6 workstations (486-based personal computers with 8 megabyte RAM and 120 megabyte hard disk), a file server, a laser printer, a Lotus Notes server, a scanning and image document filing system based on PC-Doc and an Optical Character Recognition workstation, a 3270 terminal server with data communication for Kommunedata, an ISDN (Integrated Services Digital Network) server to handle the data communication with the 15 council members (see figure 1).

The workstations at the homes of the council members are 486-based personal computers with 8 megabyte RAM and 120 megabyte hard disks and a laser printer. They are equipped with the following applications: the groupware Lotus Notes, a simple text processor called Write, PC-Doc primarily for filing and retrieval of scanned documents, and TopKit to handle key-figures about Ravnsborg's economy, population, and the administration of the municipality. These figures are statistical information extracted from information systems operated by Kommunedata for Ravnsborg and many other municipalities.

Lotus Notes is the key element and offers the council members:

* agendas with supplements and comments,
* news from the administration,
* electronic group debate,
* electronic mail, and
* on-line help.

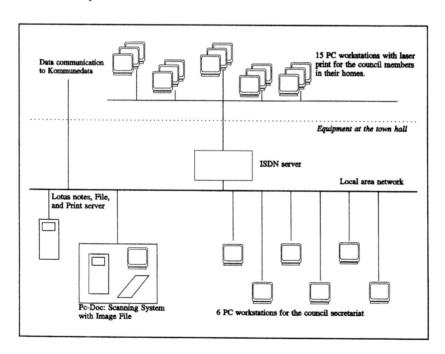

Fig. 1 : Configuration of the council system in Ravnsborg Municipality.

All workstations for the administration and the council members are operated on the MS Windows platform, which gives the user a fairly straightforward graphical interface. All data operated from Lotus Notes and PC-Doc are stored at the servers placed in the town hall.

Note that traditional modem-based data communication was too slow and too expensive, mainly because documents scanned as pictures required high transmission capacity of the ISDN network for data to be sent to the council members with acceptable response times. (One page was received within 10 to 25 seconds dependent upon its pictorial complexity.) Also the automatic handling of connections and disconnections by the ISDN network seems to make it easier and cheaper for the users to operate the system.

The security of the system is controlled both technically and organizationally. Technical security is handled primarily by limiting access to the local area network through the ISDN server. Only the 15 PC-based terminals served for the council members are organized to have access to the network, and when a terminal logs on it is only permitted access to the PC-Doc server and the Lotus Notes server. Confidential information, e.g. confidential items of the council meeting agenda, is further protected by passwords which are only imparted to council members. Organizational security is regarded as a matter of securing the servers in locked rooms at the town hall and of following the security rules established by the mayor. All activities on the systems are logged.

## 3.4. The Functionality of the Council System

Agendas and supplements for the council meetings are edited by the council secretariat which is managed by the mayor, and all this material is electronically available from the council members' workstations at home. During the preparation for a meeting the council member can annotate agenda items with comments, questions, or viewpoints. Each annotation can be personally restricted, or it can be made accessible to all council members. The system contains facilities for information retrieval in the document database to support the council members who wants further information about an issue to be raised at a council meeting, for instance to look up how similar prior cases were treated, what the main arguments were, who voted, and how. Some of the documents can be searched in their full text on a word to word basis. Others must be searched through assigned keywords or attributes, because they are scanned from paper documents, drawings, and other records.

News from the administration to council members about topical issues or ongoing projects, for example the construction of the marina, are communicated through a news database in Lotus Notes, possibly also through the email system for urgent or important news. If one needs further information the possibility of searching the electronic document database is available.

Through the email facilities the members of the council can communicate with each other and with the administration. As a special arrangement the Lotus Notes email system can support electronic group debate and collaboration. This facility was set up for only two party groups in the council, i.e. the Social Democrats (7 members) and the members of the Liberal party (4 members). It was intended as a supplement to the party group meeting for preparing and eventually deciding upon issues through an email-based group debate. In a similar way, electronic debate can be used by the council, or by the mayor who can submit an item to a hearing between the council members.

Through the application TopKit the members of the council have access to key statistical figures about the municipality's economy, the composition of its inhabitants, the salary and numbers of personnel in different parts of the administration. These figures can be compared to corresponding average figures which are calculated for the municipalities in the county and in the country as a whole.

### 3.5. The Politicians Use of the System

#### 3.5.1. Implementation and Learning

The project for the committee-less municipality started in January 1992. In April 1992 the local area network with servers was installed at the town hall, and the council members received their personal workstations at home. Because of severe technical problems with the ISDN network it was not possible to begin to use and evaluate the council system until May 1993, when the problems with the ISDN communication had been solved, and the system was operating with all its functionality. The evaluation period ended February 1994. In May 1994 the council decided to continue to use the council system and extend it beyond the council secretariat to cover also the rest of the municipal administration.

During the period from April 1992 to May 1993 council members were trained to use the workstations, the MS Windows user interface, and the text processing and TopKit applications. Before this experiment, one third of the council members had no experience in keyboards or in computing; one third had some experience in keybords but no experience in computing; the final third had used computers, but none was experienced. They attended courses which trained them to understand and use the council system; and telephone support was available to them during training at home. It was difficult to maintain members' motivation in the period when the ISDN network did not function, but this changed when the entire system was operating.

#### 3.5.2. The Actual Use of the Applications of the System

After initial implementation and the period with technical problems establishing the ISDN communication, the use of the system has been steady and it has shown satisfactory response times, practically independent of the number of users of the system.

Over a period of three months the number of connections and connection time between the council members' workstations and the local area network at the town hall were logged by the ISDN server, see table 1. After two months of operation of the whole council system the average connection time per 14 days was approximately 1.5 hours, with a great variation from 7 minutes as minimum to 5 hours as maximum.

Table 1:    ISDN connections among the council members' workstations and the local area network at the town hall measured over a period of three months (Færch 1994).

|  | number of connections per three months | minutes connected per three months |
|---|---|---|
| Average use per council member | 985 | 485 |
| Minimum usage among council members | 342 | 136 |
| Maximum usage among council members | 1,774 | 746 |
| Total for all 15 council members | 14,784 | 7.281 |

Agendas with supplements were clearly the most heavily used application of the system, on an average council members used it once a day. Next came the news and email applications which have been used regularly, once a week, by half the council members. The email application did not have much effect, because too few people were using its regularly. The electronic group debate application was used a little by the party group of 7 Social Democrats. The Liberal party group and the council as a whole did not make any use of the group debate facility. They seem to have been satisfied with the facilities of the email system. The statistical key figures of the municipality provided by the TopKit application was used very little.

After five months of operation, the pattern of usage changed somewhat. The agenda application was used significantly more, on average twice a day per member of the council. The council system made the agenda available to the council members faster than before, when it was mailed. Further, the members got extended opportunities to seek more information about specific items of the agenda, faster and more independently. Also the use of email increased considerably as more council members became regular users. Electronic group debate among all members of the council was still not used. This pattern of usage did not change before the evaluation project terminated in March 1994.

The communication between the administration and the councillors has gradually shifted towards use of email, and especially for the council secretariat, communication appears to be more efficient. During the experimental period only the council secretariat had direct access to the council system. Thus the system tightened up the normal procedure for written communication among council members and the administration. All exchange of information had to pass the council secretariat and some branches of the administration found it unsatisfactory that the council secretariat became a bottleneck in communications with councillors. This may change as a result of a decision by the council in May 1994 to integrate workstations from all branches of the administration into the email system, when the system is put in regular operation. But this decision may raise problems for the secretariat when trying to coordinate the council work effectively under the leadership of the mayor.

By the end of the project Kommunedata evaluated the council members' attitude towards the experimental council system through a questionnaire (Færch 1994). From the 14 answers received the overall conclusions were that 13 found the system useful, 11 found it gratifying to use the system, while there was a more mixed pattern in response questions on 'security' and 'confidence'. Moreover, only four out of 11 party group members stated that the system had strengthened communications within party groups in the council, although the system proved useful for exchange of information and coordination between the members during the election campaign in November 1993.

Summing up, no economic gains can be demonstrated as a direct result of the introduction of the council system. For politicians, the time saved by going to fewer meetings was used to get better information by the system and, in some cases, for improved contacts with voters. The system allows politicians greater freedom to choose convenient working hours because much more information exchange is now performed independently of the presence of other people. On the other hand, some politicians point to the fact that direct human contact, especially across party lines, has deteriorated because there are fewer meetings and because of the increased use of electronic information exchange (Politiken 1994).

### 3.6. Conclusions from the Ravnsborg Experiment concerning Computer Support for Council Work

The experiences from the experiment in Ravnsborg can be summarized as follows:

* It is possible to develop computer based tools that are considered useful by the town council and management of the administration in their daily work - the most useful functions being the communication facilities related to the agendas of the council, the personal electronic mail system, and the municipal news service.
* The computer based council system has offered an increased flexibility to some politicians in terms of the time and place of the work. Electronic mail has made communication with other politicians and with sections of the administration faster and, in some aspects, simpler. This was experienced as a relief by town councillors as well as by officials. The experiment, however, indicate that the total time used for political work by the individual members of the town council is unchanged.
* Electronic debates between all members of the council have not taken place. The facility of the system to support group discussions has been used very little and only by the 7 Social Democrats.

* Some politicians call attention to the reduction in human contact across the political party lines which has meant a deterioration of communication between the politicians.

* Some politicians point to the fact that they are better informed and have a broader outlook, thanks to the new system. The system has made it easier to locate and retrieve information.

* The introduction of the council system has created or accentuated organizational problems within the administration about the proper forms of communication and coordination between the mayor, the councillors, the council secretariat, and the administration. In particular, the use of the council system led to a displacement of the balance in favor of the mayor and the council secretariat during the experimental period. It has therefore been decided to extend the access to the system to the rest of the administration during the permanent organizational implementation of the system.

## 4. Questions for Further Studies

Following the reasoning of Hal Koch, a well-known Danish theologian and philosopher, the ideal of a multifaceted and open dialogue at both the personal level and the community level is probably at the core of modern western democracy (Koch 1945). In this sense the Ravnsborg experiment gives no strong support to the assumption that computer support for council work will stimulate local democracy. The relation between politicians and citizens has only indirectly been affected by this experiment; and the majority of the politicians do not think that the communication in the council has improved through the introduction of the CSCW system. The system has not been made available to the citizens of the municipality, although much of its information is or will be made public in paper form. The question has been raised whether these parts of the system should be made particularly accessible from workstations placed at selected locations (or even from the citizens private equipment). Such arrangements would, however, demand fairly thorough technical changes of the technical solution to secure the council system against unauthorized access to confidential files, and to prevent hacking into other municipal information systems. So far, the municipal council has abstained from introducing any public access to the council system.

   Not all members of the council have been able to make effective use of the system (Færch 1994, Politiken 1994). Politicians cannot or should not be forced to master the technical facilities that are required to operate effectively the computer systems in current use in business and administration. What they need are simpler and more intuitively understandable facilities to manage documents, including graphical information, and electronic mail and group communication. Tools with this functionality are marketed as document management systems, collaborative hypermedia systems, CSCW systems, and groupware; but very few of these, if any, are both easy to use and suffiently powerful to meet the needs of a user group with such high demands and so varied qualifications as politicians. Moreover, the integration of such tools into the existing information systems used by the administrations raises many technical problems.

However, after one year of practical use the council system in Ravnsborg is considered useful by nearly all the council members and by leading officials. It seems likely that the system has increased the effectiveness of implementing political decisions by strengthening the exchange of information and coordination among politicians and officials who are involved. The limited, yet essential problems raised by the system relate to a possible deterioration of human contacts, and to unintentional changes in the functioning of parts of the organization. Similar observations are found in other studies of CSCW systems, see for instance Markus (1994) and Grudin (1988).

## Acknowledgments

We thank the municipality of Ravnsborg for information about the experiment. We are also indebted to Pieter Tops, reviewer and editor, Claus Topsøe-Jensen, Bent Christensen, and Henrik Grunnet for careful reading and helpful comments to an earlier version of this chapter.

# CHAPTER 9

# Democracy Denied: The Political Consequences of ICTs in UK Local Government

Lawrence PRATCHETT

*Department of Public Policy & Managerial Studies, De Montfort University, Leicester LE7 9SU, United Kingdom*

**Abstract.** This chapter explores the reasons why local governments in the UK have largely ignored the democratic potential of ICTs and the consequences of this for local democracy. It argues that the democratic potential of UK local government is increasingly being frustrated and denied through the implementation of ICTs that are inherently anti-democratic. The chapter uses Langdon Winner's concept of technologies as political artifacts to argue that there are three features of local government ICT systems (their technical configuration; their organizational location; and their structural properties) that makes them innately authoritarian and anti-democratic. The argument draws upon both deterministic and constructivist models of technological development to suggest that the complex environment of local government informatization is much more deterministic in its influence over democracy than contemporary accounts of ICTs in UK local government allow for.

## 1. Introduction

New information and communications technologies (ICTs) have never offered greater potential to fundamentally alter the democratic foundations of public administration. Rapid advances in telematics - that is, the convergence of more powerful computers with increasingly sophisticated telecommunications networks - which are now being developed into concepts such as the information super-highway (OTA 1993, CCTA 1994) and the European Nervous System (Ridge 1994), have significant implications for the ways in which public services are organized, managed and delivered. More importantly, they also portend profound and sustained changes in the democratic structures and processes of government, either by engendering new forms of participatory democracy, or by further concentrating power in the hands of an elite few who become increasingly distanced from the democratic process (Van de Donk and Tops, 1992). The Orwellian or Athenian implications of informatization do not stop at the institutions of political democracy, nor indeed at the political cultures of nations or particular localities, but also extend into every facet of public administration, radically altering the relationships between public administrations and the democratic processes that govern them.

Local authorities in the United Kingdom (UK) seem as well placed as many other public institutions to take advantage of the new ICTs to both improve the delivery of local services and to enhance the democratic processes which legitimize their positions as local government. Yet most local authorities in the UK remain, at best, indifferent to or skeptical of the potential for ICTs to engender new modes of democracy, and at worst, openly hostile to such a concept. Indeed, the few schemes that have been initiated in the UK (for example, the Oxfordshire Community Information System - OXCIS) have been driven primarily by managerialist and consumerist agendas, and have concentrated almost exclusively upon the provision of information about services to citizens (Horrocks and Webb, 1994). Most ICT investment by UK local authorities (estimated as being £1.1 billion in 1993/94) has concentrated upon operational and information systems for the effective management of local government functions (SOCITM 1993). Using ICTs to engender democracy has remained peripheral to the major ICT investments of most local authorities.

This chapter sets out to explore the reasons why local governments in the UK have ignored the democratic potential of ICTs, and to examine the implications of this ignorance for the prospects of local democracy in the UK. Following Winner (1986) it will argue that, as a particular type of human artifact, ICTs can engender specific political structures and outcomes which extend far beyond the immediate situation of informatization to affect the very basis of democracy. It will suggest that the inherently political nature of some ICTs shapes and influences the democratic structure and processes of organizations, leading to a broad shift in their political culture and the democratic processes which surround them. In the context of UK local government it will argue that the prospects for increasing democracy through ICTs are handicapped and constrained by the types of technologies that local governments have often deployed with great enthusiasm. The operational and managerial systems currently being implemented in UK local government engender authoritarian and technocratic political forms that do not sit comfortably with the concepts of participatory or communitarian democracy. (The term 'authoritarian' will be used throughout this chapter as being the antithesis of democracy. It will imply a polity dominated by technocratic elites that are only influenced by democracy at the margins, and which exercises the capacity to determine policy with only limited reference to democratic processes or structures.) Indeed, they do little to enhance the traditional features of representative democracy upon which UK local government is founded and legitimized, let alone introduce new modes of democracy into local government. Consequently, this chapter will argue that if new ICTs are to be used to bring about greater democracy in local government, whether participatory or representative, it will be necessary first to address the inherently political and 'anti-democratic' nature of the existing technological infrastructure.

## 2. Informatization as a Technological Artifact

Informatization, as both a theory and a process, has been extensively defined by a number of authors (e.g. Frissen 1992, Bellamy and Taylor, 1994). This chapter is concerned with informatization as a particular form of technological artifact - that is, as something that is made or given shape by man, as opposed to possessing its own self-evolving form. Thus, it is concerned with more than simply the individual technological components of ICTs, although these could be considered to be artifacts in their own right. It is also concerned with the physical and logical combinations of ICTs and the organizational structures that support them. Consequently, as a technology, informatization includes ICT systems, the organizational structures in which they are deployed and the specialized knowledge and skills that surround them. The important point here is that the configuration of technical, organizational and human components can collectively be viewed as a technological artifact. In other words, the combinations of different elements of informatization are subject to deliberate and systematic ordering within organizations, and are specially designed to achieve desired outcomes. The fact that ICT systems often have significant unanticipated consequences and are frequently unsuccessful in achieving their original objectives, does not detract from the argument that they are deliberately crafted devices. These systems are sophisticated artifacts of man.

The argument that will be developed here is that it is not simply ICTs as technological artifacts that are inherently political and authoritarian in nature, but that the informatization process (of which they are an essential component) is itself anti-democratic. Before exploring this process, however, it is necessary to consider the broader context of local government within which this process occurs.

## 3. The Context of Local Democracy in the UK

Local democracy in the UK has a poor history. It is not that the institutions of local government in the UK are intrinsically undemocratic, although many cases for the reform of its election system have been made (Stewart and Game 1991). But it is the case that local democracy has consistently been overshadowed by national politics, and that participation in local elections is the lowest of all European Community countries (Rallings, Temple and Thrasher 1994). Less than 40 percent of the electorate turn-out for sub-national elections in the UK. Democracy at the local level has never really been considered a significant issue within UK politics. Consequently, although local government has hardly been off of the agenda since 1979, rarely, over the last fifteen years, has there been any substantial debate about the fundamental nature of local democracy outside of the neo-liberal doctrines that have demanded the establishment of a free and competitive market as the basis for democracy (Ridley 1988). During the 1980s and into the 1990s local authorities have experienced an unprecedented period of change that has affected every aspect of their structure, organization and management. This has generally deflected attention away from concerns with the democratic features of local governance, and concentrated attention on the efficiency and effectiveness of local services. During this period different forms of market competition have been introduced into almost every function of local government, through compulsory competitive tendering for most functions, but also through other mechanisms where no natural market has existed - for example, the local management of schools (in the area of education). At the same time, there have been radical changes in the financial base of local government, most notably in the substantial alterations that have been made to the local taxation system, but also through a multitude of changes to the grant system from central government. Furthermore, the rise of appointed bodies at the local level (local Quango's)[1] to replace the role of elected members in many functional areas of local governance compounds the attack upon traditional forms of representative democracy that have occurred over the past fifteen years. The consequence of these changes has been a shift away from the traditional concepts of citizenship and representative democracy, towards a more consumerist led local authority that emphasizes neo-liberal philosophies of free market competition. A corresponding consequence has also been the increasing dependence of local authorities on ICTs to deliver these changes.

More recently, however, local democracy has achieved a new primacy due to two initiatives that have come from very separate sources. Firstly, the Local Government Commission (LGC) was established in November 1991 under the chairmanship of Sir John Banham to review the structure of local government in England (with different review procedures for Wales and Scotland). The Commission has been singularly unsuccessful in achieving a consensus over the future structure of local government in England, although, somewhat inadvertently, it has been successful in highlighting issues of local community and has given renewed impetus to concerns over local democracy. Secondly, the Commission for Local Democracy (CLD) was launched in November 1993. This independent commission aims to further stimulate and influence the debate on local democracy by publishing a series of fifteen consultation papers on issues of local governance, as well as its own final report in the summer of 1995. Unlike the Local Government Commission, the CLD's focus is much more on issues of local democracy, and aims to concentrate the debate much more on how political democracy can be achieved at a local level. Both of these initiatives, however, assume a close relationship between local democracy and the traditional institutions of local government, and the proposals emerging from them largely recommend marginal alterations to the structure of the traditional institutions of local governance rather than a radical reformulation of local democracy. Whilst this assumption is somewhat problematic (not least because the traditional institutions of local government display a number of remarkably undemocratic features), it will be

---

[1]     Quasi-Non Governmental Organizations.

adopted here as representing both the collective wisdom and the likely focus for local democracy in the UK for the foreseeable future.

In analyzing the impact of ICTs on contemporary UK local government, there are two important issues that set the context of the analysis. Firstly, over the last fifteen years local government in the UK has been dominated by managerialist and neo-liberalist philosophies, which have emphasized the development of a more demand-led consumerist stance on the part of local authorities, and the development of local markets as the principal means of achieving democracy. Consequently, local governance has become increasingly fragmented and differentiated, consisting of an increasingly wide range of diverse local and sub-central governments (Gray 1994). This fragmentation has cried out for informatization to provide coordination and cohesion between disparate functions and services, and between the different elements of local democracy. Informatization has, however, concentrated upon providing improved operational and managerial systems with scant regard for the requirements of democracy.

Secondly, there has been a renewed interest in 'community' as the basis for local democracy in the UK, particularly as a consequence of the tensions created by the early tranches of the Local Government Commission (Wilson 1994) and the new focus created by the Commission for Local Democracy (Phillips 1994). It is notable, however, that issues of informatization and the deployment of new ICTs are rarely considered within this debate. The Local Government Commission has more or less ignored the potential of ICTs in developing its proposals (Blundell, de Silva and Machiavello 1994). Meanwhile, in setting out the 'terms of the debate' for the Commission for Local Democracy, Phillips (ibid) only makes passing reference to ICTs, and then only in terms of their ability to deliver 'teledemocracy', particularly in the form of 'the smart town hall'. In the reformulation of local democracy in the UK, therefore, the impact of informatization is currently being given very little attention.

## 4. ICTs as Inherently Political Technologies

Within the context of a fragmented local government that is dominated by neo-liberalist market philosophies and managerialist paradigms, and a reformulation of local democracy that more or less ignores the potential impact of informatization on both the institutions and processes of political democracy, it becomes important to understand the inherently political nature of extant ICTs in local government, and the momentum or inertia that they exert on future democratic structures. Winner's discussion of technologies as political artifacts provides a useful point of departure for such an analysis.

Winner distinguishes between two ways in which technological artifacts can have political qualities. Firstly he proposes that political qualities can emerge from the socio-political context of technical arrangements. This is the widely held belief that the impact of technologies is entirely dependent upon the social or political circumstances in which they are deployed (Street 1992). It is not the technologies themselves that engender democratic or authoritarian political forms, but the uses to which people put them. Consequently, in relation to an analysis of ICTs, computers are a politically neutral artifact that only gain political value when used for a particular purpose. The apparent flexibility of ICTs means that they can be used either to bring about democratic politics by further increasing the access of citizens to information, or to undermine democracy by further distancing citizens from the democratic process and increasing the information resources of an elite few. Within this first perspective ICTs can have the impact of reinforcing social or political cleavages and inequalities, especially where they have non-focal or unintended consequences (Sclove 1992). For example, Taylor (1994) has shown that differences in the development of the telecommunications infrastructure in urban and rural parts of Scotland is creating an uneven distribution of economic and political opportunities amongst communities. In keeping with Winner's first proposition, Taylor argues that such inequalities are not a direct consequence of the technologies employed, but are a result of the economic and political priorities that have emerged in a deregulated and liberalized telecommunications market. In this example, therefore, the impact of ICTs on democracy is a construct of their social, economic and political context rather than of the technology itself (see also chapter five).

This social-constructivist argument is widely accepted, especially in the context of supposedly malleable and flexible ICTs, and need not be further explored here. Secondly and more contentiously, however, Winner also proposes that some technologies are inherently political and inevitably engender particular political forms. His argument is that:

> ...some technologies are by their very nature political in a specific way. According to this view, the adoption of a given technical system unavoidably brings with it conditions for human relationships that have a distinctive political cast - for example, centralized or decentralized, egalitarian or inegalitarian, repressive or liberating (Winner 1986).

Consequently, in choosing technologies societies also make choices about the types of political structures and processes that are an unavoidable result of implementing that technology. This argument is effectively illustrated by the juxtaposition of two very different forms of energy generation: nuclear and solar power. Nuclear energy generation, as a form of technology, requires a highly centralized and authoritarian command structure. The high development costs of the technology, coupled with the environmental risks of radiation leaks and the security required to combat terrorism, all demand a political system that emphasizes hierarchical control and limits access. Furthermore, the centralized and authoritarian political structure engendered by nuclear energy is not restricted to the control of that technology, but transfers to adjacent social and political systems leading to an increasingly autocratic polity. By contrast, solar power offers much greater potential for democratic structures to emerge. The technology is relatively uncomplicated and cheap to install, and poses few (if any) environmental or security risks. It is also eminently more suitable for small scale developments. As a result, solar energy is more comprehensible and controllable by local communities, and is therefore, arguably more amenable to democracy. Whilst democracy is not an inevitable feature of solar technology, it is a widely held belief that a society which is based on local energy generation schemes, such as solar energy, will be more liberal and egalitarian in its distribution of power, and will develop a more democratic polity. Within this second proposition of inherently political technologies, nuclear technology is seen as being inimical to democracy whilst solar energy (along with other more localized sources of energy generation) is seen to at least offer the potential for greater democracy. In choosing large scale energy generation schemes such as nuclear energy, therefore, societies also choose a more authoritarian and restricted form of political life.

This sophisticated version of technological determinism applies particularly to large, inflexible and domineering technologies such as major energy generation technologies and rail systems. Such technologies demand authoritarian political structures in order to work, or are, at the very least, highly compatible with such structures. Being intrinsically flexible and relatively small scale, however, ICTs and the information systems that they support do not fall readily into this category of inherently authoritarian technologies. If anything, ICTs are generally presumed to support a more dynamic and democratic polity because of their apparent flexibility. As the relative costs of computerization fall, so access to ICTs is expected to increase, further supporting this supposition. But this presumption needs to be challenged. Whilst social-constructivist arguments accept that ICTs can be used to support either democratic or authoritarian politics, the concept of ICTs as being inflexible and inherently authoritarian in their application has not been fully explored. Yet it is possible to argue that in choosing to implement new information systems to support specific functions governments are inadvertently but progressively undermining democracy. In challenging the presumption of intrinsic flexibility in ICTs, therefore, it is also possible to argue that the process of informatization in public administration is intrinsically authoritarian.

The principal argument of this chapter is that ICTs in contemporary public administrations are not inherently flexible in their application and variable in their effects. Indeed, quite the opposite. When the full extent of informatization as a technology is considered, there are a number of innate features of informatization that make it intrinsically inflexible in public administrations, and remarkably predictable and consistent in its effects. For example, Collingridge and Margetts (1994) have shown very effectively how the computerization of the UK social security system developed into a highly inflexible form of technology, despite the apparent flexibility of the ICTs on which it was based. Such inflexibility is not unique to that one project. New ICTs may appear to be greatly malleable and variable in their application, offering an infinite choice of functions, structures and locations. In the context of public administrations, however, this flexibility and variability is less apparent. Within UK local government, for example, it is possible to identify a policy network for ICTs that shapes the development of ICT policies and inhibits innovation, limiting the application of ICTs to that supported by the various actors in the network (Pratchett 1994). The values and ideologies of such networks are embedded within the informatization process, and are as significant in their impact as the technical components of a system. Consequently, because ICTs in public administrations are inflexible and inherently political there is a great deal of consistency in their impact upon the institutions of government, and upon the structures and processes of democracy. For example, the 1993 survey of UK local government information technology managers found a high degree of homogeneity amongst the respondents over the key issues facing them (SOCITM 1993). Their main issues of concern focused around 13 technical problems and gave no consideration of the democratic opportunities or consequences that these issues might pose. It is possible to conclude, therefore, that for those most directly involved in formulating and implementing ICT policies in UK local government, the democratic potential (and dangers) of new technologies do not even feature upon the agenda.

## 5. The Political Features of Informatization

Before considering the political features of informatization it is necessary to question the technological determinism of Winner's argument. Winner himself does not claim technological determinism for his thesis. Indeed, prior to establishing his propositions he presents a critique of naive determinism, preferring the expression 'technological somnambulism' to indicate the extent to which societies ignore the impacts of technologies. It is nonetheless the case that his thesis is generally labelled as being a technologically deterministic one which can be contrasted with the wider degree of autonomy and choice that social constructivist positions afford (Fielder 1992). But the juxtaposition of these two perspectives is unnecessarily narrow and restrictive, confining the analysis to specific features and ignoring others. This chapter adopts a more eclectic approach, drawing upon both the technological determinism of Winner's argument and the social constructivist arguments of contemporary commentators to develop a more sophisticated framework for analyzing the democratic potential of ICTs in local government.

Rather than perceiving determinist and constructivist positions as being competing theories that are mutually exclusive, it is possible to view them as opposite extremes upon the same continuum. Technologies, especially ICTs, possess certain latent qualities that shape their impact upon individuals, organizations and society in general. For example, the ability of new ICTs to reduce the significance of spatial and temporal restraints on communication is an intrinsic feature of the technology which cannot be ignored when considering changing interpersonal or interorganizational relations. At the same time, however, the impact of these technologies is mediated and altered by the social and organizational contexts in which they are deployed, and indeed, by the very processes through which they are implemented. A wide range of social, political and economic factors combine to influence the development and impact of ICTs, with both intentional and unintentional outcomes. Hence, the impact of ICTs on communications that are constrained by geographic or temporal obstructions remains ambiguous and uncertain, being as much a factor of the social, political and economic environment in which the information flows occur, as of the technology itself. If this complexity is to be made sense of it is necessary to consider both those features that are determined by the technology, and those which are constructed by the environment in which it is developed and deployed.

The problem with combining these two perspectives on a continuum is that it is difficult to identify where the arguments of one end and the other begin. For example, the features of ICTs that are presented below as leading UK local government inexorably away from democracy appear superficially to be deterministic in their basis. Yet many of them have their roots in the organizational and political environment of UK local government and the functions for which ICTs have been used in the past, thus making them constructivist in their formulation. This problem is also a powerful advantage to the framework developed below, however, because it points to a dynamic between technologies and organizations (and society in general) which blurs the distinction between those qualities that are intrinsic to technologies themselves and those which emerge through the organizational or political location of technologies. The argument here is that there are certain features that are so deeply embedded into the institutional structure of UK public administration as to have a deterministic impact upon the development and implementation of ICTs in local government. Thus, despite apparently wide differences in their functionality and technical basis, new ICTs display a high degree of regularity and consistency in their repercussions for local democracy. As a result, ICTs inevitably reinforce dominant institutional forms and effectively militate against the enhancement of democracy within the traditional structures of UK local government. If the impact of ICTs is so heavily determined by latent organizational and political structures as to appear to be inherent to ICTs themselves, then attempts to distinguish these characteristics from those which are innate to the technology become irrelevant. It is much more relevant to identify those characteristics that are implicit within the informatization of local government either because they are inherent to ICTs themselves or because they are structurally embedded into the environment in which the technologies are to be implemented.

This is not a tautological contradiction that simply moves the argument back into the social-constructivist position of Winner's first proposition. Instead, it suggests that the effects of information and communication technologies are so inseparable from the political and organizational framework of public administration that they appear to be an intrinsic feature of all new ICT based systems. Hence, although this argument acknowledges the social constructivist basis of many features of informatization, it places a much stronger emphasis upon the deterministic impact of these features than is ordinarily the case. In order to engender democracy through ICTs it is necessary to address more than simply the technical components of a system. It is necessary to consider all features of informatization that give rise to the technological momentum of authoritarianism.

There are at least three features of informatization in UK local government that implicitly engender anti-democratic and authoritarian politics: Firstly, the technical configuration of the ICTs that provide the infrastructure of the polity. Secondly, the organizational and institutional location of the technology that give it purpose and meaning. Finally, the structural properties of the technology that arise from its focus on information. Each of these will be dealt with in turn.

## 5.1. Technical Configuration

The technical configuration concerns all components of a system that can be classed as ICTs. It includes the various hardware, software and network components which collectively comprise an information system. On their own, none of these components are intrinsically authoritarian in nature. Indeed, it is possible to see many different ways in which they can be used to enhance democracy, hence emphasizing the mutability and flexibility of such technologies. But there are two features of the technical configuration of ICTs in public administrations that make them highly compatible with authoritarian political structures, and militate against a more democratic use of them. Firstly, it is an inherent feature of these technologies that they are not implemented in isolation from other technical features of an organization, especially within the large multi-functional organizations of public administration. Consequently, new ICTs have to deal with the technical legacies of previous ICT investments, either by providing an appropriate interface with them where they link to other systems, or by supplanting them in some way. In the technological design process (Scarbrough and Corbett 1992) the legacies of the technical infrastructure of public administrations provide the main focus of development, and foreclose upon other more innovative options that may engender more democratic uses of information systems. The complexity of ICT systems, coupled with their scale in relation to the available expertise in most public organizations, forces the development process to concentrate upon the detail of the system (for example, concentrating on resolving some of the operational problems created by the previous system), leaving little or no room to consider moral or political enhancements. This is not a trivial issue: overcoming the legacy of existing systems is a major concern for those involved directly in the informatization of public administration, and acts as a major distraction in the design process. Distracted in this way, system designers tend to emphasize managerial enhancements and system efficacy over democratic improvements. In the increasingly complex environment of fragmented local governance the management functions of existing systems take precedence over the flexibility of new ICTs.

Secondly, ICT systems in public administration are characterized by higher risk and complexity in their design and operation (Willcocks 1994). This is due in part to the organizational and technical legacies of previous systems, and also to the multi-functional nature of most public organizations. It is further compounded by the multiple and ambiguous purposes of many ICT systems in public organizations which are designed not simply to deliver particular operational features, but also to meet specific organizational or political peculiarities. Informatization, with its emphasis upon the integration of information from a range of different sources (Bellamy and Taylor 1994) is both a contributor to this technical complexity and a means of making sense of it. The implications of such technical complexity are manifest. The control of ICT systems, and the process of informatization in general, becomes dominated by a technocratic elite which emphasizes neo-positivist principles of rationality and efficacy, and which infers democracy to be an imperfect and deficient decision making process (Fischer 1990). If ICTs are as important to the future of public administration as many suggest (e.g. Willcocks 1994) then control of that technology is fundamental to the future of democracy. Consequently, even where ICTs are used to enable greater participation in political decisions, or to improve access to information, this is undertaken through the limitations and direction imposed by the technocratic elite who control the deployment of ICT resources. As Danilo Zolo has argued:

> ...power in information-based societies should be envisaged as a means of communication through which certain agents 'reduce complexity for other' by pre-emptively limiting the choices open for their decision and thus by restricting the horizon of their possibilities. If this is true, then it is clear where, in such societies, the hidden and uncontrollable core of inner power is concentrated (Zolo 1992).

The consequence of technical complexity in the informatization of public administration is a form of 'subtle authoritarianism' (Fischer 1990) in which the neo-positivist epistemology of the ICT technocracy becomes self-entrenching (Hickman 1992), leading inexorably towards more technocratic and authoritarian political structures.

*5.2. Organizational and Institutional Location*

Related to the authoritarian features of their technical configuration, ICTs are also inherently political because of their organizational and institutional location. The size, complexity, functional differentiation and overt politicization of many public organizations collectively make the context of informatization in these institutions radically different. Willcocks and Harrow (1992), for example, identify 11 different features that distinguish public sector IT projects from those in the private sector. Most information systems that are used in public administrations are developed specifically and exclusively to meet a particular functional need and are not easily transferred to other organizations (with the obvious exception of routine automation systems such as payroll). This claim is not restricted to major systems such as the (UK) DSS operational strategy, but includes most of the functions of local government and other public agencies. For example, the 'local management of schools' in the UK has spawned a proliferation of systems and software companies that exist specifically to support this initiative. As ICTs are deployed in more complex environments to fulfil more challenging roles, so this specialization of administration systems can be expected to increase. Informatization in the public sector, therefore, must be seen as being a differentiated process that is dependent upon a unique sub-set of information and communications technologies. This uniqueness emerges from the organizational and institutional location of the informatization process.

There are at least two reasons why the organizational and institutional location of ICTs engenders authoritarian and anti-democratic politics. Firstly, it can be argued that the organizational and institutional location of ICTs acts as a powerful source of inertia against moves towards greater democracy through the use of ICTs. The public choice literature that has underpinned many of the managerial changes in UK public administration, and especially Dunleavy's 'bureau-shaping model' (Dunleavy 1991), emphasizes that bureaucrats are self-regarding and concerned mainly with maximizing their own personal benefit. Dunleavy argues that bureaucrats will choose from a number of bureau-shaping strategies, including hiving-off of some functions, in order to secure the long-term interests of the organization and their own personal careers within it. Within such a framework the use of ICTs to engender democracy can be seen as a threat to the autonomy of bureaucrats to pursue the most appropriate bureau-shaping strategy that maximizes the benefit to the organization. Whilst in public, bureaucrats may support calls for greater democracy, bureau-shaping strategies are likely to be recalcitrant and inimical to any activities that will undermine the authority or influence of the bureaucrats. Democratic initiatives that are based in ICTs are only likely to be successful if they suit the long-term and intrinsically authoritarian needs of the bureau, especially as defined by the top bureaucrats. In an environment in which political interest in ICTs is at best limited (as is the case in UK local government), the bureau-shaping model suggests that regardless of the overarching political culture of an organization, the maximizing strategies of bureaucrats are likely to subvert the democratic potential of new ICTs to benefit their own interests.

A second and distinctly different reason why the organizational and institutional location of ICTs engenders authoritarian politics derives from the ability of technologies to exert symbolic and cultural influences on organizations. This argument holds that technologies are symbolic of particular cultural values and ideologies. For example, Sclove argues that nineteenth-century New England factories and schools were designed to resemble churches, in order to 'symbolically impress upon workers and children the need to maintain at all times the same quiet, order, and deference to authority that they were taught to exhibit at worship' (Sclove 1992). The technologies of information and communication are teeming with symbolic inferences for organizations. In particular, ICTs are symbolic of modern, efficient, progressive, innovative, even 'leading-edge' organizations. This symbolism is widely supported by the media, from a range of advertising images through to the messages of contemporary pop-music (it would be unthinkable for an advertiser to portray a modern business without visual and verbal reference to ICTs. Similarly, much of the recent 'rave' music has associated itself with the technological ascendancy of youth culture - '*techno-techno!*'). Symbolically, ICTs appear to be socially and politically good. But nowhere within this symbolism is there evidence of enhanced democracy, beyond the artificial democracy promised by instant referenda, push button voting and other aspects of teledemocracy (McLean 1986). Indeed, if anything the symbolism of ICTs implies a clinical and rational world that emerges from their increased deployment, that has no room for the inefficiencies and inconsistencies of democracy. This has prompted authors such as Jacques Ellul (1992) to argue that the logic of technology and the logic of democracy are contradictory and mutually exclusive. This is particularly true at an organizational and institutional level, where issues of democracy are subsumed by an emphasis upon the efficacy and rationality of ICTs.

## 5.3. The Structural Properties of ICTs

A reference to the structural properties of ICTs is generally concerned with the inability of new technologies to overcome social, economic or political inequalities, and indeed, their tendencies to reinforce any such cleavages (McLean 1989). This is a valid argument that is particularly apposite for attempts to enhance democracy by using new ICTs to deliver more information to citizens. Hence, Zolo suggests a 'cognitive differential' in which:

> Those agents who possess greater cultural, economic and political resources find that they can put the information they receive to good profit, while those who are less gifted simply find themselves unable to decode it or to extract any benefit at all (Zolo 1992).

New ICTs are structurally biased, therefore, serving only to further enhance the asymmetrical distribution of power within society.

In the context of ICTs in public administration, however, it is another feature of this structuralism that is important, that associated specifically with the unique properties of information. In other words, it is the informational specificity of ICTs and informatization that is of interest here. As Coombs *et al.* (1992) have argued, information is characterized by two distinct features: the distribution of information between groups or individuals; and the meaning attached to the content of that information. New ICTs in public administrations are primarily targeted at improving or altering the first feature, by influencing information flows within or between organizations. They play a role in the second feature, however, by influencing the ability or means by which information can be interpreted. Consequently, it is necessary to recognize that information is not of an ordinal value, but is heavily context dependent. The value of information is only apparent in relation to other information, and indeed, can only be realized if the actor has the resources and capacity to act upon it. It is shaped by both spatial and temporal dimensions with the result that its value changes over time and according to its geographical context. These features are widely recognized by news agencies, who levy different charges for news reports, depending upon the age and geographical significance of that news. They seem to be largely ignored, however, by those who wish to improve democracy through increased information. Most importantly, information is 'culturally mediated' by the recipient, which leads to informatization having variable effects in different cultural or political contexts. Hence, information contains inherently structural properties that cannot be divorced from either the technologies or the processes of informatization.

These structural properties are manifested in public administration by concerns over privacy and the protection of sensitive information. The increased information flows of informatization are counter-balanced by anxiety over the sensitivity of information, either because information systems contain personal details about individuals, or because the information is commercially sensitive. Within local government, information systems contain a range of highly sensitive information about individuals, ranging from Social Services details about 'problem families' through to financial details about benefit claimants (e.g. for housing benefit purposes). There are strong moral, as well as logical arguments, for restricting access to such information. The introduction of competition in to every function of local government also makes aggregate information much more sensitive. Information about how functions are organized and the costs for undertaking them are now highly sensitive. Anxious to protect their services, local authorities again restrict access on a 'need-to-know' basis. This type of information has become increasingly valuable, both to the local authorities who wish to retain functions 'in-house', and to the private companies who aim to compete with them.

The inherently sensitive nature of information at both an individual and aggregate level means that structurally the informatization process encourages local authorities, and other public administrations, to be defensive and protective of their own information. This protectionist stance is an inevitable feature of the new technologies that are being deployed. In making information more easily manipulable and more freely available, ICTs also encourage organizations to adopt a more possessive and covert attitude towards information resources. The consequence is that far from engendering greater democracy through the improved distribution of information, ICTs are encouraging public administrations to become more secretive and defensive about their information. The democratic utopia expected from the widespread distribution of information throughout society, therefore, is thwarted by the greater need for privacy and guardianship of information resources. This emphasis upon privacy and protection leads ICTs to inherently authoritarian, as opposed to democratic, political structures.

## 6. The Consequences for Local Democracy in the UK

The possibility of ICTs acting as the catalyst for renewed local democracy in the UK do not look good. As the foregoing analysis of informatization in UK local government indicates, the authoritarian nature of ICT applications in contemporary public administration appears to be inescapable. In developing the concept of ICTs as inherently political, however, this argument has maintained an explicitly eclectic approach, drawing upon both determinist and constructivist models of technological development. Hence, it has accepted the importance of such features as organizational location and the ability of individual actors (or bureaucrats) in shaping the impact of ICTs on public administrations. But it has placed particular emphasis upon the deeply entrenched features of informatization that make its implementation in local government appear to be deterministic in its impact. This is not technological determinism in its most extreme form, but it is, perhaps, as Winner would argue, a form of technological somnambulism in which the institutions of local government sleepwalk through the nightmare of increasing authoritarianism.

It is also part of this argument that the authoritarian features of ICTs in public administration are not clearly articulated in most debates about democracy. Yet this is a major omission. The impact of informatization on public administration and the institutions of democracy is too profound to be ignored. Accordingly, the consequences of inherently authoritarian ICTs for local democracy can be seen as being twofold.

Firstly, the authoritarian nature of ICTs that emerges as a result of the three features identified above is all-pervasive. Within local government, therefore, the emphasis is upon information systems that provide improved managerial control for the various technocratic professional networks that dominate local government (Rhodes 1988), and which deliver efficiency or effectiveness that corresponds to the bureau-maximizing strategies of the main technocratic elites. It is true that much of the impetus for these systems comes from outside of the immediate scope of informatization, especially in the form of legislation and the neo-liberalist new public management that is currently dominating UK public administration. But the point here is that the overall form of the technologies that are being implemented within the institutions of UK local government is much more compatible with authoritarian political structures than it is with democratic processes. In all functions of local government the informatization initiative is concentrated around improving the ability of managers to control, and in improving the quality of service to 'customers'. Initiatives that share information between functions in order to improve the quality or efficiency of local services are widely encouraged, but initiatives that seek to provide information to the local community or to engender greater citizenship are marginalized. Consequently, any schemes that attempt to move informatization into the local community occur at the periphery of local government, rather than at the heart of it. For example, the Manchester and Kirklees Host systems, which aim to provide a low cost telematics infrastructure for business and community use have emerged from economic development sections rather than corporate IT departments, and are managed by an external company rather than the Councils own IT staff (Ducatel 1994). Thus, the authoritarian nature of extant informatization has become self-entrenching by transferring to adjacent political processes, reinforcing the technocratic nature of local government. New ICTs, therefore, are becoming part of an authoritarian legacy which may well defeat future attempts at engendering democracy.

Secondly, because the authoritarian features of informatization are so pervasive, this has implications for any attempts to engender local democracy. From the technical legacies and complexities of information systems, through to the symbolism of ICTs and the intrinsic defensiveness brought about by the informatization of local authorities, there is an inherent authoritarianism in the use of ICTs. Any reformulation of local democracy, even if it does not depend wholly upon the traditional institutions of local government, must address the inherent authoritarianism that is reinforced by the ubiquitous use of anti-democratic ICTs in public administration. Local democracy must make use of informatization, not ignore it. At the same time it is also necessary to critically analyze current ICT based proposals to develop local democracy. Proposals for teledemocracy that are based in optimistic uses of interactive technologies, and even those schemes that aim to enhance democracy by improving the information available to local communities are too fragmented and unsystematic to address the authoritarianism sustained by existing technologies. Proposals for using informatization to increase local democracy must address the inherently political nature of ICTs as a whole, rather than deal with informatization in a piecemeal way. Fragmented attempts to engender democracy will only founder against the systemic authoritarianism of contemporary ICTs.

# CHAPTER 10

# Democracy and Virtual Communities

*An empirical exploration of the Amsterdam Digital City*

Kees A.T. SCHALKEN and Pieter W. TOPS

*Tilburg University, PO Box 90153, 5000 LE Tilburg, The Netherlands*

**Abstract.** The Amsterdam Digital City has been inspired by the American and Canadian Free-Nets. These are community-networks which are also called virtual communities. Anything that happens in the real world, also happens in such a virtual community, albeit digitally. Digital cities have been made possible by the development of network technology. They give a new dimension to the discussion about the relationship between democracy and ICTs. The discussion goes beyond the classic opposition between direct and representative democracy. New forms of discussion and democratic organization seem to become possible. Digital cities appear to transmit an impulse to new forms of communitarian democracy. However, for the time being the population of the Digital cities is rather one-sided: people are predominantly male, young and highly educated.

## 1. Introduction

For a long time the discussion on the relationship between information and communications technologies and democracy has been dominated by one perspective: technology was to bring the ideal of direct democracy within reach. The necessity to organize the democratic process in a large-scale society with many participants by means of systems of representation, would become obsolete; technology would make it possible to consult the citizens involved on any subject at any time (see chapter ten). In a way the dominance of this idea of direct democracy is connected with the specific characteristics of first and second generation information technology. Big central computers, which could administer huge data files, were typical of these generations. They have been made for better and faster computations, a capacity which led to speculation about instant stock-taking and aggregation of individual citizens' opinions.

The assumed relationship between technology and direct democracy has always been a point of criticism. Somewhat disparagingly, there was talk of a push button democracy, in which citizens would be invited to cast relatively ill-informed but decisive votes on any subject at will. This would mark the end of the conscious and meticulous stock-taking and weighing of interests of representative democracy, in which the position of minorities is constantly being taken into consideration as well. The crucial, consultative moment in democratic decision making would come under pressure and maybe even give way. This could lead to a sort of populist drilling of democratic decision making (Depla 1995).

Meanwhile we are beginning to deal with a new generation of ICTs. The integration of information and communications technologies is typical of this one. Not only does this technology make for better and faster computation, it also brings about new types of communication. It is especially the rise and development of network technology that gives a new dimension to the discussion on the relationship between democracy and technology. In this chapter we shall discuss one of the concrete experiments that have emerged from this development: 'The Digital City' in the Dutch town of Amsterdam, an initiative modelled after the American Free-Nets. It is an experiment that goes beyond the classic definition of direct democracy, appearing, as it does, open the way for new means of forming public opinion and a new democratic organization. The chances are that 'virtual communities' will arise, which may act as a spur to public decision making, but which may also raise some thorny questions.

In this chapter the 'Digital City' project will be discussed; at first attention will be paid to the history of the North-American Free-Nets (2) Then we will give a brief description of the Amsterdam Digital City (3) and of its inhabitants (4). Some bottlenecks in the Digital City will then be analyzed (5). After that, we will describe some issues in the relationship between the digital city and democracy (6). In doing so, some of those thorny questions will emerge.

## 2. Free-Nets in the United States and Canada

The Amsterdam experiment with the Digital City does not stand on its own. The initiators of the Digital City were inspired by the Free-Nets in the United States and Canada. Free-Nets are so-called 'community-networks', also known as 'virtual communities'. Everything that happens in the 'real world' also happens digitally in this virtual community.

The first Free-Net system was founded in Cleveland in 1985 by Tom Grundner, who at the moment is managing director of the NPTN (National Public Telecomputing Network), the umbrella organization of all Free-Nets in the world. The Cleveland Free-Net has meanwhile grown to become the biggest in the world, with over 24,000 participants.

A Free-Net possesses certain specific characteristics. One is that the Free-Net concept was developed and implemented by representatives of the social domain (the 'grassroots movement'), not by government organizations. The Free-Nets in the United States and Canada are founded, arranged and administered mainly by representatives of social organizations. In this respect, then, the primacy of citizenship holds for the Free-Nets. On these social organizations' initiative, information needs in the local community are taken stock. They see to it that sufficient capital is raised (in many cases by subsidies from local government, social institutions and users) to acquire the necessary equipment. Also, the volunteers see to it that information and data files that are administered by local governments, libraries and other institutions, are opened up to the general public. Anyone possessing a computer and a modem can subsequently call in for free (barring telephone charges). Public access terminals are also made available to make sure that those who do not have the necessary equipment can access the system in a public space.

An important aspect of the Free-Net system is that not only information is made available, but also that new means of communication are being created. In conjunction with this an on line connection with the Internet is made. For instance, in a Free-Net system there are ample opportunities for communication through electronic mail (email), newsgroups and on line, real-time discussion groups (also known as IRC or Internet Remote Chat). An advantage of the connection to Internet is that the Free-Nets can be linked up with existing networks. With that, the scope exceeds the geographical area that the Free-Nets applied themselves to in the first place. Local, federal and national data banks are unlocked for a large group of people in this way. Additionally the Free-Nets provide the opportunity to visit other Free-Nets, thus creating a nation-wide network.

This combination of collecting information from a social initiative and offering it for free, together with the provision of communication facilities has proved a clear success in the U.S. and Canada. The Cleveland Free-Net was soon followed by the Denver Free-Net (in the U.S.) and the National Capital Free-Net (Ottawa, Canada). Meanwhile the development of these Free-Nets has boomed in the U.S. and Canada. Already 42 systems are linked up with the NPTN. Apart from that there are contacts with some 142 foundation committees in North-American cities.

Meanwhile national and local governments in North-America have embraced the concept of Free-Nets. The Clinton-Gore administration has awarded a $ 20 million grant to the NPTN to erect a so-called Rural Area Network, which is supposed to enable also the less urbanized areas to set up their own Free-Nets. The Canadian province of Manitoba has awarded the Winnipeg Free-Net $ 40 million to carry through a network of local phone-in points, which is to facilitate the installation and administration of a Free-Net for each town in the province.

## 3. Amsterdam's Digital City

With the sending of an email message to the American Vice-President Gore on 15 January 1994, the Amsterdam alderman De Grave opened the Digital City. The Digital City was developed by the cooperation of the Amsterdam cultural center 'de

Balie' and the computer activists' corporation 'Hacktic Netwerk' (recently renamed the corporation 'xs4all', pronounced as 'access for all'). The city was developed on the model of the Free-Nets discussed above.

Like most Free-Nets the Digital City can be reached in three ways: through a personal computer with modem; through the Internet; or through one of several public terminals that have been opened in the city. Interest in the Digital City was overwhelming in the initial phase. The 20 modem lines that were made available appeared insufficient already in the first week. Despite cutting back the log-in time from an hour to half an hour, and despite the hurried installation of additional phone-lines, waiting times for the Digital City remained substantial. As a result, reports were quick to make mention of a 'traffic jam' at the entrance to the Digital City. Meanwhile the Digital City has over 15,000 participants and the system is accessed daily over 3,000 times (state of affairs per December 10, 1994).

The Digital City boasts a post office where you can send and receive electronic mail; a central station where world travel through Internet (the world's fastest-growing international datanetwork with (estimated) over 20 million users) can be accomplished in a matter of minutes; a plaza with cafés where you can contact friends in Japan or the U.S. through the IRC (Internet-Relay-Chat), and there is also a business district where one can get information on institutions of such diverse character as the Anne-Frank Foundation or the anarchistic Nomen Nescio. In Town Hall a connection has been made with political parties, the personal workplaces of civil servants and two municipal datafiles; the public information system PIGA and the administrative information system BISA. Within these systems information can be directly accessed by means of search keys. The information files on offer in the Digital City are frequently consulted (BISA, for example, was consulted over 9,000 times in the first ten weeks).

Besides various possibilities for seeking and finding information, the Digital City also offers a variety of discussion platforms under such subject headings as 'Schiphol and its extensions', 'Construction and Demolition in Amsterdam', and 'Crime'. The stimulation of public debate has always been one of the most important objectives in the design of the Digital City. This is why the choice was made to carry out the experiment during the period immediately before and after the local government elections of March 2, 1994. The various discussion platforms are attended to in differing degrees. The discussions under the headings 'Technopolis' (a discussion about the relationship between information technology and democracy), 'racism and the multicultural city' and the discussion about the Digital City itself, attract a group of about 60 participants who regularly contribute to the discussion.

## 4. Who are the inhabitants of the Digital City?

The Digital City offers something for everyone: information, communication, amusement and even possibilities to enter into social relationships. The 'experimental' character of the Digital City remains prominent here. Many applications still have to crystallize, and many questions remain therefore unanswered for now.

As the Digital City has been enthusiastically received - witness the media attention and the unexpectedly high number of participants - , the question of how this group of users is constituted is an important one. For, according to a frequently made criticism, the Digital City is mainly a toy for 'technojunks' and 'cyberpunks'.

To answer the question a Digital City survey was conducted in cooperation with the Digital City organizers. In it, the following questions were asked: who are the city 'inhabitants', why are they participating in the experiment, what do they do in the Digital City; and how do they evaluate it?

In April and the first week of May 1994 an option 'QUESTIONNAIRE' was added to the main menu of The Digital City. After choosing this option one was informed about the objectives of the questionnaire and one could decide to cooperate (every inhabitant could only fill in the questionnaire once). A total of 1,197 inhabitants filled in the questionnaire completely (about 1/10 of the total population). Due to the fact that this kind of electronic research has not often been conducted, it is difficult to assess the representativeness of the sample.

### 4.1. Sex

No less than 91 percent of the city 'residents' are male. The general image has always been that information and communications technologies is a man's world, and the male majority in the Digital City is overwhelming. However, this is not a problem that is exclusive to the Digital City. Conservative estimates on female participation on American Internet providers such as Compuserve or America Online show a similar image: only 10 to 15 percent of the online population are female (Trouong *et al.* 1993).

### 4.2. Age

The Digital City is a young city, not only in terms of the city itself, but also in terms of the age of its inhabitants. Table 1 reveals around 58 percent of the residents to be thirty or younger. The youngest resident claims to have been born in 1986 (i.e. 8 years old). Over 38 percent of the inhabitants are to be found in the 31-50 age category. Older people are strongly underrepresented in the city. Only 3.4 percent of the residents are over fifty. The oldest resident in the survey registers 1918 as the year of birth (a respectable 76 years of age).

Table 1                              AGE

| | |
|---|---|
| 8-18 | 5.9% |
| 19-25 | 29.0% |
| 25-30 | 23.3% |
| 31-35 | 15.7% |
| 36-40 | 10.9% |
| 41-50 | 11.8% |
| 51 or older | 3.4% |

## 4.3. Education and Occupation

The residents of the Digital City are highly educated. No less than 72 percent of the inhabitants have had, or are currently following, Higher Vocational Training or university education (table 2).

Table 2                              EDUCATION

| | |
|---|---|
| primary school | 1.1% |
| lower vocational/secondary school | 3.9% |
| O levels - A levels | 23.1% |
| college | 24.7% |
| university | 47.3% |

The less-educated are poorly represented in the Digital City. Apart from the large population of higher educated people in the Digital City, students and school pupils are also strongly represented. In reply to the question about their current position, 31 percent of the respondents indicate that they are at school or studying.

Table 3                              OCCUPATION

| | |
|---|---|
| government/semi-government employed | 21.2% |
| private sector employed | 27.3% |
| self-employed | 12.4% |
| domestic duties | 0.1% |
| student/school pupil | 31.0% |
| unemployed/unfit for work/pensioner etc. | 7.7% |

Clearly students form the largest category in the Digital City. They are closely followed, however, by those employed in the private sector (27.3 percent).

## 4.4. General Interests

In order to determine the Digital City inhabitants' specific interest areas, they were asked what those were. More than one area of interest could be filled in.

| Table 4 | INTERESTS |
|---|---|
| Computer technology | 76.6% |
| Art and culture | 43.3% |
| Politics and democracy | 41.0% |
| Social sciences | 31.3% |
| Economics | 27.2% |
| Sport | 22.5% |
| Other | 24.4% |

It will come as no surprise that computer technology tops the list. The Digital City is of course a computer system, to which computer enthusiasts are more easily attracted than others. Yet over 23 percent of the city's residents indicate they have no particular interest in computer technology. The fact that a certain degree of computer skill is a pre-requisite to participation in the Digital City is apparently no handicap for them.

## 4.5. The Digital City Resident Profile

The figures above present an image of the average Digital City resident. The total picture is rather one-sided. Most Digital City residents are young men, highly educated, frequently still studying or working in the private or public sector, with a great interest and ability in the use of information and communications technologies. Women, older people and the less-educated are strongly underrepresented.

The Digital City is still in an experimental phase, in which it is mainly the 'early adapters' who take to the network. It is therefore possible that, with the passing of time, the user profile will change and become more balanced.

## 4.6. New Developments in the Digital City

An important instance of progress on the Internet is the development of a graphical user-interface. In 1993 information on the Internet was almost exclusively available as text. Text could be consulted through protocols as 'telnet', 'ftp' and 'gopher'. In accordance with the then state of the art on the Internet, the first version of the Digital City presented only text to its users. The software program 'FreePort' took care of the necessary linking of the different Internet protocols.

The year 1994 saw the rise of a standard for the Internet, which does not only integrate the different protocols in one program, but also offers a graphical interface. The latter can handle text, image and sound as an integrated whole. The standard that was developed for this is known as the 'World Wide Web' (WWW).

The fact that the second version of the Digital City also raises huge interest appears from the most recent figures. In October the number of visits stood at a daily average of 3,000, and in the first three weeks 680,000 pages were queried and consulted.

## 5. Bottle-necks in the Digital City

In the first year of the Digital City's existence some bottle-necks have come to light. These concern the accessibility and vulnerability of the system, the professionalism of the organization and the way in which discussions are being conducted.

* *System accessibility: traffic jams on entering town*
  Because large numbers of people try to log in to the Digital City at the same time, users are likely to face long waiting periods. Even though the number of modem-connections and phone-lines has been expanded to 50, the traffic into town is still congested. The arrival of the new graphical interface has made the problem even more serious. The retrieval of graphical information burdens the system heavily. As a result, the processing of commands is slowed down. An extension of phone-connections, storage and memory capacity can alleviate these problems in the future.
* *System vulnerability*
  The short history of the Digital City has exposed the system as still very vulnerable. Already in the initial phase the city was paid a visit by a 'burglar' ( a so-called 'hacker') who deliberately corrupted a number of files.
  The Digital City hardware itself is also vulnerable. In November 1994, a crash of the hard disk that contained the Digital City led to the instant disappearance of a large part of the town archives, including all newsgroup contributions. It turned out that no backups of these files were available. Also, some inhabitants appear to derive great pleasure from requesting an account under a forged name in order to contribute to discussions anonymously or under somebody else's name.
* *Professionalism of the organization*
  Because the Digital City was set up as a ten-weeks experiment, little thought was given at first to its internal organization. A small steering committee supported by a number of (technical) staff was believed to be adequate. Some of the staff are working for the Digital City as volunteers. The success of the Digital City, however, faced the steering committee with a sizable number of inhabitants, informati-

on providers and other interested parties. To maintain the stability and reliability of the organization, a certain professionalization of the organization is called for.

This will require a way of doing things that may easily conflict with the volunteer spirit of the organization. All kinds of laborious discussions on financing and 'commercialization' are in the offing, as the experiences in North-America confirm.

* *Discussion inside the Digital City: digital flame-throwers.*

In the Digital City discussions are held on all kinds of subjects. These discussions are very different in kind. On the one hand there are constructive discussions, on the other there are also aggressive and sometimes even very unpleasant personal discussions. The latter phenomenon is known on the Internet as 'flaming', after the digital flame-throwers brandished by the participants in the discussion. Digital discussions have a characteristic trait that makes it possible to react instantaneously to messages on the screen. In that sense they resemble a real discussion between people. However, the contributions made by the participants are stored and can be read and re-read by everyone. In that way the digital discussion combines the elusiveness of a face to face discussion with the perpetuity of an exchange of letters. This creates a dynamic that can easily lead to so-called 'flame-wars'. These usually last for about one or two weeks, and frequently end with requests from inhabitants who are not directly involved to terminate the discussion or continue it through email.

## 6. The Digital City and Democracy: Some Issues

Van de Donk en Tops have analyzed the meaning of ICTs in three different models of democracy (see chapter two in this volume). In direct democracy ICTs are seen as facilitating decision making by citizens directly (referenda, opinion polls). In representative democracy ICTs are seen as in instrument to improve contacts between citizens and representatives (opinion polls, communications technologies). In communitarian democracy ICTs are supposed to support informed discussion and deliberation among communities of citizens. For those last two models the Free-nets and digital cities are especially relevant. They create new ways of communication between politicians, civil servants and citizens and they are breading new life into the formation of communities of citizens. But by doing this, they raise some interesting new questions about the organization of democracy. In the next sections we will present an exploratory analysis of the issues and questions involved.

## 6.1. Politics and Democracy in the Digital City

The Digital City can function as a platform where (local) governments can get in touch with citizens and vice versa. Government services can use the system to provide information (like in the Digital City the Amsterdam BISA en PIGA system and the information from political parties around the elections). Electronic addresses are being published, with which citizens can contact civil servants or administrators. Also, platforms are being set up in the Digital City, where discussions can be conducted on local issues. Among other things, the Digital City can contribute to the following:

* Providing and acquiring information. Through the Digital City citizens can be kept in touch with policy intentions and activities of the Amsterdam municipality. Conversely, through the Digital City the municipality can acquire information from the citizens. An example of the latter is the questionnaire on employment initiatives that was included in the city.
* Reporting station for questions and complaints. Politicians and civil servants can be directly approached through the Digital City. Citizens can aim their questions and complaints straight at the right person. An ombudsman could enter the Digital City.
* Discussion and the forming of public opinion. Discussions are conducted in the Digital City in various ways. As different kinds of information can be linked to new means of communications in the Digital City, informed discussions are possible on different subjects. Such a discussion is being held at the moment on the shaping of a city-province of Amsterdam.
  In this way the Digital City can play a role in the development of innovative forms of participation and democracy. A network like the Digital City can also have consequences for the ways in which political parties arrange their work procedures. Several options are at their disposal.
* The Digital City can help political parties to become more widely known. Persons as well as viewpoints can be displayed  Parties can open their own party office in the city. Here they can give information about party viewpoints, announce activities and congresses, and open the way for communication with anyone interested. One example is the way in which GroenLinks (the green party) is presenting itself in the graphical version of the Digital City.
* In the Digital City political parties can take part in the discussions that are conducted there. They can also put themselves forward as the moderators of the debate. A medium like the Digital City makes it very simple to link existing interests and expertise for each subject. However, the very peculiar dynamics of an electronic discussion should be pointed out here. Discussions can be of the very constructive kind, but as often as not they degenerate into so-called 'flame-wars', in which slurs and abuse are launched back and forth across the screens.

\* Political parties can also use the facilities provided by the Digital City for shaping their internal communication. So-called 'mailing-lists' can support internal discussions on local subjects. Without having to call a general meeting every time, party members can be consulted electronically.

Apart from its effects on the functioning of political parties, the Digital City may also have other consequences. For instance, the structure of the network of which the Digital City constitutes a part, is fundamentally non-hierarchical. A municipal organization, by contrast, is organized on hierarchical principles, with politics at the top. The consequences this will have for the contacts and discussions that arise across the network, are not clear. Questions will be raised, for instance, about the responsibility of civil servants who get involved in the digital discussions. Should they operate within the existing framework of political responsibility? This issue certainly needs to be looked into, if politicians and civil servants wish to take a more active stand in the Digital City.

### 6.2. *The Digital City as a Community Network*

The Digital City can serve as a boost for the social structure of the real city. In this way the Digital City may function as a community network, supporting the local community. Some considerations on 'the individualization of society' point out the fact that citizens' sense of being part of a community is dwindling. Traditional meeting places appear to lose their function in present city life. A computer network may give new shape to this function.

An important element of a community network is the possibility to communicate. A community network will give rise to a tightly-knit 'virtual community'. It is also possible to get connected to the network from the world of associations. For instance, a great number of 'Special Interest Groups (SIG's)', ranging from the Bird-Watchers-, Cooking and Eating-, the Gardeners Exchange-, to the Islam-, Christianity-, Baseball-, Curling- and Cricket-SIG have found their niche in the Canadian National Capital Free-Net. They use the Free-Net to exchange information, but also to have meetings, get communication going, and to conduct serious discussions with members and anyone interested.

The Digital City was set up for the Amsterdam region in the first place. The Digital City contains the public and administrative information systems of the Amsterdam municipality. In the several discussion platforms discussions could be held on such typically Amsterdam issues as the appointment of the new mayor, construction and demolition in Amsterdam and the extension of Schiphol (even though the latter goes beyond the Amsterdam region in scope).

The Digital City contains the local political party programs, and the office district offers a link with a great number of local institutions. Finally, the Digital City was financed in part by the municipality of Amsterdam.

However, this does not imply that the Digital City cannot transcend its own community. Through the national or international network, contacts can be made from the local community with all kinds of locations in the world. A 'virtual community' like the Digital City has no fixed spot on the map. People from outside Amsterdam equally had the opportunity to call in (or log on through the Internet using telnet). Many of them did. Some 50 percent of the Digital City users reside outside the Amsterdam region.

The above clearly shows that the computer networks can provide a new incentive to the establishment of community networks. So, instead of further contributing to atomization and fragmentation, they actually open the way for new forms of community action. These will be less limited in place (and time) than before. The new community networks are functional in nature, and not restricted to particular locations. By contrast, the organization of political democracy is still strongly determined on a geographical basis. There is a certain tension between this territorial foundation of existing democracy and the functional orientation of the rising virtual networks.

## 7. Conclusions

In this chapter we have dealt with some issues that relate to the rise of the Free-Nets and the Digital Cities. We have shown them to throw new light on the discussion about the relationship between democracy and technology. The link with direct democracy (instant referenda) that was initially made, has faded into the background somewhat. Alternative forms of organization and discussion are coming into being. Digital Cities are giving incentives to the shaping of communities. However, the virtual communities are not tied to time and place, and therefore transcend the classic, geographical orientation of our democracy.

An initiative like the Digital City also introduces new ways of communication between citizen and administration, both in the sphere of services and in the more political relationship that exists between them. However, this development is not neutral, but questions existing relations and organization patterns. One question, for instance, would be whether it is not getting time that the classic, hierarchical relationship between politics and bureaucracy was modernized.

Thus it becomes evident that a number of classic issues and principles are being questioned by the way in which the possibilities of information and communication technology manifest themselves in the Digital City.

# CHAPTER 11

# Political Parties in the Digital Era. The Technological Challenge?

Paul F.G. DEPLA and Pieter W. TOPS

*Tilburg University, PO Box 90153, 5000 LE Tilburg, The Netherlands*

**Abstract.** New technology has entered the world of politics. The introduction has a gradual character, but political parties make more and more use of the applications of information and communications technologies. This chapter discusses the influence of this 'creeping revolution' for the role and position of political parties. ICTs challenge their traditional organization, function and culture. The technology offers new opportunities for two 'successors' of the classical mass party: the modern cadre party and the professional electoral association.

## 1. Introduction

Political parties seem to be on the decline. The end of the political party is regularly forecast in scientific and journalistic publications (Tromp 1985: 21). In a further analysis of these publications the decline seems to concern mostly the classical mass parties, as described by Duverger (1964). These parties, founded in the 19th century, originate in emancipation movements. They are the political branches of broad social movements, that concentrate on certain socio-economic or socio-cultural groups in society. Mass parties are not organized around a person, but based on an ideology; they have a highly programmatic rather than a personalistic character. A solid network of local and regional branches enables a strong organization, which is centrally managed. Mass parties have a great number of members, who contribute actively to the party as volunteers. A flourishing 'club life' is the last characteristic of a mass party.

For a long time, the mass party was considered the example of a modern party organization (Koole 1992: 25). Apart from a small number of liberal and conservative parties, which usually do not form part of an emancipation movement, political formations have often had the character of a mass party, especially in Western Europe. However, from the 1960's tide began to turn. The successful emancipation of large groups in society, the crumbling of tight-knit social networks and the decreasing appeal of ideologies as *grand designs* affect the basis of the classical mass parties. The most obvious symptoms of the decline of classical mass parties are a decreasing number of members, lesser enthusiasm for 'club' activities, programmatic disorder and a less natural involvement of voters to one particular party (Commissie-van Kemenade).

In several countries, political parties are looking for an answer to their diminishing appeal. In The Netherlands the reports from the Van Kemenade (1991), the Van Laarhoven (1991) and the Duyvendak (1993) commissions are examples of this. These commissions have presented proposals for the organizational renewal of political parties. These proposals have drawn on political science and sociological publications regarding the position, organization and functioning of political parties. In the past three decades, several 'successors' of the classical mass party have been announced. In 1966 Kirchheimer foresaw the rise of 'catch-all-parties', while in the 1980's Panebianco (1988) saw a future for political parties mainly as 'professional electoral associations'. Finally, Koole (1992) considered the 'modern cadre party' to be the successor of the classical mass party.

In this chapter the possible influence of the rise of new media on the position and functioning of political parties is analyzed. Does the application of technology in the political process lead to a natural 'heir-apparent' of the classical mass party?

Before this question is answered, in the first paragraph we describe how new media enter the political stage. To do so, we refer to several initiatives and projects where technology plays a role in the political process. In this, we concentrate on the situation in the Netherlands. Furthermore, we analyze the character of the new media, after which we describe its implication for the political system. Finally, in the last paragraph we discuss the challenge the rise of new media involves for the position, functioning and organization of political parties. To illustrate this challenge, two scenarios are described, which may result from the political applications of the new media.

## 2. The Political Entrance of ICTs

Is it really an interesting question whether ICTs have significance for political parties? Are new information and communications technologies being applied at all in Dutch politics? Future visions expressed before, like the one of a paperless public administration, have not come true. Nevertheless, one can observe that the new technologies have found a place in the world of politics. The introduction has a gradual character, and is rightly known as a creeping revolution. The following inventory gives an impression of the multiform development of ICTs in the political scene in the Netherlands.

| CDA-TEL,<br>PDVA-BBS. | These are data banks of the CDA (Christian Democratic Party) and PvdA (Dutch Labour Party) which contain all kinds of topical information about both parties. People who have a computer and a modem can consult these data banks. |
|---|---|
| BRINKMAN-VIDEO | To involve viewers more in political broadcasts, the CDA has given them the possibility to ask their personal questions to the intended party leader Brinkman. |
| CDA INFO-LINE | A special telephone line from the CDA. For the amount of forty cents a minute, the caller can ask all sorts of questions about the CDA. By now, every day about a hundred people call this number. |
| PEP (PVDA ELEC-TRONIC PROFILE) | An electronic program to easily organize a survey among the party members or parts of the electorate. |
| PVDA INFO-DISKETTE | This information diskette contains information about, among other things, the party's history, illustrious party members, portraits of members of government and administrators, the current electoral program, important addresses and the organization of the PvdA. |
| CDA ELECTORAL PROGRAM DISKETTE | By putting its model electoral program on diskette, CDA has made things easy for its local party organizations in the 1994 local elections. To compose a local program, all the local organizations have to do is order the diskette and add the name of their own municipality. |
| MAILINGLIST GROENLINKS | GroenLinks (Green Party; Libertarian Left) has created a mailinglist on Internet, to stimulate the discussion within the party. Interested members and non-members can subscribe to this list, thus receiving all contributions to the debate on the mailinglist. |
| THE ELECTRONIC PVDA BALLOT PAPER | The representatives at the 1993 PvdA congress could vote with an electronic ballot paper. The computer made it possible that the result of the vote was known within half a minute. Because of this, the congress had a more 'flashy' media-sensitive character than before. |
| THE DIGITAL CITY | An electronic reflection of city life (in Amsterdam). Almost anything that takes place in an ordinary city, can happen in the Digital City. Political debates can also be organized through the Digital City, for example about the desired profile of the new major of Amsterdam. |

| GROENLINKS ON THE WORLD WIDE WEB | GroenLinks has put a homepage on the World Wibe Web. All people interested can inform themselves via Internet about the standpoints and activities of this party. Homepage users can also 'click through' to pages of organizations related to GroenLinks. |
|---|---|
| CABLE EXPERIMENT HOOGVLIET | With the help of two-way cable, teletext can have an interactive character. Inhabitants of Hoogvliet (Rotterdam) can obtain all sorts of information about their district via their tv screen and by using a special remote control. The administration of Hoogvliet used the interactive teletext to put all kinds of questions to its citizens. |
| AMSTERDAM CITY-CONVERSATIONS | Television debates on local television about political and social issues. By reacting to statements viewers can influence the program. |
| RADIO-REFERENDUM RIJNMOND | The local radio station canvasses the opinion of the population on a topical political subject. During the program, supporters and opponents of a proposition about this subject speak. Listeners can respond to this. By asking a few extra questions, the station hopes to be able to draw a (rather) representative picture of the opinions of the population. |
| CITY CONSULTATION NIJMEGEN | An 'instant referendum', which can be held quickly. The municipality has developed a scenario, so that at any moment two thousand inhabitants of Nijmegen can be asked about their opinion on a certain political issue. |
| CITY PANEL DELFT | On the basis of a large survey, the wishes of citizens and their judgements of the activities of the local administration and the public services are being determined. Also, by using the city panel the public support for proposed policies can be considered. |
| AUTOMATIC REGISTRATION OF MEMBERS | A kind of 'office automation', which is used by almost every political party. It is thus possible to add extra data to the registration of members, to make profiles of the membership file. By using specific keys it is relatively easy to trace, for example, all youths, all members with interest in sports or all members with management positions in business. |
| OMROP FRYSLAN, RADIO WEST, RTV-OOST, AT5 | (Frisian Broadcasting Company, RTV-East, Amsterdam Television 5) Four local or regional tv stations. These new tv stations - which leave behind the 'amateurish' experiments of the '70s and '80s - aim their programs and news coverage at specific geographic areas. |

| DIRECT MAIL | In spring 1993, the city council of Amsterdam decided to build a large tennis ground at the borders of a recreation park in the 'Amsterdamse Bos'. This decision, which would make disappear part of the Vietnam-weide ('Vietnam meadow'), raised enormous protests. Almost six thousand inhabitants of Amsterdam lodged a complaint at the local authorities. Their addresses were stored in a computer file. GroenLinks (Green Party; Libertarian Left), which supported the council's decision, used this file to explain the party's point of view to all the people in a letter. |
|---|---|
| COUNCIL INFORMATION SYSTEM IN THE HAGUE | Data bank for members of the council. This data base contains information that is relevant to the work for the council: documents, minutes of meetings, votes, the composition of commissions, the municipal budget and information about the municipal system. |
| EMAIL VOORBURG | Councillors of this South Holland municipality acquired a personal computer and modem, due to the 'pc at home plan'. With the modem they can contact the mainframe computer at town hall. Via the modem councillors can confer with one another or send one another documents - like motions - and comment them. |

Table 1 : Multiform development of ICTs in the political scene in the Netherlands.

This review shows that ICTs make their entrance in Dutch politics both on a national and local level. In some of the initiatives technology is very emphatically present, like in the PvdA information diskette, the mailinglist and the homepage of GroenLinks, the council information system in The Hague, the CDA electoral diskette or the *email* in Voorburg. In some other examples, ICTs are less prominent. The city consultation in Nijmegen, the Vietnamweide letters of GroenLinks, the radio referendum Rijnmond: in these examples the new technology is less visible for users and outsiders. Here, the new media are important in a supportive way. However, without technology these initiatives could never have been applied in politics in their present form. The boom in opinion polls proves this. Even without computers, opinions and preferences of people can be listed, but not with the frequency and intensity at which this is happening at the moment. In short: in a both 'visible' as well as an 'invisible' way, new technology enters the world of politics.

## 3. Characteristics of the New Technology

The new technology has a number of characteristics, which influence the way information processes go (Abramson *et al.* 1988). They have implications for the political process in various ways.

### 3.1.  Amount of Information

The amount of information that can be collected, handled, processed, analyzed, stored and asked for has increased strongly, thanks to computers, cd-rom, *bulletin board-systems*, teletext and videotext. Not knowing belongs to the past; not knowing becomes not wanting to know.

Politicians can inform themselves better by using the new technology. The results of the investigations among citizens make the wishes and meanings of the population and the own electorate clear to politicians. Meanwhile, they can inform themselves via data banks about the nature of social problems and the possible reactions. The The Hague council information system is an example of such a data bank, which politicians can use to increase their knowledge. The new media can also be used to inform citizens more about political parties. Regional tv stations can inform citizens of local politics, while political parties can inform citizens through all kinds of direct mail-actions of the standpoints they have taken. The letters GroenLinks sent to the people who had lodged an objection against the building of tennis grounds in the Vietnamweide illustrate in what way political parties can inform citizens about political considerations and choices.

In a number of ways, more information seems to have a positive influence on the political process. At the same time, the new media make the danger of an *information-overload* topical. The new media can further broaden the present information flow. However, there is a possibility that receivers are flooded with an amount of information they can never manage to handle and use: 'the more I see, the less I know'. Moreover, it is not in the least certain that citizens are more involved in politics when the political news coverage is at top speed. The public political tiredness that appears after a few intensive election campaigns seems to point in that direction.

### 3.2.  Speed of Information Processes

Besides having an effect on the amount of information, ICTs also influence the speed at which information can be collected, handled, analyzed and exchanged. Time and space are hardly barriers any longer. With a fax or via an electronic network, written documents - of whatever size - can be spread very fast over the entire world.

The development of the computer, with more and more capacity, makes it possible to quickly process and analyze a great deal of information. The importance of this for politics can be made clear on the basis of opinion polls. On the one hand, it is possible to see at any moment of the day how the population judges an event, a political decision or something a politician has said. A few days after the parliament's decision on the future of the Rotterdam airport Zestienhoven, it is clear how many people agree with this decision and what the judgement of the parties' own electorate is. Thanks to these opinion polls, politicians can anticipate public opinion very fast.

On the other hand, the results of opinion polls might, at a certain point, completely dominate the activities and standpoints that are taken in politics. Because of opinion polls tumbling over each other, increasingly on the political agenda there is only a place for another new reaction to another new survey among the population. Initiatives such as the radio referendum and the city consultation hold this risk to some extent.

### 3.3. Careful Selection of Receivers of Information

Under the influence of ICTs, radio and television become less and less unaimed mass media. To an increasing extent, television and radio channels differentiate to clearly defined groups of viewers and listeners with specific interests and characteristics; Radio One as a news-station, Radio Three for young people, Radio Four for classical music, Radio Five for minorities, RTL IV for the family and RTL V for the young educated male. These are just some examples that illustrate that television and radio gradually become massive information sources for specific groups of people, a development strongly stimulated by the rise of cable. Via cable, many more tv and radio stations can be offered than via the air. Because of this, it is easier to differentiate the channels, so that different groups can be served with programs that suit them. Regional television stations are examples of channels directed at a (geographically) selected group of viewers. In Anglo-Saxon literature (Abramson *et al.* 1988), this development is characterized as *narrowcasting* instead of *broadcasting*.

This *narrowcasting* is not confined to radio and television. This phenomenon appears in the sending and collecting of information in a broader sense. Information is sent to groups which are defined with increasing precision. The South Africa Committee for example has asked the leaders of the Labor Party party leaders to approach all its members in a letter, asking for a contribution to the ANC Campaign.

The increasingly precise approach of receivers of information is becoming even more sophisticated, due to the computer's ability to link or *match* large data files. These data files can be of a very diverse nature, for example, the subscribers to a magazine, the contributors to a good cause, the members of a social organization, or customers of certain shops. To an increasing extent, these files are stored in computers and are digitalized and thus can be linked together, so that specific profiles of groups of people can be constructed. Expressing interests, hobbies, buying power, holiday destinations, sex, age and social orientation.

Because of the various activities people undertake, they voluntarily - but mostly unconsciously - make data about themselves available. Because of the digital traces that people leave behind in nowadays' society, they can be 'identified' as persons that meet a specific profile and, consequently, they can be 'bombarded' with very accurate information. Door to door brochures and advertisements in newspapers will disappear, and direct-mail campaigns, such as the one GroenLinks did during the decision making process concerning the Vietnamweide, will take their place. In the information exchange between for example customers and retailer, citizen and administration and electorate and the elected, a great deal of unnecessary dialogue can disappear. The chance that the information actually reaches the receiver increases, but the sender of the information is, as it were, fishing in an aquarium.

As mentioned before, politicians can use these information profiles as well. They can provide specific parts of their own electorate with the information on issues they take special interest in. The general TV commercial will be replaced by political reports, specifically aimed at young liberal homosexuals or elderly businessmen. Because the information suits their own interests, receivers will probably feel better disposed to the message.

Because of the increasingly accurate definition of specific parts of the electorate, a certain 'balkanization' might occur, with people only being approached on matters of their own interest and standpoints. From the point of view of the maximization of votes, politicians can use the possibilities of *narrowcasting* to speak to the electorate with a forked tongue. The elderly are told that the AOW (Old Age Pensions Law) is 'sacred', while employers are promised that all social security benefits will be frozen, so that the public expenditure can be tempered. An alternative to the possibility of better informed citizens is the danger of citizens being more informed about less issues. One only watches or listens to the information channels that suit one's own interests.

## 3.4.  *Decentral Use*

The possibilities for the decentral use are the fourth mutual characteristic of the new media. Because of the 'miniaturization' of technology, decisions about the applications and use of ICTs can be taken decentrally. The growth of local tv and radio stations discussed before is interesting in this respect. However, the possibilities of the application of new media go beyond this.

In this respect one could think of the development of the *cam-corder* as an example, which, in principle, makes everybody a film producer. All kinds of events can be recorded with this camera. This makes more and more things accessible for a larger audience. While - certainly in unexpected matters - television cameras often arrive when an event is already history, such incidents might be filmed by an 'accidental' passer-by with a video camera. This might have serious political and public consequences. In 1992, for example, the acquittal of some police officers in Los Angeles lead to extensive riots, because a home-video had recorded the very rough way in which they had arrested Rodney King.

For the decentral use of ICTs, besides the video recorder, the development of the personal computer is of interest. By now, the PC has such capacity that it can handle almost every activity that used to take an entire *mainframe*. For example, a computer can be equipped with a statistical program, enabling the user to analyze all sorts of input data. The computer becomes a fast, automated punch card reader, while the individual user becomes a 'researcher'.

The development of the modem also gave an impetus to the decentral use of new information and communications technologies. With the help of a modem, a person behind his desk can communicate with people who are on other locations. For example, in Voorburg, members of the council receive all necessary documents from city hall by modem. In this respect, the modem can be considered to be an electronic postman. Through the modem, communication within political parties may get a different character. Via the modem the PvdA and CDA *bulletin board* systems can be used by everybody. Thus, members and people who are interested can be informed quickly and in great detail on the standpoints of a party. Moreover, users can ask each other questions and inform others about their own activities.

Finally, the possibilities of decentral use of ICTs are strongly expressed in the flourishing of *local area networks*. In these networks personal computers can be linked to a *mainframe* (or *server*). By doing so, all sorts of possibilities of the *mainframe* are available for the individual user. Having his own 'station', he can use all these possibilities decentrally - from behind his own keyboard. The importance of this is increasing, because these *mainframes* can be linked to worldwide networks. Consequently, the individual user can consult large data banks, in which a great deal of information is stored - such as the catalogue of the Library of Congress - from behind his personal computer. The development of the *Internet* is very important in this respect. Through this network, members of organizations, such as staff members of universities and hospitals, can communicate with others, without ever meeting each other. 'Virtual' discussion groups are created, examples of this being. The mailinglist of GroenLinks and the Digital City which have its own forums. The electronic networks - as mentioned before - are also used for the development of council information systems, like those in The Hague.

This miniaturization, which creates opportunities for decentral use, brings the new media within the reach of many people. As a consequence, information processes can democratize themselves. The importance of informal networks of, for example, experienced councillors who possess a great deal of information, decreases. New councillors can collect the necessary information through an information system. In the United States, according to Frantzich (1982), the automated information systems in Congress have had a similar effect: in a computerized Congress the 'Old Boys' networks had less grip on discussions and the taking of standpoints than before.

At the same time, one should bear in mind that the availability of technology does not garantee its use. For many people, the new media remain unknown, especially when they are not user-friendly. If the application of ICTs in society increases, then there is a chance that these people will miss any benefits. Some express the fear that a new elite of *whizz-kids* and computer-adepts will arise. Since accessibility has always been considered an important condition for discussions and decision making in politics and democracy, attention should certainly be paid to these possible exclusion-mechanisms of the new media.

## 3.5.  *Interactive Use*

A final characteristic fundamentally distinguishes ICTs from present information and communication channels, which is that the new media can be used interactively. The development of fibre optic cable, which is used for telephone and television is illustrative in that respect. These cables make it possible to transmit a great deal of information, while at the same time citizens can response to the information they receive, creating 'interaction' between the senders and receivers. As it were, a shift of roles takes place; receivers of information become senders as well. In these interactive applications of ICTs the users are able to influence the information exchange.

The telephone is also an interactive communication medium, for callers respond directly to one another. This does not make the telephone a variation on new information and communications technologies, since unlike the telephone, ICTs enable massive interaction. In this respect, ICTs are comparable to mass media such as radio and television. Many individual computer users can join in the discussions which are being organized within an electronic network. Through interactive teletext many citizens can respond to questions the local administration asks them, or viewers can give their opinion on propositions that are put forward during a television debate. The Amsterdam city-conversations and the cable experiment in Hoogvliet are based on this principle of massive interaction.

In this respect, ICTs combine the interaction possibilities of a communication medium like the telephone, with the large-scale character of mass media such as television and radio. The new media bridge the world of personal communication and mass communication. They unite the advantages of direct interaction with those of the massive exchange of information. This combination contains the unique, and for political applications probably the most revolutionary, element of the new technology. The massive use of the interactive characteristic makes ICTs suitable for introducing new kinds of political participation. Citizens are no longer addressed as passive voters. Interactive applications such as 'teleconferences' and 'instant referenda' give citizens new opportunities to get actively involved in political and social discussions. The question remains though, whether these applications will lead to a massive involvement of people in political discussions. If there is no will to create a political community, it cannot be created under the influence of the new media.

Moreover, mass media are rather unaimed. In spite of the fact that with ICTs certain target groups can be carefully selected - for example on *bulletin board systems*, where there are separate forums aimed at specific topics - there is a danger that with a massive application, ICTs maintain a rather unaimed character. This may have consequences for the nature of the discussions, which have a somewhat 'passing' character; one often responds quickly to one another. Here the term *flame wars* is used as a description; people are mostly responding to provocative parts with ditto reactions. Discussions in which arguments are put forward and discussed, on the basis of which finally a certain consensus is reached, are rarely found. Such discussions only take place when participation is limited to a group of people who have a relationship in some way or another, perhaps trough a business relationship or a mutual interest.

This causes a dilemma in the political applications of ICTs. In political discussions and in political decision making, their massive accessibility makes the new media very suitable for enabling new forms of political participation and communication, but the massiveness seems to lead to a certain unaimed communication, which does not seem to suit the 'appeal' and 'quality' of the political discussion and decision making very well.

## 4. The Challenge of ICTs for Political Parties

New media have five characteristics. Characteristics that are especially important to the way processes of data -collecting, -handling, -processing and data storage go. In the last paragraph we have shown how these different characteristics are important to politics. With this, we have not yet analyzed the way new media could change the character of politics. As indicated before, the introduction of the new technology provokes all kinds of spectacular futuristic views. Both democratic heaven and democratic hell are held out to us: Athens next to Orwell (see chapter two). Some people put the political significance of ICTs into perspective and argue that political issues are not made or broken by technical changes in the political process. Although it is good to consider any 'tall' stories about the revolutionary significance of ICTs with scepticism, one's eyes need not be closed to some consequences for the political system - especially for political parties - which in the long term seem to be attached to the introduction of ICTs.

### 4.1. *New Opportunities for Direct Democracy*

Firstly, forms of direct democracy seem to get new opportunities because of the applications of new media in the political arena. Time and place are no longer barriers to take part in political decision making. From their living room citizens can give their opinion on all kinds of propositions about current political issues which reach them through their television screen or computer monitor. By using the re-mote control or the telephone, the entire population can take part in votes about these propositions. In other words, with the help of ICTs it becomes rather simple and cheap to organize instant referenda.

Since these electronic plebiscites are a realistic option, the natural necessity of the representative democracy is being put under pressure. The new technology simplifies consulting the entire population. Intermediary organizations such as political parties and interest groups will then lose one of their main functions: the representation of interests. In principle, the population can administrate itself and no longer has to delegate decision-power to political representatives. ICTs make an 'electronic Athens' possible.

Although in literature it is often stated with great fuss that ICTs enable direct democracy, the actual change that ICTs have brought about in politics has so far been restricted to changing the red pencil for the ballot machine. This machine makes sure that the votes are counted faster; an important factor on election night. However, neither the character nor the number of elections will be influenced by it. It is just the romance of long exciting election nights on which the results from the different polling stations come trickling in one at a time, that will disappear.

The new technology has not yet been used to organize formal consultations. On the other hand, ICTs have been of importance in a number of somewhat 'informal' consultations. Here one could think of radio-referenda, the city consultation in Nijmegen and the city panel of Delft. In all these initiatives, in which technology has an important supportive role especially in the background, the 'people's voice' is consulted. Hopefully it can play a role of importance in political discussions and decision making.

On a local level particularly, the citizen seems to be discovered by the city council. In different ways, opinions, wishes and experiences of citizens are listed. This revival of the consultation of citizens, as a specific kind of direct democracy, may have consequences for the position of local politicians and political parties. While in political science handbooks articulating the interests of the people was one of the main functions of political parties, this function is made somewhat redundant by the consultations of citizens. With these investigations, a profile of preferences and opinions of citizens can be constructed as well, which in a number of respects is probably more accurate than the image politicians can represent. In this respect, the consultations can be considered competitors for political parties. A few negative reactions at the introduction of the Delft city panel show that local politicians are not always too pleased with this competitor. Some councillors said the panel was not necessary because 'the council was the city panel'.

### 4.2. New Forms of Political Debate and Participation

The direct democracy which could develop thanks to the new media, is being criticized from different sides. With instant referenda, the democratic process would be too much restricted to passively registering standpoints and preferences of citizens. There is no room for forming an opinion nor for discussion in which the parties concerned can give their view. Because this is supposed to be essential in prudent decision making, it is expected that the introduction of instant referenda will result in a democracy of a poorer quality. Criticism of direct democracy is reflected in the way the electronic referenda are judged. It is said to be a *push-button-democracy*, in which political involvement of citizens is being reduced to periodically pushing a button of the remote control or the telephone.

Some of these objections can be overcome by other interactive applications of the new technology. Then the use of ICTs in politics does not necessarily lead to passive forms of political participation. The interactive use of cable television, telephone and computer networks enable alternative forms of political discussions and forming of opinions. The city-conversations in Amsterdam show this. These conversations are an initiative to stimulate discussions on social and political issues. Where it is intended to make politics more attractive and accessible for citizens and to give them an active role in the political discussion. This contribution of the citizens can make sure that the public and political debate are geared to one another. Apart from that, the city-conversations give the parties the opportunity to contribute to the public debate. With this application of the new media, the political parties can not only get in touch easily with the electorate, but they can also give a new interpretation to their opinion forming function.

### 4.3. Responsive Representative Democracy

Of old, direct democracy encounters a great deal of resistance. The representative democracy, with its inherent patterns of checks and balances, deliberations and compromises, is mostly considered a superior form of political decision making. Nevertheless, it is beset with some important problems. It is often stated that there is a large gap between citizens and politics, and that politicians' standpoints less and less in line with those of their own electorate. The introduction of ICTs in politics can lead to a more responsive representative democracy. The boom in opinion polls is an important example of this. Political parties use the services of research agencies more often to investigate the citizens' opinions. With it, the electoral position of a party can be determined, but also insight can be acquired into the standpoints of the population regarding topical political issues and policy proposals. Politicians can be inspired by this knowledge in their attitude. Because of this, there is a chance that citizens will recognize themselves more in 'their' representatives.

However, opinion polls can also be a threat to established politics. A continuous flood of polls can make politics less stable, since short term results begin to dominate, bringing a pressure on politicians to follow the citizens' opinion as shown in the polls. There are normative objections against this development; the autonomous position of representatives - who are expected to work without burden - is being put under pressure. Instead of being delegate, more and more a mandatory role will be imposed on them. The continuous flood of opinion polls can thus lead to a 'staccato' democracy, in which populist parties would have better chances than a party of principles.

## 4.4.   Targeted Campaign

Opinion polls redefine interaction patterns between politicians and citizens. In addition to this, ICTs enable a more direct communication between elector and the elected. As mentioned before, through the linking of data files digital profiles can be constructed. These profiles, in which for example social activities, interests and environment are expressed, can be used by parties to provide carefully selected target groups with specific information. General, rather untargeted campaigns will be replaced by a detailed information distribution, which suits the receivers' perception of their environment.

In nowadays' society, political parties can use the digital profiles in a different way as well. It is often said that processes such as individualization and the declining importance of ideologies have caused a fragmentation in society. Because of these developments the supporters of political parties have a less homogeneous character; the support consists of various social groups with different interests and standpoints. This makes it difficult for political parties to direct campaigns to the entire group of supporters. The digital profiles seem to offer a solution for these problems of political parties. Different parts of the own electorate can be reached with a diversity of information and campaigns. Because of this, political parties can organize and mobilize different groups of the electorate.

From an electoral point of view, such strategy may have great value. A the same time, the increased possibilities to reach specific groups with detailed information can lead to a situation in which politicians take less trouble presenting a more general perspective, in which the different interests of society are weighed. The capacity to somewhat reconcile these differing interests and to sublimate the differences in a specific definition of the public interest, a classical function which distinguishes political parties from interest groups, may be gradually affected by this.

Because of the development of technology, politicians are increasingly able to control the information. To do so, political parties can for instance use so-called *bulletin boards*. These electronic bulletin boards are used to send and receive information, calls, announcements or messages. Through these bulletin boards, politicians can - without interference of intermediate channels like newspapers and tv stations - inform citizens of standpoints, speeches, reports and activities. The media no longer have to be a messenger, acting as a mediator between politicians and citizens. In this respect the use of ICTs creates the possibility of unmediated politics. Consequently, the information about politicians and political parties is no longer coloured by interpretations of 'independent' journalists.

The possibilities to control the provision of information on a decentral level make the new media attractive for political parties. However, these possibilities are not without danger. After all, the parties are no longer a necessary link in the communication between citizens and politicians. Politicians no longer need the parties to directly make contact with the population. Therefore, the new technologies give politicians the opportunity to 'emancipate' themselves from political parties. Politicians will no longer need parties to convince and mobilize citizens. To reach a great deal of voters, it will not be necessary any longer for politicians - supported by a large staff - to organize a great deal of meetings or to canvass extensively. The Ross Perots and Silvio Berlusconi's show, that, with the help of some ICT applications, rather 'partyless' politics are possible. Because politicians can act more independently from political parties, the application of ICTs seems to stimulate a further personalization of politics.

Opinion polls play an important role in this development too. Polls can show which individual characteristics politicians should and should not emphasize to make a positive impression on the electorate. Besides, candidates can use opinion polls to acquaint themselves with the population's opinion on different political issues. Even without a coherent program, they can, on the basis of opinion polls, put forward those views that will be the most favorable to them in an electoral way. Then the politician is no longer a political leader who tries to influence the public discourse with a general platform, but has become a 'broker in majorities'(see Van de Donk and Tops, p. 25).

### 4.5. Internal Party Organization

So, in some respect the introduction of information and communications technologies puts the position of political parties under pressure. In addition to this, applying ICTs in politics will probably have its influence on the internal organization of the parties. The communication between national party organizations and members is an example of this. ICTs offer national party organizations all kinds of possibilities to influence the discussions in the own organization more strongly. The national party organizations can control the information supply to members with a number of ICT applications. In this respect, the PvdA information diskette is illustrative. The diskette informs members and people who are interested of the PvdA's standpoints. Furthermore, GroenLinks can inform members and interested people on its standpoints and activities through the Internet homepage. With this information supply, the national organization can also somewhat 'streamline' the discussion and points of view. The CDA diskette containing the model electoral program for the 1994 local elections illustrates the way ICTs can be used to gear the standpoints in a party to one another. This was not the intention of the diskette, yet it was an effect. Since the new technology can be used decentrally, the individual members and local party organizations are able to somewhat adapt the information of the national organization. A local party organization does not have to restrict itself to introducing the name of the municipality concerned, but can also adapt the national standpoint on housing to its own views.

Moreover, when gathering information or organizing discussions, the party leadership no longer need to direct themselves primarily to existing channels. *Bulletin board-systems* and organizing opinion polls are alternative sources for the party leadership. Also in decision making, political parties are no longer depending from the activities of local party organizations. Via electronic referenda, within a party decisions can be taken in a time-saving and a to all members accessible way. Furthermore, within a party alternative forums can be organized. For example, bulletin boards enable teleconferences, with which interesting experience has been gained in the United States.

Within political parties the same applications are possible. Members, and non-members as well, who are interested in specific subjects can be organized according to such a subject through computer- or teleconferences. Thus, for political discussions on a party level, members are no longer dependent on the activities of their local organization. These applications of the new media will undoubtedly have enormous consequences for the organization and functioning of political parties in the long term. For example, for both national party organizations as well as individual members, the need for a an elaborate structure of local organizations is decreasing. A number of functions which have made local party organizations essential to both members and the national organizations for a long time will become redundant because of, among other things, the applications of ICTs.

In this respect the experience of the German SPD is worth mentioning (Bogumil and Lange, 1991). In this party ICTs have not only been of importance in increasing the internal efficiency, but also in attempts to modernize the party. Being a mass party, the SPD has to deal with an increasingly heterogeneous and fragmented support, which makes traditional functions, such as integration, reaching a consensus and mobilization more and more difficult to fulfil. As a reaction to this, the SPD started looking for new kinds of party loyalty, trying to reach new *Zielgruppen*. In this, ICTs play a supportive role, for example through the creation of data bases with information about relevant political and social issues and the people involved. This makes it easier to reach those people and involve them in party activities, such as organizing professional conferences. To an increasing extent, discussions and the forming of opinions take place on a functional party level. Consequently, the position of local party organizations is undermined; the gusto to become active on a local level decreases.

## 5. The Future: Two Scenarios

ICTs have entered the political stage. The examples discussed in the first paragraph make clear that in various activities in the political process, services and products are used which have been made possible by the arrival of the new media. Technology is used for election campaigns, communication with the electorate, internal party organization, parliamentary occupations, and for the preparation and implementation of policies. It is often stated that the new media have qualitative consequences for the character and course of the activities in the political process (Depla 1995).

The rise of technology also seems to affect the position of political parties. In the previous paragraph, for example, the changing forms in which discussions and the decision making in the political process can be organized is pointed out. Technology makes it possible to take a certain distance from the existing structures, procedures and routines in political parties. With this, the rise of new media is relevant for the discussion on the future of political parties as well (Koole 1992: 16).

As concluded in the first paragraph, in political science there is a debate on the successors of the classical mass party. These arguments mainly address socio-economic, socio-cultural and political developments, and no attention is being paid to the rise of new media. The publications seem to have a 'blind spot'. As illustrated in the previous paragraphs with Dutch examples, the entrance of new media in the political system may have consequences for the future position and functioning of political parties. On the basis of the consequences discussed, two scenarios can be described. We will conclude this chapter with a description of both of them.

In the first scenario the new media contribute to a modernization of the functioning and the organization of political parties. Technology is applied to enable, for instance, new forms of political participation. People are addressed to on the basis of their interest or knowhow. With the development of a *bulletin board-system* or the creation of a mailinglist on the Internet, members and sympathizers can be invited to take part in discussions on specific issues. In this way, functional discussion forums are created, in addition to the existing territorial relationships between local and regional branches. The rise of these functional discussion groups have at least three advantages for political parties. Firstly, members and voters can commit themselves to the party. When politicians join in and the results have an effect on the course of the party, discussion groups may have a high appeal. Secondly, discussion groups are a source of social information for political parties. During the discussions, social issues and feelings among voters come forward. Parties can use this information when defining their standpoints, so that their role in parliament is more recognizable for the electorate. Finally, parties can give an interpretation to their role as a forum on which relevant views are aired and exchanged (Commissie-Van Kemenade 1991). The existing party organizations hardly seem to fulfil this function anymore. Social discussions mostly take place outside political parties. Social organizations, media, and companies organizing congresses have taken over this function from political parties. According to De Haan and Duyvendak (1993) political parties have slowly, but surely, run into social isolation. The debate forums facilitated by the new media could make an end to this.

Furthermore, in this scenario the new media are applied to introduce new kinds of decision making. Technology makes it possible for many more members to have a vote in every decision of a party, and the vote for the list of candidates during the PvdA congress is an example of this. This kind of decision making would never have taken place without the availability of new media. With the development of an electronic voting-program (e-Vote), decision making can, in principle, even be organized through a *bulletin board-system*. In that case, truly all members can give their opinion on the lists of candidates or programs. With such party forums, direct democracy is introduced. This development has got a paradoxical effect on the relationships within a party. As members speak out, the influence of the national party organization on the decision making increases. Since in the 1960's a great deal of parties have introduced an internal democratization, decision making in a classical mass party is mostly indirect. Hence, the regional party-elite can leave its mark on the decision making within a party. With the rise of new media, the need for indirect decision making disappears; the party leaders can let members co-decide on standpoints of a party, without interference from regional leaders.

In the first scenario, technology is also used to improve communication with voters. Thus, parties can communicate directly with their grass roots. Parties no longer have to announce their standpoints to voters via journalists. With a *bulletin board-system, a faxed bulletin* or a mailinglist on Internet, parties can manage the information flow to voters. The news coverage of a party is then no longer 'coloured' by journalists. With direct mail-actions, such as the one of GroenLinks concerning the Vietnamweide, parties can inform voters on a certain standpoint. With these actions, which can be organized easier because of the rise of the new media, parties can obtain support and understanding for difficult decisions. In direct mail-actions, specific parts of the electorate are approached. The communication with voters can be aimed better, since with new media profiles of voters can be made. General campaigns are replaced with information that is geared to the perception of those receiving the information. This helps parties to approach and bind the different parts of their increasingly heterogeneous group of supporters.

Finally, in the first scenario parties use new media to determine their standpoints. Technology makes it easier for the parties to be informed about the views and opinions of their voters. In this context the new forms of political participation discussed before are interesting. Furthermore, to an increasing extent parties attach importance to research. Political parties organize more and more opinion polls. The results of these polls make clear which politicians are popular, what the image of the party is, which parties are the major competitors, which issues are important for their own electorate, and what the wishes and views of the voters are. This knowledge has a strategic importance for parties. By being informed of 'the people's voice', parties can distinguish themselves and make sure their politicians and standpoints are recognizable for the electorate. Since general political programs seem to have less cogency, parties may be able to attract voters in this way.

In the first scenario, new media contribute to a renewal of the participation, the decision making, and the communication in political parties. The new media enable parties to renew themselves in such way, that they are appealing for voters again. In this scenario technology brings about a revival of political parties, which occupy a prominent position in society and social debate. They are not classical mass parties, but a kind of modern cadre party (Koole 1992: 407-408), focused on issues and political leaders. The national leadership has a great influence on the party. However, members can participate in (functional) discussions and (direct) decision making. Their number is limited; 'club'-life is no longer very important. The modern cadre party wants to involve sympathizers in discussions with a highly open character. Finally, research is one of the principal supporting services. The profile of modern cadre parties depends mostly on quantitative and qualitative results of opinion polls.

The development towards a modern cadre party is but one of the possibilities. New media can also contribute to a continuing marginalization of political organizations. In the second scenario party organizations disappear and are replaced by electoral associations (Panebianco 1988). To illustrate this scenario we present a fictional newspaper article, published by one of the authors in 1992 (Depla and Schalken, 1992).

*Traditional parties wiped out*

# Jordan First Black President

Washington, 12 November 2000.
**For the first time in history, citizens of the United States of America will have a black president.This sensational result of the elections was obvious as the first results from the Eastern states were made known. In most states, the 'independent' Michael Jordan had built a comfortable lead over both Cuomo, the current president, and Kemp, the Republican candidate.**

At ten p.m. local time Cuomo accepted his defeat, while Jordan was celebrating his victory with a group of supporters in Chicago. In his first comment Jordan, the former basketball-professional who was extremely successful with the 'Bulls' in the 1990's, pointed out the serious consequences of the result for American politics. It was not just the first time ever a black president was elected, it was also a long time since the monopoly of Republicans and Democrats had been broken by an independent candidate. The new occupant of the White House concluded satisfied that 'traditional parties were swept away'.

**An excited Jordan**

### Independent president

From the first analyses of the results, it appears that Jordan has appealed to both Democrat and Republican voters. Running mate Johnson, who was a

great support for Jordan especially in the Western states, stated therefore that Jordan 'will not be representing the voters of a single party, but will act as a genuine independent president'. The future of political parties was the main topic in a great deal of comments of politicians on the election results. The Democrats attribute the success of the independent candidate to Jordan's charisma. 'Jordan's media-performance is unique', says former senator Kennedy, 'however, there is a small chance that future candidates will be able to beat the powerful organizations of the political parties'. Others think the future for American political parties is less bright. They point out a number of successful elements in Jordan's campaign, which may affect the position of established political parties in the long term.

### 'Electronic campaign'

In Jordan's campaign, for example, an enormous amount of money was spent in the so-called JEP-project (Jordan Electronic Panel-project). In every state, a few thousand citizens received a computer and modem. Periodically these citizens were asked some questions on topical issues. Furthermore, they could indicate which political issues they had discussed with family, friends or acquaintances in the past week. By linking the computer to a network, their answers could be quickly processed by Jordan's staff members. In this way they were able to anticipate on the shifting trends in public opinion. Jordan had an important advantage on the traditional parties, which also organized opinion polls. He did not have the burden of a party program, and of sensitivities of parts of the traditional grass roots. Therefore, Jordan was able, more than other candidates, to react directly and adequately to changing views of the American electorate.

## Video profile

Furthermore, Jordan's campaign team had developed electoral profiles, based on a number of socio-economic, cultural and political background variables such as education, unemployment figures, age, degree of urbanization, voting behavior-patterns and leisure activities. For every profile a specific videotape was made. Then a database was set up by purchasing various mailing lists, from, among others, union members, churchgoers, members of sportsclubs and contributors to environmentalist groups. By linking the different lists, profiles were created which fitted 'seamlessly' in one of the videotapes of Jordan. During the election campaign, many Americans received a tape which fitted their own perception and views. For elderly Americans in Southern states a tape was recorded with the emphasis on the work ethic in Jordan's career, while the tape for the young blacks on the East-coast accentuated the success of the 'slumkid' Jordan. So, every electoral group was presented a 'specific Jordan'. Thus Jordan succeeded in obtaining the support of very diverse electoral groups. Jordan proved to be a skilful broker in majorities.

## Satellite

In addition to this, Jordan used the possibilities of satellite to make his campaign successful. Every day, Jordan made a number of recordings for individual states, in which attention was being paid to some topical issues. A broadcast for Texas dealt with the consequences of the third oil crisis, while a recording for New Jersey exposed criminality. Via satellite these recordings were sent to the different states. Therefore, local tv stations, focused on election news concerning their own state, reported on a regular basis on Jordan's standpoints. Without leaving his headquarters in Chicago, Jordan was able to dominate the political news in the individual states. Furthermore, Jordan used the satellite to get in touch with the electorate in the different states. Thanks to this new medium, for half an hour he could answer questions from viewers of a local tv station in Alaska without leaving his study. Next, a local tv station in Florida was contacted. In this way, on one day Jordan was able to communicate with voters from various parts of the United States.

## Dark Horse

Finally, Jordan's campaign was refreshing, since he joined the election campaign at a late stage. While Cuomo and Kemp have campaigned to secure their candidacy for more than a year, Jordan confined with a three-month hit-and-run-campaign. The electorate has been seduced by the disarming features and the new ideas of the so-called 'dark horse' Jordan.

The way in which Ross Perot and Silvio Berlusconi have emerged, illustrates the meaning of the described scenario of Jordan's election. The development of new media offers opportunities for the rise of the phenomenon *professional electoral association*. Parties are then organized around a single political leader, who distinguishes himself on his characteristics or on one single issue. For the elections a union or project organization is created, which is aimed only at the mobilization of voters. Campaigning is its only activity. After the elections the union disappears, to reconvene for the next campaign, if the politician concerned is a candidate.

## 6. Conclusion

The meaning of the rise of new media for political parties is ambiguous; the two scenarios described express this. The future will tell what the empiric value of the scenarios is. However, we will discuss the scenarios in a speculative way.

The question whether the application of new media will lead to the rise of modern cadre parties or professional electoral associations depends partly on the way in which technology is used in the political system. Which characteristics of technology are used, and probably even more important, which actors use the technology, seem crucial questions. For the future of political parties, for example, it will be of importance whether or not the interactive features of the new media are used. With these features, political parties are able to bring up discussions and to involve members and sympathizers in their organization in a new way.

However, it is likely that eventually the meaning of new media for the position of political parties is also dependent on a number of political factors. For instance the character of the political system seems to be of importance. Some countries have a highly personalistic oriented system. This may be the result of the electoral system or specific historic conditions (Barrington Moore 1984). America and France are examples of this; in the first practically every politician is elected directly by the people, and in the latter the emancipation movements arose after the introduction of universal suffrage. In these countries there is a fair chance that with the rise of new media, the second scenario comes true. When parties traditionally have a rather fleeting organization and have not been able to dominate the political process to a great extent, people can apply the technology to bid for the voters' favor without the help of existing political formations. In these countries, the - not so strong - political organizations can slowly but surely be replaced by professional electoral associations.

In countries where political parties are indeed deeply embedded in the political system, it seems likely that, due to technology, a modernization of the political formations takes place. Thus political parties can reinforce their position in society. According to this line of reasoning, in for example, Germany, Austria, Scandinavia and the Benelux countries, where parties leave their mark on the political process, the application of technology will most likely go together with the rise of modern cadre parties.

Although it is probable that technology will reinforce the position of parties in the political system, this idea requires refining. The rise of new media makes the political system more sensible to external conditions. This goes mainly for systems in which political parties have a powerful position. In case of a serious political crisis, the availability of technology enables individuals to carry out an election campaign, independently from existing political formations. When the individual concerned can use the new media to obtain detailed information on voters and address the electorate directly, it is possible to make a bid for political power. The quick rise that Silvio Berlusconi made after the loss of the Italian Christian-Democrats and Socialists, illustrates that in a democratic political system in crisis the presence of new media can lead to an impetus towards more personalistic politics. This example also makes clear that such an individual must possess the necessary means to guarantee access to the (new) media.

# CHAPTER 12

# Information Technology, Openness of Government and Democracy

Stavros ZOURIDIS

*Tilburg University, PO Box 90153, 5000 LE Tilburg, The Netherlands*

**Abstract.** In several ways Information and Communications Technologies (ICTs) may contribute to the openness of government ('technology of freedom'). Access to electronic government information and the development of automated systems, which support the information services of government (and therefore enhance the transparency and accessibility of government) are examples of this. In this chapter two automated public information utilities are reviewed. The issue of access to electronic information in Dutch and U.S. law will also be addressed. New communications technologies seem to offer possibilities for faster, more effective and efficient dissemination of government information. ICTs may also threaten the openness of government. Protection and deletion of information are easier with ICTs. A lack of disclosure facilities poses another threat to the openness of government. Finally, the applicable law in the United States and the Netherlands contains a number of legal gaps. Therefore, ICTs function as a 'technology of secrecy'.

## 1. Introduction

In this chapter some implications will be explored of the introduction and use of Information and Communications Technologies (ICTs) for the openness of government and public access to government information. First, the significance of public access to government information for the future of democracy will be addressed. Two elements of democracy will be distinguished, namely a representative and a participative element. It appears that public access to government information performs a number of functions that pertain to both elements.

Openness of government is conceptualized as a specific point on a continuum that ranges from complete secrecy to complete openness of government information. The extreme positions on this continuum are, at one end, that the law ordains that all government information be accessible to the public and, on the other, that all government information has to remain secret. With the enactment of the Act on the Openness of Administration of 1980 (which was revised in 1992), the Dutch legislator introduced the principle that all government information should be accessible to the public. The Act also mentions some situations in which government information should be withheld from publication. For example, the Act states that government information should be withheld from the public when publication of the information might damage the security of the state. The Act on the Openness of Administration also states that the interest of publication of government information should be weighed against interests like privacy or criminal investigation. Openness of government and public access to government information can thus be defined as a specific situation with a certain degree of secrecy and openness. This situation may not be the same in countries with different public access (and secrecy) laws, like the American Freedom of Information Act, the Swedish Freedom of the Press Act and the Canadian Access to Information Act. Differences are found in the way in which the obligations are phrased, the way in which public access rights are designed, and which exceptions are allowed.

In this chapter, the implications of the use of ICTs for the legal framework in which the openness of government is laid down, will be analyzed within this conceptual scheme. On the one hand ICTs may lead to a shift in the existing situation in the direction of openness (the 'technology of freedom'). On the other hand the introduction and use of ICTs may lead to a shift of the situation, which implies that more government information is confidential. In these cases ICTs are referred to as a 'technology of secrecy'.

The study of the implications of ICTs is hindered by the fact that ICTs are developed in a socio-political constellation. Guthrie and Dutton conceptualize the development of automated information systems as making political decisions (Guthrie and Dutton 1992). These political decisions are made within the organizational, political, legal and economic constraints of the government agency. These contingencies affect the way in which ICTs are designed and thus these contingencies also affect the implications of ICTs. A specific conception of 'openness' and 'information supply' (which is defined as disclosure and dissemination of government information) will lead to a preference for certain 'technological paradigms' (see Guthrie and Dutton, 1992). When this decision to adopt a certain technological paradigm is made, one implicitly chooses an information system with particular functionalities. The implications therefore cannot be ascribed to ICTs only. The specific (economic, political, legal and organizational) environment of ICTs must also be taken into account.

For the sake of clarity two concepts have to be defined, namely 'public access' and 'government information'. In this chapter 'public access' is defined as an enforceable right of all citizens in a community to take notice of information which is at the disposal of government agencies in that community.

When we describe this right of 'public access', two different types of government information will be distinguished (Beers 1992), namely 'documentary information' and 'non-documentary information'. "The former comprises any record or recording that can be read, listened to or otherwise comprehended by means of technical aids. By the latter is meant any information not documented on a record or a recording which can be obtained when one is present at a meeting or a proceeding, as well as by visiting a building or some other facility. Examples are statements which are made during a meeting or a proceeding but are not put on record, unrecorded facial expressions of members of committees, the atmosphere in a courtroom, and the conditions in a prison. The availability of both documentary and non-documentary information can be secured by a right of access to records and recordings as well as to certain meetings and facilities" (Beers 1992: 181).

## 2. Democracy and Public Access to Government Information

In many ways openness of government and public access to government information are related to democracy. When the Act on the Openness of Administration was discussed by Parliament, a number of these connections were mentioned. First, public access to government information was said to be necessary for citizens' participation in governmental policy processes. Citizens' participation presupposes the disposal of adequate government information. Second, public access to government information is important for public accountability, supporting the political accountability of government to parliament. Openness of government would also be important for citizens when they want to initiate legal action against government decisions and for the security of law. To appeal to a court citizens must be informed about the applicable law and the reasons why the government chooses to interpret the law in a certain way. Thus, public access to government information serves the legal protection of citizens. Finally, public access to government information is related to the exercise of a number of fundamental rights, such as freedom of speech. Some commentators even speak of public access as an (emerging) fundamental right (Beers 1992).

The Dutch democratic system combines two kinds of elements of democracy, namely participative and representative elements. To analyze the significance of openness of government for democracy, the functions of public access to government information will be connected with these elements.

First, the democratic system in the Netherlands is characterized by representative elements. Citizens elect representatives, who represent the entire population without consulting them. Parliament decides for the people. Citizens supervise parliament by means of regular, free elections. An increasing degree of diversity and emancipation of the population have made a purely representative democratic system obsolete. In contemporary society it is not possible to force citizens into a passive role when they are confronted with policy processes which concern their personal lives. The sixties, which were a manifestation of these societal changes, led to different forms of participation of citizens in policy processes, which vary from opportunities for citizens to give their comments on government decisions, to particular kinds of co-production of policy between citizens, companies, pressure groups on the one hand and government agencies on the other.

Public access to government information is important for the functioning of both democratic elements. With regard to the representative element, public access to government information can be important for public accountability. In a pure representative democracy, where citizens are not involved in decision processes, parliament and government have to account for the decisions they make. On the basis of that kind of information (which opinions are related to which party?) citizens are able to decide to which party or representative they give their votes.

Public access to government information is also important for the functioning of a direct democracy. Information supply precedes different forms of citizens' participation, for example co-production by citizens and government. Citizens, companies and pressure groups are only able to participate in decision making processes when they are informed about which alternative decisions are possible, which consequences are related to certain decisions, and to what degree the alternative decisions are feasible. One of the problems of the 'traditional' forms of citizens' participation (a form in which citizens are able to give their opinions about decisions) in the Netherlands was a lack of openness in politics and administration, which caused a lack of information and therefore an asymmetrical power relationship between citizens and administration.

For the functioning of democratic systems a certain degree of openness of government is necessary. Information supply by government agencies, as it is legally codified in the Dutch Act on the Openness of Administration, contributes to the continuity of democratic institutions and the realization of democratic values.

## 3. Openness of Government and ICTs

In this chapter openness of government is conceptualized as a specific point on a continuum, which ranges from complete openness to complete confidentiality of government information. The introduction and use of ICTs might change this existing situation in different directions. Both potential shifts will be explored and confronted with the Dutch conception of openness of government, as it is laid down in the Act on the Openness of Administration. In the elucidation of some legal aspects we will refer to the American Freedom of Information Act (FOIA).

### 3.1. The Dutch Act on the Openness of Administration

The Act on the Openness of Administration contains general rules on confidentiality and the public nature of government information. Specific acts, for example the Urban Planning Act ('Wet op de ruimtelijke ordening') and some environmental acts (e.g. 'Wet milieubeheer'), contain specific regulations on public access to government information and information supply (disclosure and dissemination of government information) by government agencies. However, the most important Act in this area is the Act on the Openness of Administration. Despite the wide range of this Act, the legislator made a number of fundamental choices when it developed the Act. These choices have implications for the objectives, functions and instruments of the Act. They also cause a number of tensions in the functioning of the Act in public administration practice (Frissen *et al.* 1994).

One of the most important choices of the legislator concerns the way in which the public access right is designed. Which right is vouchsafed to citizens? Should the government be obliged to publish documents which are at its disposal (a document [record] system), or does one opt for a public right to government information, which may or may not be written down in documents? The latter is called an information system. In the Netherlands the legislator chose an information system but limited it to information which is laid down in documents. The FOIA in the United States is an example of a record system. FOIA obliges government agencies to publish records, while the Act on the Openness of Administration in the Netherlands gives citizens a right to the information. However, in the United States the opinions on this matter seem to be shifting. With regard to the introduction and use of ICTs, the Office of Technology Assessment (OTA) raises the issue of whether 'the FOIA should continue to be viewed as an 'access to records' statute, or whether it should be perceived more broadly as an 'access to information' statute' (Office of Technology Assessment 1988: 20).

Another policy choice was made when the legislator connected the voluntary disclosure and dissemination of information (information supply) by government agencies with the peoples' right of access to government information. These are two different matters. Information supply has to do with political decisions. When they voluntarily supply information, government agencies want to attain certain goals, such as informing citizens or influencing certain citizens' behavior. Openness of government has to do much more with a rule (a 'fundamental law'). In the Netherlands that rule ordains that government information is of a public nature. In public administration practice these two overlap. In both cases government agencies supply citizens, companies or pressure groups with information.

A third choice was made when the Dutch legislator did not choose a fundamental constitutional public access right. In Chapter 1 (civil rights) of the Dutch constitution one cannot find a fundamental public access right to government information. However, article 110 of the Constitution (the Chapter on 'legislation and administration') does contain an obligation for government agencies to practice Openness of Administration in accordance with the law. The phrase 'the law' refers to the Act on the Openness of Administration and specific legal regulations on openness and secrecy.

The legislator wanted to pursue two objectives with the Act on the Openness of Administration. First, the Act fulfills the government's above mentioned constitutional obligation of article 110. Second, the Act is used as an instrument to attain a 'good and democratic administration' (preamble of the Act on the Openness of

Administration). The Act makes it easier for citizens to request information about administrative decision processes, the organization of government and any other matter which is related to policy.

As regards content the aim of the Act is thus to stimulate a 'good and democratic administration', by trying to be (as) open (as possible). This aim is abstract and also broad. It includes both participatory and representative elements. The Act's contribution is to supply citizens, companies and pressure groups with government information. Since the enactment of the law in 1980, the meaning of this objective and its practical consequences have changed. Initially, the emphasis was on the legal instruments of the law, especially the public access right to government information. From then on attention shifted towards the degree to which public administration is committed to openness.

The Act on the Openness of Administration contains two instruments to realize the above mentioned goals. With regard to these instruments the Act has a limited scope. First, only those government agencies which are listed in the Act are subjected to the Act's obligations. Second, the information has to be laid down in a document. A document is defined as a written material or other material containing information, which is under the custody of a government agency. Third, the information must concern an administrative matter. Administrative matters relate to the policy of a government agency, including the preparation and the implementation of this policy. The person requesting information must indicate on which administrative matter he or she wishes to be informed. It is impossible to request information on an unlimited variety of administrative matters.

The two instruments can be summarized as follows. First, everyone may request information laid down in documents and concerning an administrative matter. When an agency is confronted with an information request, it has to decide within two weeks whether or not to comply with the request. When the addressed agency does not have the information, it is obliged to pass the case on to the agency which does have the requested information. When the request does not fulfil the above mentioned criteria (the scope of the Act), the agency turns down the request. Of course, the denial has to be motivated. When the information request can be subsumed under one or more exceptions, which are mentioned in the Act, the agency also turns down the request. Finally, when the request fulfills the criteria and no exception is applicable, the agency has to comply with the request. This can be done in different ways, namely by (1) giving a copy of the document or providing the literal content of the document in other ways, (2) allowing the questioner to acquaint himself with the content, (3) providing a summary of the content of the document, or (4) giving information about the requested document. The government agency chooses between these different ways to comply with the information request, but it has to consider the preferences of the person requesting and the progress of the government's work. Thus the decision on these different forms of information supply is ultimately reserved to government agencies.

The second instrument is voluntary information supply. The government agency concerned directly is obliged to voluntarily supply information about its policy, when revealing the information serves the interest of a good and democratic administration (article 8, paragraph 1). This obligation furthermore contains a number of legal requirements. The information has to be disseminated (article 8, paragraph 2) (1) in such a way that citizens can comprehend the information, (2) in such a way that interested citizens and citizens who have interests are reached as much as possible, (3) with such timing that citizens can give their opinions on the decisions to which the information is related (article 8, paragraph 2). Especially by the latter requirement the connection is made with the participation of citizens in policy processes. Examples of this instrument are leaflets and brochures on specific policy programs and newspaper announcements of the city council's meeting.

The Act lists a number of exceptions, both for decisions on information requests and voluntary information dissemination. Article 10 contains two types of exceptions, namely absolute and relative exceptions. When one of the absolute exceptions is applicable (for example when information dissemination might damage the security of the state), the information is confidential. In these cases publication of the information conflicts with the Act. When one of the relative exceptions is applicable (e.g. when it concerns the relations of the Netherlands with other states, criminal investigations and privacy), the government agency has to weigh the interest of publication against the interest or interests mentioned in the Act.

## 3.2. Information and Communications Technologies (ICTs)

When the implications of ICTs for the openness of government are explored, it is necessary to define ICTs. At least it must be clear which elements characterize ICTs and why new media or new technologies are anything special at all.

ICTs can be recognized by the basic technologies used. These basic technologies include micro-electronics, computers and telecommunications networks (Bouwman and Jankowski 1989: 9). Micro-electronics contribute to the increased possibilities of existing information and communications systems, which are becoming more reliable and cheaper. Computer technology makes it possible for users to improve their control on mutual communication. Computers create possibilities to send, store, manipulate, and reproduce messages. Telecommunications networks make it possible for users to communicate with others on different locations at the same time. In this chapter, ICTs are defined as the use of these basic technologies.

ICTs are characterized by a number of elements, which may have specific significance for the openness of government, politics and democracy (Abramson, Arterton and Orren 1988, see also chapter two and five). First, ICTs cause a huge increase in the quantity of available information. This characteristic is related to the storage capacity. The storage capacity grows exponentially when ICTs are used. The second characteristic of ICTs is a huge increase in the velocity at which information can be gathered, disseminated and retrieved. Gathering and disseminating information is hardly limited by the dimensions of time and physical distance. The third characteristic, is the increased control of information by those who receive the information. When ICTs are used, the possibilities of selecting information are expanded. Those who disseminate or disclose information keep control of its contents. With ICTs, those who supply information are also offered more possibilities for selection, especially with regard to the dissemination of information (information targeting). A fifth characteristic of ICTs is decentralization. This characteristic is ambiguous, because the use of ICTs can also lead to centralization. Decentralization therefore takes place within a frame of centralization, because transparency of networks offers possibilities for central control of decentralized processes (Abramson, Arterton and Orren 1988, Snellen and Van de Donk 1987, see also chapter two).

Finally, ICTs are characterized by interactivity. This characteristic may have specific implications for democracy and politics. Interactivity is defined as the measure of control of participants in a communications process on the mutual discourse, and the possibilities of changing roles within the mutual discourse (Bouwman and Jankowski, 1989: 10). The mutual discourse concerns the possibility that a communicative act is based on a series of preceding communicative acts. This mutual discourse can be described thoroughly by three basic elements: change of roles, control and participants. The change of roles makes it possible for individual A to place himself in the position of individual B and thus conduct the communicative acts of B, and vice versa. A and B respond to each other's communicative acts, and their roles are exchangeable. Control implies that it is possible for an individual to determine timing, content and sequence of the communicative act, make alternative choices, insert data, which can be used by others, and if necessary develop new applications. A participant in this definition can be both an individual and a source of information. When information and meaning are exchanged, transmitter and receiver have equal roles.

These characteristics may be used as tools to analyze some implications of the introduction and use of ICTs for the openness of government. The existing point on the continuum, which ranges from complete openness to complete confidentiality, might shift in both directions when ICTs are introduced.

## 3.3. 'Technology of Freedom'

The introduction and use of ICTs may enhance the openness of government in at least two ways. First, ICTs may have implications for the accessibility and the (enforceable) access to government information. This will be demonstrated by the characteristics of ICTs. The huge increase in velocity and storage capacity improves the possibilities for disclosure and dissemination of government information. Interactivity may lead to changing information relations between citizens and administration. Second, automated systems are developed which support the disclosure and dissemination of government information (and the interaction of citizens with government agencies). These kinds of systems may improve the accessibility of government information. Generally, enforceable access to electronic government information causes a change in the existing situation and therefore leads to enhanced openness of government.

It appears that the inherent characteristics of ICTs make it possible to improve disclosure and dissemination of government information. The huge storage capacity causes an increase in the quantity of information which is available to the public. The limited significance of dimensions like time and physical distance with regard to the information supply as such may increase the accessibility of government information (ceteris paribus). Requests for certain information can be processed more quickly because less time is needed for searching for and retrieving information. Improved file structures can also enhance the quality of the supplied information. The accessibility of the information which is present at government agencies is thus improved. Also modern communications technologies improve the dissemination of government information and a specific kind of interaction between citizens and government agencies by which both government and citizens supply information (interactivity).

The issue of whether or not the improved accessibility enhances the enforceable access to electronic government information can only be addressed when the public access laws are taken into account. To answer this question the above mentioned distinction between an information system and a document system is relevant, because at the most fundamental level, new technologies are obscuring the boundaries between record and nonrecord material. As information technology evolves, records become more difficult to conceptualize in terms of discrete, tangible documents. Information technology is, in a sense, 'detaching information from its embodiment' (Grodsky 1990: 21). An example may be found in computer programs or models for calculation. When these are written on paper, the original copy can be read and copied. When information is stored with help of ICTs, it is virtually impossible to recognize an 'original' copy of it. It is very easy to separate information from the original embodiment. In public access laws which are based on an information system like the Act on the Openness of Administration in the Netherlands, the introduction and use of ICTs is not problematic on this issue. In the Dutch Act an enforceable right is laid down to information regarding administrative matters which is contained in documents. 'Documents' are defined in the Act on the Openness of Administration as a written paper or any other material containing data which is held by a government agency (article 1, sub b Act on the Openness of Administration). In public access laws which are based on a record system an enforceable access right to 'information' does not exist, since only documents (records) are made available to the public. To maintain the existing situation on the continuum when ICTs are introduced, it is necessary for the concept of 'document' to be interpreted in a flexible manner. The 'Citizens Guide on Using the Freedom of Information Act and the Privacy Act of 1974 to request Government Records' states that 'any item containing information that is in the possession, custody, or control of an agency is usually considered to be an agency record under the FOIA. (...) The form in which a record is maintained by an agency does not affect its availability. A request may seek a printed or typed document, tape recording, map, photograph, computer printout, computer tape or disk, or a similar item. This flexible interpretation of 'record' is established and followed by court decisions (see also Beers 1992: 204).

Public access laws contain the obligation for the public administration to publish available information (or 'records'). The issue of 'availability' is especially interesting when ICTs are introduced and used. Government agencies are not under the obligation to create new information. One may question whether the difference between searching for or retrieving information or records and creating information or records is unambiguous when ICTs are used. "What constitutes a search for available records?" (Beers 1992: 205). With regard to this issue the differences between 'computer searching' and 'computer programming' are important, 'considering any new programming or program modification to be analogous to record creation and therefore not required as part of the FOIA 'search' process (Grodsky 1990: 26). In this view searching for information (or documents/records) is enforceable, but a government agency cannot be forced to create or modify computer programs to retrieve information. The Act on the Openness of Administration in the Netherlands states that everyone has a right to request information which already exists and which is under the custody of a government agency. The question can be redirected to the issue whether citizens are only able to use the existing facilities for disclosure of government information. When the existing facilities for disclosure of information are not adequate to disclose the requested information, reprogramming may be necessary to guarantee access to existing, but currently unretrievable information. Preservation of this legal guarantee requires that government agencies take into account public access laws when they store information or design automated disclosure facilities. If this does not happen, chances are that the introduction and use of ICTs will affect the citizen's access right to government information.

The development of flexible automated systems may also improve disclosure of government information and thus enhance access to government information. These kinds of systems have been developed in the Netherlands, just as in the United Kingdom (Bellamy, Horrocks and Webb this volume), the United States (Guthrie and Dutton 1992), Denmark (Hoff and Stormgaard 1991), Germany (Liedtke 1990) and France (Lenk 1990). Two Dutch examples will be described.

The Information Project Almelo (IPA) started in 1988 (see also Van Delden and Roelfsema 1989: 20). Together with a number of non profit organizations and the public library of Almelo, the municipality developed an automated (videotex) public information system. In this system the municipality has its own information facility, which is based on two components. First, an application was developed for 'service and reference' information. This component deals with questions like: what does one have to do to obtain a passport, where and when does one have to apply for a certain grant? This component contains information about the services offered by the municipality. The other component contains information on administrative decision processes, for example electronic information on dates of meetings of the city council and a number of other documents, such as the decisions of the Mayor and Aldermen, (summaries of) important bills, et. At a number of places in the city the municipality has installed terminals, where everyone can have access to the files. This project is no longer operational in Almelo, and has become an independent organization and moved to the municipality of Hengelo.

The municipality of Amsterdam has two public information utilities which contain municipal information. The Public Information Municipality of Amsterdam (PIGA-system) was designed to be a municipal facility for the dissemination of information to the public (Gemeente Amsterdam 1994). In this project the 16 districts of Amsterdam and the municipality cooperate to refer citizens directly to the right address. This system contains information about municipal institutions (address, phone numbers, hours of business, tasks and products), administrative municipal organs (organizations, working field and schedule of meetings) and non-municipal institutions in the area of social work, culture, education and recreation. Besides, a part of the system is reserved for municipal bills, regulations, brochures, etc. Only a short summary is included, as well as the address where one can obtain these documents. By means of a keyword (which is included in a thesaurus) this information can be retrieved. The information is kept up to date by the participating organizations. These have 'local editorial boards', which are responsible for the information contained in the system. The PIGA-system is supplemented by the Administrative Information System Amsterdam (BISA). This system, which in terms of design is comparable with PIGA, contains administrative information, such as the minutes of meetings of city councils, written questions of members of the city council, letters which have been sent to the city council (since 1989), the decisions of the college of the Mayor and Aldermen (since 1990), and the regulations of the municipality of Amsterdam. This information is disclosed by means of keywords. When, for example, one inputs 'canary', one gets the written questions of council member R.H.G. van Duijn with regard to the death of '*Canary Joop*', whose owner was the bureau of management support of the municipality of Amsterdam. The canary died after cleaning the carpets (with some toxic cleaning material) of the bureau. Both the PIGA-system and BISA participate in the project The Digital City (see chapter ten).

Besides these examples many different initiatives could be mentioned which fit into this framework. As well as the publication of the 'municipality' and 'province' disks (De Graaf 1992), which contain general (legal and factual) information about these institutions, the videotext-services of central government in the Netherlands must also be mentioned. The Dutch national government offers various information services on videotext (for example the tax revenue bureau, the Ministry of Housing, Urban Planning and Environmental protection and customs). The national government also offers a videotext service P.O. Box 51 (the central information agency of the government, comparable with the Government Printing Office in the United States), where one can order written government publications (and video tapes). This service does not include administrative documents. Only public information documents can be ordered which are summaries or popular versions of administrative documents and records. The national government also has a system for informing the press by electronic mail. This system disseminates press releases electronically among the newspaper journalists (Schoenmacker 1994). Finally, a number of municipalities are experimenting with automated systems for information supply to citizens, such as the municipalities of Zoetermeer, Rotterdam, Eindhoven and Tilburg. This can be done by information systems for city councils, which disclose administrative information to citizens. Besides government agencies, commercial publishers also offer electronic government information. For example, Elsevier, a publishing company, offers the tax disk, which contains the income tax regulations. With this disk, citizens can calculate the amount of tax they owe the government and apply tax deductions electronically.

ICTs thus contribute in different ways to an enhancement of the openness of government. A huge increase in velocity and storage capacity improves the disclosure and dissemination of government information. ICTs may also improve the accessibility of government information (and service delivery by government agencies). Structural electronic public information facilities are designed to enhance public access to government information.

### 3.4 'Technology of Secrecy'

In two ways at least the introduction and use of ICTs threaten the existing legal situation as regards openness and confidentiality of government. First, ICTs may create gaps in public access laws which impede access to electronic information. ICTs also make it possible to impede accessibility of government information. For example, ICTs facilitate the quick and untraceable deletion of information.

The first gap in public access laws is linked to the access to electronic information which was addressed in the former section. In an information system the medium (written or other material which contains information) is not relevant, and in the document system of the United States 'record' is interpreted in such a way that it contains electronic information. Still, electronic access remains problematic. Supplying the information in an electronic format (or a specific electronic format) sometimes affects the value of the information which one receives. In a certain case in the United States, i.e. the National Archive vs. CIA, a pressure group requested from the Central Intelligence Agency (CIA) an index of the available documents under the Freedom of Information Act (Beers 1992: 209). The pressure group wanted this index in an electronic format, so that they could analyze the information. The CIA refused to supply the information in the requested format and produced a printout of 5,000 pages (about one metre of paper). The appeal of the group that the quantity of the information in the given format made analysis of the information practically impossible was rejected by the court with the argument that the information was supplied in a reasonably accessible format. One of the reactions of commentators was that because the information was not supplied in an electronic format, the CIA had refused the request, because an essential element of the request was the format of the information. The information should be supplied in a format which made it fit for analysis (Sorokin 1990).

Theoretically, this problem can also arise in the Netherlands. In section 3.1 of this chapter the different forms of information supply under the Act on the Openness of Administration were mentioned. Electronic formats are not mentioned explicitly in the Act. Electronic dissemination of information fulfills the criteria of one of the forms mentioned, namely supplying the literal contents. However, supplying the information in a non-electronic format also meets this criterion. The Act states that government agencies should take into account the preference of the requester and the progress of government work when they choose between these different formats. The government agency thus decides on the basis of an abstract and undetermined criterion, and is legally allowed to opt for dissemination of the information in a non-electronic format, even when an electronic format is requested. In fact it appears that a legal gap is created, which can only be removed by changing the Act. As long as this gap exists, the introduction and use of ICTs threaten the existing public access rights to government information.

The introduction and use of ICTs in public administration may cause legal tensions (Beers 1992: 212). First, information requests do not always correspond with the way information is structured by government agencies. This may imply that creation of new information is necessary to comply with the information request. This activity is not obligatory in Dutch public access law (and also FOIA). A connected problem is that citizens always request information ex post (after the information is generated, gathered and stored), while computer systems require structuring of information in advance or together with the development of automated systems. Facilities to disclose and disseminate government information also attract very little legal attention. In public administration practice many initiatives for disclosure of information are observed, for example the PIGA-system and BISA in Amsterdam. These systems do not contain facilities for combining information, and analysis of the retrieved information is sometimes impossible. Citizens are only able to trace which information is available. Without ICTs, citizens generally do not know which information is available. Because information requests have to state which information is wanted (a limited administrative matter), government agencies in the Netherlands can withhold information which is under their custody. During the last couple of years different commentators in the Netherlands have been advocating the development of a database which contains an index of available government information. In the United States, the issue of a 'government-wide information index' was raised by the Office of Technology Assessment (Office of Technology Assessment 1988: 17).

Finally, sometimes electronic information is concealed by the government. Electronic mail can be defined as a 'record in being', despite the fact that it contains crucial administrative information which is relevant to the public (Grodsky 1990: 37). During the Iran-Contra affair Lt.Col. Oliver North tried to delete some electronic mail. Because of the automatic electronic backup in case of 'electronic power surges', the electronic mail was retrieved eventually. In the Netherlands, electronic mail may be defined as a 'personal policy belief', which is exempt from the obligation to reveal government information.

These legal gaps can be removed by taking into account the requirements of public access laws when ICTs are used. Flexibility, which is defined as the possibility of disclosing information in different ways, is crucial for the maintenance of the existing public access rights. In the Swedish public access law this requirement has already been codified.

It is inherent in the introduction and use of ICTs that a technical threshold is created (Hoff and Stormgaard 1991). Information may not be disseminated by written documents anymore, which could imply that a part of the population is not informed (Sorokin 1990: 278). To maintain the existing point on the continuum the information might provisionally be made available both in electronic and non-electronic format.


## 4. Conclusion

When ICTs and the openness of government are explored, we are confronted with the ambiguity of ICTs and their implications. On the one hand, ICTs make it possible to enhance the accessibility of government information, as was demonstrated by the increase in speed and storage capacity of computers. The accessibility of government information may be enhanced by the introduction of ICTs. ICTs also facilitate an exponentially increased dissemination of government information.

Various examples of systems which contribute to the utilization of these possibilities have been described in this chapter. Although these systems are being developed by more and more government agencies, the extent to which they are used by citizens not always meets the expectations. Apparently citizens are not eager to use these new tools, which was also demonstrated by experiments with videotext systems (Ministerie van Economische Zaken 1991). The fact that these systems are mostly developed without citizens being consulted may contribute to this. Citizens' demand cannot always be presupposed.

On the one hand, ICTs may thus lead to an enhancement of openness. On the other hand, ICTs are a potential threat to the existing legal situation, because of the lack of flexibility when automated systems are developed. When one develops automated systems, one also has to take into account the requirements which are prescribed by the law on the openness of administration. ICTs facilitate the untraceable and easy manipulation of information. The Act on the Openness of Administration in the Netherlands contains some gaps which threaten the openness of government when ICTs are used in public administration. Legal regulations can obviate these threats. ICTs serve as a technology of secrecy when the requirements of public access to government information and the accessibility of government information are not met during the development of automated information systems.

Besides the adaptation of legal regulations, the commitment of government agencies to openness is relevant to the structural implications of ICTs. To what degree do civil servants and politicians commit themselves to doing their jobs in the public's eye? Do they still want to conceal as much government information as possible, despite public access laws? ICTs are designed differently in organizations with a commitment to openness than it is in organizations with a culture that is characterized by secrecy and the concealment of relevant information. In some municipalities in the Netherlands, which are committed to political and administrative renewal, politicians and civil servants are eager to utilize the possibilities of ICTs to enhance accessibility of government information. The automated systems in the municipality of Amsterdam have been developed in the framework of administrative and political renewal, among other things to enhance citizen involvement with local democracy (Gemeente Amsterdam 1993).

The decision to use ICTs and a certain design of ICTs may be conceptualized as policy choices. Does one opt for one-way or two-way communication? Do only politicians and civil servants have access to the automated documentary information systems, or does one develop an application which is available to the public? Does one emphasize the accessibility of government information or does one want to develop a kind of management information system (Guthrie and Dutton 1992)? These policy decisions are made within the context of public access regulations, which makes explicit attention for legal guarantees to maintain the existing, but delicate situation with respect to openness and secrecy of the utmost importance.

# CHAPTER 13

# Connecting Orwell to Athens?
# Information Superhighways
# and the Privacy Debate

Charles D. RAAB

*Department of Politics, University of Edinburgh, 31 Buccleuch Place,*
*Edinburgh EH8 9JT, Scotland*

**Abstract.** This chapter describes the proposals for 'information superhighways' in
the United States, Canada, the United Kingdom and the European Union in terms
of their perceived implications for democracy and the protection of privacy. It
looks at recent discussions of democracy and privacy in the context of information
and communications technologies, and posits a close relationship between the two
values.

## 1. Introduction

The concept of the 'information superhighway' (ISH) has been framed as a new
departure that promises great benefits and few disadvantages. The development of ISHs
is firmly on the ICTs (information and communications technologies) policy agenda,
fuelling much hyperbole. The United States' National Information Infrastructure (NII)
is the most prominent proposal (Information Infrastructure Task Force 1993). It is being
watched with interest abroad, for the NII will have global implications. Similar
initiatives are also underway in other countries, such as Canada and the United
Kingdom, and in the European Union. There are lively debates about ISHs in
governmental and business circles, academia and the media (Dutton *et al.* 1994).

This chapter considers these initiatives illustratively, in terms of their conceptions of
democracy and of privacy. ISHs hold out both the promise of the one and the threat
to the other, posing anew the question of the relationship amongst different values in
an expanding information sphere which is difficult but necessary to regulate. The
chapter also argues that, rather than being inimical to the openness of information and
communication that underpins democracy, the protection of privacy is itself an
important value in a democracy, as well as sustaining the use of personal data by
business and public agencies. First, some competing visions must be assessed.

## 2. Democracy, Privacy and the Information Super Highway

Information highway proposals seek a legal and material framework for a commercially and governmentally important infrastructure of interactive communications through the merger of separate technologies. Some see ISHs as fulfilling ancient democratic dreams by enabling citizens to forge politically relevant links with each other, to receive information from government and give information to it, and to participate more effectively in policy processes. Apocalyptic visions see the ISH in the light of post-modernist themes that include post-industrialism, in which ISHs offer the prospect of a new *economic* order based on ICTs, moving from manufacturing and service industries to information-based ones; and *social* reorganization, moving from family, class and other social solidarities to the creation and recreation of more fluid and permeable structures. They also include the reconstruction of *political* institutions and processes, leaving behind the hollow shells of parliaments, parties, and perhaps even states themselves as a new, direct democratic order is realized. In all, these prospects envisage a cultural and personal revolution.

The 'information economy' and 'information society' paradigms have thus been joined by that of the 'information polity', which most concerns us here. However, Taylor and Williams' (1991) formulation of this notion is neither utopian nor deterministic in its discussion of the ways in which computer networked information systems may affect public administration, including the provision of public services to the citizen, and they enumerate several *caveats*. They lend no support to any beliefs that ICTs are about to usher in a golden age of perfect administration or of benevolent bureaucracy - two conceptions about which Hood (1976) and Yngstrom *et al.* (1985) have given reasons for skepticism.

Bellamy and Taylor (1994) argue for systematic research into the information polity with regard to public administration or management. This construes the 'polity' more governmentally than politically: more in terms of the effect of information systems upon the organization of government and its outputs, and less in terms of the citizen's political role as a provider of inputs. Dutton (1992) observes that political scientists abandoned an interest in the political aspects of 'teledemocracy' and lapsed into recycling utopian or dystopian speculations. Yet a thriving, mainly transatlantic literature on ICTs and democracy is surveyed by Dutton (1992), and also by van de Donk and Tops (1992), (see also chapter two) and need not be separately described here. Whereas 'electronic democracy' discourse often assumes the bankruptcy of conventional politics and is uncritical of high-tech methods of returning power to 'the people', these academic observers' balanced approach identifies several components in the development of ICTs or ISHs and evaluates their separate implications. Dutton (1992) notes emergent applications of ICTs in politics and in service provision: broadcasting government information, transactions with members of the public, access to public records, interpersonal communication, and surveying and monitoring. Van de Donk and Tops (1992) consider the variety of political uses of ICTs, including electronic plebiscites, improvements in representative democracy, pressure group and parliamentary applications.

Like the curate's egg, applications of ICTs and the use of ISH infrastructures may therefore be 'good in parts', but only investigations of the parts can advance our knowledge - and judgement - of them. Miles (1988), too, notes the polarization of those who see the future as either utopian ('concordists') or dystopian ('antagonists'). But he also identifies an orthogonal axis along which are those who see likely change as limited ('continuists') and those who think it will be profound ('transformists'). His argument for a 'structuralist' approach views change as far more complex and dynamic: there are many possible 'information societies' and no single vision of the future, for a great deal is open to decision making. Equally, we may envisage many 'information polities' or 'electronic democracies', depending upon how ICTs are shaped by legal, historical, cultural, organizational and other factors, and upon how political actors learn and choose. The result may well be unexpected effects and incrementalism rather than fundamental change (Van de Donk and Tops 1992).

Local government research shows the part played by democratic goals in shaping public access systems (Dutton and Guthrie 1991, Guthrie and Dutton 1992). Political culture only partly explained the kind of public information system adopted in Southern California. Innovations depended upon developers' and designers' subscription to ICT paradigms that embody different conceptions of, and support different communication practices for, the relationship between the citizen and public authorities, and of citizens to each other. Extending Laudon's observation (1977), Guthrie and Dutton note that different forms of information polity, including democratic and participatory elements, could be promoted by the particular system adopted. For example, participatory democracy, with horizontal communication amongst citizens and their role as 'inputters' to authorities, conforms to an electronic mail model, as in Santa Monica's PEN scheme; whereas a broadcasting model, in which citizens receive information from the 'top', relates to a different (but not necessarily incompatible) idea of an informed citizenry (Guthrie and Dutton 1992). Thus PEN's public terminals appealed on egalitarian grounds that might be absent in less democratic places. If the information polity is open to human agency acting within technological, social and political possibilities and constraints, it is important to unpack its dimensions and avoid either euphoria or pessimism (Lyon 1994).

What can be said about privacy in the developing ISHs? The 'Orwellian' prospect sees the ISH as a surveillance system in the broad sense of the term, in which any advantages of electronic service delivery (Dutton *et al.* 1994, OTA 1993), teleshopping or teledemocratic voting are overshadowed by the increased risks to privacy and information security that arise from the necessary 'capture', and the possible misuse, of personal data that are involved in achieving many ISH objectives. It should be noted that 'privacy' in the context of information practices is best seen as an expanded concept that involves human dignity, 'personhood' and identity, and is so understood in the theory and practice of privacy and data protection, in which the ability of individuals to control the use of personal information is the fundamental issue at stake (Lyon 1994). The dawning of the 'computer age' gave rise to literature, debate, and some twenty-five years of policy and legislation aimed at protecting privacy in the use of ICTs and information systems. But the global, multimedia nature of the ISH moves the problem of control, and hence of privacy, into a new dimension beyond the already severe difficulties associated with regulating power relationships in the era of automatic data processing. The realization of this problem helps to explain why privacy issues are being debated at all in regard to ISHs. It does not, however, determine any particular scenario or the relative importance of privacy as an ISH issue.

Three prominent views can be identified. The most paranoid vision is that ISHs are conspiracies to perfect the means of surveillance so that a malign public order can be enforced. In the second, and less dramatically, they merely facilitate 'Big Brother' (or, more realistically, the interconnection of many 'Little Brothers') by enabling states or organizations to move in that direction, and such movement may occur through political decisions to combat real or perceived threats, such as terrorism, fraud, street crime or drug-smuggling. Third, and more subtly still, the interests and pressures generated by the undoubtedly beneficial business and state applications of ICTs along the superhighway incrementally erode personal privacy and its associated human values, either by devaluing their importance in the face of the benefits of the ISH ('the price you pay'; 'a price worth paying'), or by denying that they are being eroded at all ('I have nothing to hide'). Privacy is therefore, and respectively, impossible, politically negotiable, or meaningless.

However, bureaucratic and marketing visions of the superhighway embody interests that are likely to be more powerful than other values in shaping the ISH's infrastructure and regulations. The provision of goods, entertainment and public services is more likely to be the main ISH achievement. These benefits are not negligible. But if their provision shapes the infrastructure and use of the ISH in ways that constrain democracy-related applications, then these political values can only be achieved on the ISH against heavy odds, and only with any prospect of success as second-rank benefits if they are supported by a public eager to practice them, although the provision of a democratic infrastructure requires action from above as well. Democratic inputs may therefore only be a by-product of infrastructure decisions taken on other grounds. As for privacy protection, users of personal information in providing goods and services may come to see some protection of their customers' or clients' data as consonant with their own commercial or governmental interests. As we shall see, there are signs that this symbiosis is becoming more clearly understood in ISH debates. Thus, as with democracy, privacy may be less likely to be protected directly as a result of normative deliberations in technological or governmental circles, or through laws and enforcement agencies - however crucial they are (Flaherty 1989) - than it is from the perception that good privacy protection means good business or good government, and that it can be built into technologies rather than thrown round them like a fetter. Sophisticated ICTs managers seem to be adopting this view on grounds of economy, efficiency, and public relations.

This is possibly reinforced by a growing public awareness of surveillance and some resistance to it. There seems at least to be some understanding that goods, services, state administration and entertainment carry a price-tag of risks to privacy that may occur through the misuse of personal data collected for providing these. Although public concern over privacy invasions may be relatively low or sporadic, the development of data protection in a number of countries has been stimulated by public anxiety over real or imagined breaches of privacy. National censuses, as for example in Germany and the United Kingdom, have been jeopardized by public uncertainty about confidentiality. Privacy issues concerning the media have also been aired in public. Although the interpretation of surveys is difficult, much of it indicates that privacy is not a negligible value in many countries (Ekos Research Associates s.d., Equifax 1990, Holvast, van Dijk and Schep 1989, Székely 1991). As with public access technology, the shaping of privacy protection in particular settings involves several cultural, administrative, legal and other factors (Bennett 1992). A repertory of tools is available, from state regulation to organizational selfregulation via codes of practice, to individual selfprotection by means that include privacy technologies, for reducing the Orwellian likelihood (Bennett 1992, Chaum 1992, Industry Canada, 1994b, Raab 1993).

With this brief exploration in mind, we can now investigate how democracy and privacy protection are considered in current ISH initiatives.

## 3. Recent Developments

The position of democracy and privacy in relation to the main economic and governmental impetus hangs in the balance as technical and regulatory infrastructures are formed. Developments in the United States (US), Canada, the United Kingdom (UK) and the European Union (EU) illustrate the state of thought and action about 'Athens' and 'Orwell'.

### 3.1.  The United States

The US's National Information Infrastructure (NII) initiative was launched late in 1993 (IITF 1993), although Vice-President Gore, its leading political protagonist, had signalled the idea some time before (Gore 1991). The government wanted a policy for the further growth of an ISH that was already being developed by private means. It saw a crucial role for government action, as catalyst and rule-maker, to enhance and complement the private sector. Nine principles and objectives were to guide official action. Although economic goals predominated, anti-Orwellian ideals but not much of Athens found their way into the NII principles of universal service, ensuring that information resources are available to all and are affordable; the easy and equitable provision of public access to

government information; and network security and trustworthiness, thus protecting
privacy.

Among the benefits envisaged were 'civic networking', by which the NII "'could be
used to create an 'electronic commons'" (IITF 1993: 15), but here the paradigm was
more that of the provision of information and learning opportunities to citizens through
local networks than the facilitation of citizens' political action. Other NII objectives also
bore upon the themes of democracy and privacy, although less directly. Thus the
promotion of seamless, interactive and user-driven applications by reforming rules and
policies has implications for the free flow of information that is vital for democracy, but
that may also endanger privacy if unaccountable and uncontrollable transfers of
information across networks evade privacy rules. Likewise, the aim of coordination with
other levels of government and with other nations is to remove obstacles to the flow
of information in order to help US industry. The formation of an *internationally*
accepted (and multi-level) privacy protection system may be a coordination issue.
However, the lead in shaping such a system has been taken by Europeans, whose
proposals have been nervously regarded in US circles because of the proposed 'high'
level of protection for personal data in transborder data flows (Raab and Bennett 1994).

To develop the NII initiative, an Information Infrastructure Task Force (IITF) was
established, representing 'all the key agencies involved in telecommunications and
information policy' (IITF 1993: 19), working under the auspices of the White House
Office of Science and Technology Policy and the National Economic Council. IITF
committees and their working groups were set up, bearing as well on the
informatization of the federal government itself under the National Performance
Review, in which the reinvention of government was to include electronic benefits
transfer and the use of kiosks for access to services and information. IITF working
groups dealt with privacy, ways of disseminating government data, universal access,
intellectual property rights, and the application of IT by government agencies. An
Advisory Council brought the two sides of industry, other levels of government,
academia and public interest groups into touch with the IITF. It is noteworthy that
Congress's Office of Technology Assessment has also investigated electronic service
delivery, and has researched open government issues and privacy implications of the use
of personal identifiers, smart cards, profiling and data matching (OTA 1993). Thus these
topics have received considerable governmental and public attention. Although privacy
is protected through a profusion of federal and state laws dealing with particular sectors
and applications of personal data (Plesser and Cividanes 1991), US data protection is
generally conceded to be inadequate insofar as the machinery for implementation is
largely absent or weak, leaving aggrieved citizens to find legal remedies. Most crucially,
data privacy in the non-governmental sector is only regulated in certain industries; there
are no general data protection laws covering the private sector in North America outside
the Canadian province of Quebec. These gaps have been most relevant, and at issue, in
the current EU creation of a supposedly higher standard, which might have serious
adverse consequences for US interests. Thus the outcome of IITF work on privacy is

important for the crucial judgements that other countries will make about the permissibility of transborder data flows to the less-well-protected environment of the US, as well as in the domestic politics of the NII.

In May, 1994 the IITF's privacy working group issued draft privacy principles. The document sought to 'provide the framework from which specialized principles can be developed' (IITF 1994: 1) for particular sectors and circumstances. It recognized that the NII meant that 'large amounts of sensitive information will be on line, and can be accessed, perhaps without authority, by a large number of network users' (IITF 1994: 1), and that 'the threat to personal information privacy has never been greater' (IITF 1994: 2). The report made the point that the NII's full success depends upon the proper protection of privacy so that citizens can have confidence that risks do not outweigh benefits: 'adherence to these Principles...is critical to developing trust between data users and data subjects in the electronic information age' (IITF 1994: 4). The working group sought to update and extend the 1973 Code of Fair Information Practices - which helped to shape the 1974 Privacy Act - to cope with an ICT environment. Moreover, because the ISH will be interactive, with individuals generating large amounts of personal data and using them to access information, obligations were to be placed on individuals as well as organizations.

The privacy working group's framework embodied general principles that resemble those that are found in national and other laws as well as in international conventions and guidelines. These cover not only the security of personal information, but its accuracy, timeliness, completeness, and relevance for the purpose for which it was collected. They include transparency, in which data gatherers explain to individuals the purpose and nature of the collection, the intended use, its confidentiality, and the means of legal redress. Data users were urged to assess the impact of their practices upon privacy, to educate themselves, their employees and the public about information practices and risks, to provide 'subject access' and to allow persons to withhold consent to further and incompatible uses. The principles will not be legally binding; regulations will be made and tailored to specific sectors and circumstances. This sectoral approach is also found elsewhere, sometimes embodied in extra-legal codes of practice (e.g., The Netherlands or the UK), and was mooted in the proposed EU Directive. But however pragmatic, sectorization is open to the charge that the boundedness of sectors is questionable in the business world, and perforce regarding the flow of personal data; even the basic distinction between 'private' and 'public' sectors is less cogent in the information age. Apart from reporting on principles, the Working Group also looked into the creation of a privacy agency - long a bone of contention in the US - and other control mechanisms, as well as identifying gaps in the law.

However, the report was severely criticized by activist groups and others interested in privacy and technology issues, and was being revised in late 1994. The Electronic Privacy Information Center (EPIC) declared the recommendations to be 'a surprisingly weak set of standards that does little to protect privacy or even to recognize some of the emerging privacy issues brought about by network communications' (EPIC 1994: 14).

It found the IITF wanting in the areas of encryption, informed consent, unique identifiers and enforcement, and inadequate to cover transborder data flows. Although its critique was unsystematic and sometimes drew questionable conclusions from its interpretation of the IITF document, EPIC thought the latter actually weakened the 1973 Code, in part by shifting responsibility for privacy protection from organizations onto individuals (although the working group did argue for an 'ideal symbiotic relationship between data collectors and data subjects' in line with 'the true interactive nature of the NII' (IITF 1994: 5). EPIC advocated principles that allocated responsibilities and rights more clearly and with less burden on citizens, and for which there was some means of enforcement. Also, it wanted to address problems arising from unique personal identifiers, and it encouraged encryption and other devices.

Whatever the merits or faults of the working group's or critics' arguments, privacy has become a serious item in NII deliberations. Democracy is also evident in the formal agenda, although mainly in terms of improving public access to government information. Thus an electronically accessible Government Information Locator Service (GILS) was launched in December, 1994, to be developed within and among government departments and agencies. But those parts of the infrastructure that are already in regular use, such as electronic mail, bulletin boards, the Internet and the World Wide Web, also carry much message traffic and information that illustrates the ISH's importance to democratic inputs, as increasing numbers of American citizens - and others, for these networks are global - talk to each other about public issues, mobilize political and pressure group activity as well as receive government's policy-related information. Such communication brings pending legislation to the notice of interested communities and enlists their support or opposition, and shows how named elected representatives can be lobbied electronically. A profusion of official publications, reports and documents can be purchased, read or downloaded.

Of particular interest is the availability of discussions and possible political pressure over privacy itself. Electronic newsletters and bulletin boards talk about impending legislation or administrative activity, exchange views, advertise conferences of activists, academics and practitioners, etc. A dramatic issue has been the 'Clipper Chip' controversy over the government's attempt to allow only the export, as a putative world standard, of an encryption device that can be accessed by federal law-enforcement and intelligence agencies for surveillance or industrial espionage (Association for Computing Machinery 1994, Holderness 1994). A petition with over 40,000 signatures against this was electronically organized by a privacy pressure group.

## 3.2. *Canada*

A 1994 government discussion paper (Industry Canada 1994a) focused on policy issues involved in the creation of an ISH infrastructure. Industrial, economic, cultural, and private and public service objectives were emphasized, and distinctively Canadian interests and circumstances were highlighted, including implications for sovereignty and cultural identity. Because Canadian industry competes with US, Japanese, and European firms in providing an information infrastructure for Canadians, government leadership was seen as necessary. Not unlike the NII literature, the discussion paper was thin on representative or participatory democracy, but universal access was given as one of three key objectives, and the improved delivery of services includes some 300 InfoCentres that have been opened to provide one-stop shopping for government information and services. Among fifteen policy issues that were canvassed, one concerned copyright and intellectual property, and another concerned the propriety of censorship and other controls on information in Canada's 'democratic society' (Industry Canada 1994: 27). The values of free speech and freedom of association were thus invoked, and alternative possibilities were mentioned for exercising a gatekeeping role. An issue was how the ISH can improve public access to government-held information; another concerned the re-engineering of government - an 'information polity' issue on the 'output' side. But the closest the paper came to addressing the role of the active citizen on the political, or 'input' side, was in asking whether the ISH should be 'deliberately designed to provide a public space for information sharing, public debate and electronic democracy' (Industry Canada 1994a: 28).

Privacy protection was one of four principles in the development strategy, but was presented in a low-key initial remark that 'it is in the best interest of industry to take appropriate action. However, the government is prepared to take the required measures to ensure that privacy concerns are addressed, should this be necessary.' (Industry Canada 1994a: 14). Incisive privacy-related questions were asked, revealing a depth of consideration for relevant issues that are not only germane to Canada, and that are thus worth quoting at length:

> 'Does government need to take stronger measures to protect the privacy and security of information?...can we continue to rely on voluntary compliance...? Is a uniform national level needed to cover all types of personal information...? Do we understand exactly what information privacy means to various users of the network, and agree on what level of privacy is required for different tasks? How can the government ensure that Canadian privacy protection standards meet international norms?...Should one of the factors influencing the choice of technologies and standards for the information highway be the implications for privacy protection or erosion? Are there affordable technical solutions...? Who should pay for improved privacy protection - network or service suppliers, or individual citizens? Will governments need to intervene to regulate the use of electronic surveillance and the subsequent or third-party use of transactional data generated by use of credit cards and government services? What measures should be adopted to ensure the security, reliability and integrity of the information highway network? What kind of encryption protection should be provided and who should pay for it?' (Industry Canada 1994a: 28-29).

Subsequent deliberations have taken place in official and other national settings, including a government advisory council which, in turn, created five working groups. A discussion paper of October, 1994 set forward possible approaches for privacy protection, outlined current efforts in Canada and abroad, and sought public comment as part of a debate on the social and economic impact of the ISH (Industry Canada

1994b). The idea of developing a privacy standard was the most novel approach. Four years earlier, the Canadian Standards Association (CSA) had already begun to formulate a standard that might also meet the ostensibly higher level mooted in European harmonization. The CSA involved in its deliberations many federal departments as well as major players in industry, commerce, the world of ICTs, and consumer affairs. This work engaged high gear in 1994, in parallel with official ISH statements. An important aim was to ensure that privacy standards would bear upon ISH technology, and not be merely an ineffective afterthought, in order to mitigate the effects of transactional data gathering and associated surveillance upon privacy.

Recent thinking inclined towards a mixture of approaches to privacy protection that include not only regulatory legislation - overcoming the existing Canadian patchwork - but also voluntary standards and codes of practice, the use of privacy technologies such as public-key encryption (Chaum 1992) as well as altering the technology of, for example, telephone billing systems or video cameras, and consumer education. Industry Canada was cooperating with the Organization for Economic Cooperation and Development (OECD) in investigating encryption systems. Under CSA auspices, other data protection research aimed at recommendations expected in 1995, and interest was shown in the sectoral code experience of other countries, such as The Netherlands (Bennett 1994). The CSA was developing a model code, with a minimum national standard for fair information handling practices which would also meet increasing foreign expectations of protection for transborder data flows. Sectoral codes may follow this. A mixed strategy of privacy protection for the new ISH world would be more robust and flexible, without relieving data users of their obligations and placing them on the individual; yet persons, through privacy technology or through awareness of their rights and of how to exercise them, would continue to play a role in self-protection. The interaction of the strategies in the 'mix', however, would seem to need special attention for privacy protection to be an effective 'coproduction' (Raab 1993).

### 3.3.  *The United Kingdom*

In the UK, a CCTA (The Government Centre for Information Systems) consultative document in May, 1994 dealt with  possible public sector applications on the ISH (CCTA 1994). Because this paper was thus specialized, it did not deal with the range of issues found in the US or Canadian examples. As another current initiative is to promote more open government (HMSO 1993), including public access to information through the Citizen's Charter and its sectoral offspring, the ISH document blended into that area of policy discourse by emphasizing better public 'consumer' services though electronic and digital means. The CCTA is, indeed, in the Office of Public Service and Science (OPSS) which spearheads the open government initiative, thus reinforcing the connection between the latter and the ISH. 'Open government' is important to democracy, but it can be doubted whether the government's idea of it is adequate (Raab

1994). Moreover, open government embodies mainly a 'broadcast' paradigm (Guthrie and Dutton 1992), and does not engage the question of citizen cross-talk or political input; neither did the consultative ISH document, except for a few interesting illustrations.

The paper's main focus was on the nature of the ISH as it might pertain to government, and on identifying specific applications. It saw ISH as a new term for an old concept that had taken root in commerce and government. What was new concerned data compression and multimedia infrastructures, expanding the potential for interactive services. Electronic correspondence between individuals and departments, public access to service information, electronic mail, and remote booking of appointments were given as general ISH service categories. Government would give a lead by 'harnessing these opportunities for public sector applications so that public services are improved' (CCTA 1994: 11). The private sector, which was already providing goods and services electronically, would be involved, but Whitehall stakeholders needed coordination. First, departmental opportunities to improve services, exploit technologies, and increase openness would be reviewed.

The CCTA explored the attributes required for successful electronic service delivery systems, and listed many possible governmental applications, with the *caveat* that these 'are only examples and are not necessarily under consideration' (CCTA 1994: 17). Many concerned public access to information, and a large number dealt with 'remote forms handling' in services such as passport applications, tax assessment, and job-finding. Also mentioned were such democratic 'input' innovations as electronic messages to the Prime Minister, the Cabinet, and MPs; questionnaires from the Citizen's Charter Unit to the public; and electronic voting on referendums and in general elections. This last application would be most significant in a country with a constitutional aversion to referenda, and in which election ballots are not computerized. The prospect of medical diagnosis and consultation on the ISH, as well as the transmission of medical records, fingerprint and photographic images, personal financial data, and the information contained on forms, raise questions about privacy protection and data security. The CCTA saw these as ISH issues. Compliance with the Data Protection Act was important, and 'information providers will need to balance the requirement for freedom of information versus intrusion into personal privacy/information' (CCTA 1994: 21) - more the recital of a typical *mantra* than a contribution to a very vexed question of information policy, and in contrast to the paper's greater detail on technical and economic aspects of the ISH. Other issues that touched on democratic themes included international access to information and the problem of different national rules regarding freedom of information, involving the need to agree on international laws for cross-border issues 'to stimulate common freedoms for citizens in a globally networked community' (CCTA 1994: 22). The resolution of intellectual property issues were also mentioned.

The House of Commons Trade and Industry Committee had meanwhile been investigating a major ISH component, optical fibre networks and services, and how the broadband network might be regulated (HMSO 1994a). Here, too, the services exemplified were a mixture of commercial and other interactive ones. The Committee worried about falling behind in the international race. The report dealt mainly with economic issues, competition policy, and broadband infrastructure. With an eye to US ambitions in service development and universal access, it wanted government to take a more active, coordinated approach to developing public sector applications, thus apparently underlining the CCTA's approach. It also touched on the question of regulating the content of networked material. It was not in the Committee's remit to look at democracy and privacy issues, so these were absent from the written evidence it received, but Microsoft Corporation highlighted privacy, security, and the protection of intellectual property as requiring government's attention (HMSO 1994b).

Thus, in the UK's airing of the prospects of an ISH, there has been only a modest degree of exploration of democracy and privacy protection, apart for the important widening of public access to information. This is not too surprising, given the provenance of the reports surveyed here. However, the CCTA hosted a large consultative meeting on ISHs in November, 1994, at which proposals were set out for creating a number of short-term electronic discussion forums ('collaborative open groups', or COGs) to carry some major issues forward, and to coordinate developmental thinking. COGs were established for topics that included open government; data protection, copyright and pricing of public information; security; local government; and others. It is interesting to note that UK Government information, including certain documents, speeches, departmental descriptive material, the Chancellor's Budget, and details about the Data Protection Act and Registrar's Office, became newly available on the Internet in October, 1994 through the CCTA's Government Information Service. Later on, OPSS Ministers' speeches emphasized the role of the ISH in fulfilling the Citizen's Charter and Open Government policies, and in making government 'open for business around the clock'.

## 3.4. *The European Union*

A European Commission Communication of July, 1994 on the 'information society' - an Action Plan (Commission of the European Communities 1994) - crystallized thinking. Its background included existing EU activity on information and telecommunications issues. Chapter XII of the Maastricht Treaty had provided for the development of trans-European telecommunications networks, and there was also action concerning integrated broadband communications. The fourth framework document included significant resources for ICT research. Directorates-General III (industrial policy) and XIII (information technology and telecommunications) were restructured and coordinated under the direction of Martin Bangemann (Eckstein 1993). In addition, two important Directives - a general data protection one and another on privacy in ISDN - were still some distance from adoption, but the issues of privacy protection and access to public sector information, as well as other legal problems of the information market, had been under continuing investigation in the IMPACT and PUBLAW programs.

The Edinburgh Summit in December, 1992 mooted the development of information networks towards a Common European Information Area to promote growth, competitiveness and employment. This went further at the Copenhagen Summit in June, 1993; at the year's end, the Brussels Summit adopted a White Paper on these aims, emphasizing the role of ICTs (Carpentier 1994, Commission of the European Communities 1993), and including privacy protection as one of the regulatory means to making public services available faster, more selectively and less impersonally. A Task Force was mandated to put in hand further action in terms of a report on the information society. Its two Working Groups dealt with economic and technical aspects, and with regulatory and political aspects. Its report was presented at the Corfu Summit in June, 1994, (Europe 1994), which moved to set up a permanent coordinating instrument across Member States, embracing the private and public sectors, in order to establish a regulatory framework for development. This framework was to consider access to markets, network compatibility, intellectual property rights and data protection; the uses for an ISH included health care, traffic management, teleworking, city information highways and administrative networks, among others. Bangemann's May, 1994 Report (CORDIS 1994), adopted at Corfu, emphasized the importance of a coordinated approach, with a 'seamless interconnection' of networks and interoperable services, for the quality of life of citizens and consumers, and for social equality. Universal access was necessary, lest individuals' rejection of the new information culture pose a danger to it. Public authorities were to establish safeguards and to promote fair access. New markets for goods, information and entertainment were envisaged, but a regulatory environment must ensure full competition.

Some policy issues concerned privacy and intellectual property. Bangemann recommended EU action towards a regulatory framework for these in Europe and even internationally. The report also grasped the important pragmatic point about privacy protection, that without the legal security of a Union-wide approach, lack of consumer confidence will certainly undermine rapid development of the information society.' Pointing to Europe's leadership in data protection, it warned against nationally disparate approaches in the face of new technologies and services, and urged a rapid decision on the long-awaited data protection Directive. In view of the ISH's envisaged road traffic management, administrative and health care applications, this recommendation seemed timely. Bangemann also discussed encryption as a privacy tool and favored its harmonization, but a legal framework would be needed against hacking. However, and in light of 'Clipper Chip', it is significant that the report saw that 'governments may need powers to override encryption for the purposes of fighting against crime and protecting national security', thus potentially raising fears about Europe-wide surveillance on the ISH. The improved provision of public services apart, specifically democratic applications of a European ISH were scarce in the report. The 'information polity' concept has not penetrated thinking, which was framed in terms of a European 'information society' or economy, although the ISH infrastructures will obviously allow its realization. The formation of a trans-European public administration network was seen first as a link amongst agencies in the fields of tax, customs and excise, statistical, social and health data - with privacy implications, as personal data are communicated - and later as a link between them and citizens. The proposed city information highways - up to five by 1997 - will carry few democracy-related messages, except for 'access to information services' by 'consumers'.

The Commission's July, 1994 Communication invited EU institutions to support and debate the issues. It outlined further steps that would be taken through EU machinery to act on the recommendations. On privacy, it aimed to have the general Directive adopted within 1994, but thought it was necessary to consider how general principles related to specific new technological situations. An encryption proposal was to emerge by September, 1994. EU work on the public administration network was already far advanced, and the Commission would stimulate pilot development of city information highways. But the Communication was silent on democratic benefits. At the end of 1994, the Essen Summit acknowledged the importance of the Action Plan, looked towards a 1998 liberalization of telecommunications, and called for the rapid creation of a legal framework including data protection; a common Council position on the latter was still awaited.

## 4. Democracy and Privacy: Mutual Reinforcement

This brief survey indicates that ISH policies include - although perhaps insufficiently - some consideration for political and social values for which new developments have consequences. But these values should not be construed as separate agenda items, for they bear upon each other. The relationship between democracy and privacy can only be briefly and hypothetically explored here. The main argument is that each is an important supportive condition of the other. More specifically, democracy cannot be truly enhanced by ICTs if there are inadequate safeguards against the surveillance possibilities of the systems that are used for this; and privacy safeguards are only possible in a democracy, where public authorities are held accountable. It is thus not a question of developing the resources and techniques of each in isolation, or merely of a 'balance' or trade-off between democracy and privacy, but of achieving both with a recognition of their mutuality.

This requires some discussion. A democratic political system presupposes as well as ensures liberty of expression and communication among citizens themselves and between citizens and the state. This condition is threatened by official secrecy and censorship. One of the liveliest debates about civil liberties on the ISH concerns censorship on the Internet, in which providers of bulletin boards have sometimes exercised editorial control to exclude certain participants from the openness of discourse that characterizes the ISH. As Kapor (1991) points out, the ambiguity of the public or private status of these discussion groups means that controversies over the permissible latitude of free speech are likely. The issues are ones of law and etiquette, but in regard to the ISH they are debated in a grey area in which the applicability of established rules and norms is very uncertain. Yet free speech in a democracy may be subject to limits, for not only do 'loose lips sink ships' in wartime, but libel, defamation and obscenity, for example, also cannot enjoy legal protection.

However, democratic liberties may also be hindered by the actual or suspected presence of surveillance, because the latter has a 'chilling' effect on communication or expression. Surveillance thrives in authoritarian regimes that are not exposed to public debate and criticism. When it is used in political systems that are called democratic, it is legitimized and restricted on grounds of necessity and special justification, as with censorship. The covertness or unaccountability of its operation is regarded as a blemish with overtones of authoritarianism, and libertarians argue for adequate safeguards. Thus a legal requirement to obtain a warrant for wiretapping, and some form of accountability to legislatures for such practices, are ways in which covert surveillance may be reconciled - however tenuously - with democracy. In a related discussion, Mellors (1978: 109) argues that 'the best safeguard is not that they know less about us, but that we know more about them; and that we are aware of what they know about us and how they use such information.'

Surveillance may isolate individuals, disrupting social intercourse and communication. Isolation is far different from solitude and privacy. Democracy cannot exist where persons are isolated; it can, however, where they are private, and some democratic institutions - for example, the secret ballot or the ability of political groups to converse in conditions of privacy - that underline the connection are regarded as hallmarks of democracy. ICTs can promote communication, the expression of political opinion, and political action amongst citizens who cannot meet in person if they can trust the security of electronic communications and the integrity of these media against surveillance. If it appears (or is convincingly suspected) that, say, supposedly secure messages are being monitored by authorities, that discussants on ISH media are being targeted and profiled because of their unorthodox views, or that personal information that is disclosed for one purpose finds its way into other uses without one's knowledge or consent, then the ISH's potential as a trusted medium for democracy may suffer. So, too, may its effectiveness or reliability in providing services or goods, where such transactions require the gathering of one's personal details. This is why ISH proposals, as we have seen, consider privacy and data security to be important if the administrative and commercial advantages of the ISH are to be realized.

A problem arises for the proposition concerning the mutuality of democracy and privacy when, in practice, certain forms of surveillance enjoy popular or parliamentary support, thus opposing democracy to liberty. Democracy then is in danger of becoming the tyranny of the majority. Contemporary surveillance devices such as video cameras in public places raise this dilemma, although the object here is normally the apprehension of criminals, not the suppression of political expression. Its careless, arbitrary or unaccountable use in crime control may alienate even those who support it for limited and specific public-order purposes. However, where the object shifts - as it may do in the grey area of violent political protest or in the targeting of suspect social groups or categories - then it becomes repugnant to the idea of democracy. Public authorities themselves, including the police, have sometimes been reluctant to have wide surveillance powers, and have even resisted identity card schemes for fear of becoming alienated from society unless democratic accountability rules were also in place, even minimally. Although such scruples are often overcome, a crucial distinction is that they are never even entertained in authoritarian regimes; their relaxation in a democracy may be the result of a lengthy debate.

The affinity between democracy and privacy is reinforced through the idea of *consent*. In democratic theory, authority enjoys the consent of the governed; similarly, privacy protection requires one's consent to the use of her or his information. Consent to government is more confidently given where government is publicly accountable and its actions reasonably transparent. This is why 'open government' is seen as necessary: the public accessibility of, for example, official statistics, evaluative reports, policy documents, and public financial accounts. ISHs are likely to assist democracy by making much more non-personal information available to many more people. For the reasons already touched on, democracy also requires transparency about the use of personal data. An important assumption in data protection systems is that consent to the use of one's personal data may be genuine only to the extent that data users are transparent, and thus accountable, about what they are doing with one's information. On the other hand, it also requires that there be limits on who can know what about whom. ISHs make these limits much more problematical, but make privacy safeguards all the more necessary on pragmatic grounds.

For both democracy and privacy to be enhanced - or at least not damaged - by ISHs, effective rules of the road for treating non-personal and personal information would have to be created. It is too crude and rhetorical simply to say that the better the privacy, the better the democracy, and vice versa; and the better the provision of commercial or governmental outputs as well. Although it may be sounder to talk about minimum prerequisites for each, that would presuppose an ability to measure the extent of privacy safeguards and of democracy: a problem which cannot be discussed here, but which needs consideration if the postulated mutual entailment is to be normatively persuasive and practically possible (Raab 1991).

## 5. Conclusion

ISHs are being developed primarily for their likely benefits to the economy and the state, and to the involvement of the citizen/consumer in both. These benefits include industrial development, employment, financial gain, better consumer service, public service provision and the reorganization or 'reinvention' of government. The improvement of democracy is important as well, but it is more a side-benefit or luxury than a motive force for ISH infrastructural development, although democratic goals play some part in its strategy of political salesmanship. Democracy is involved in the ISH in two senses. First, it is a purpose served by it through, for example, 'electronic democracy' applications such as voting, opinion polling, the facilitation of information flows amongst citizens and between them and government. Second, in the sense of open and equal access to electronic and information infrastructure, so that there are no 'haves' and 'have-nots', and so that information resources are available to all on the same terms. But democracy in either sense may be marginalized by the stronger economic and state emphases, and it may exist more in rhetoric than in reality. As we have seen, the democratic 'input' voice is muffled in ISH discussion documents and official papers. On the other hand, the networks are already used by citizens for political purposes and for opinion-shaping discourses that are vital to democracy. If democracy is to hold its position both as an objective along the ISH and as a principle of its operation, it will need political support and pressure, as well as demonstrable achievements in enhancing democracy. It will also need a legitimizing ideology through which traditional democratic theory is restated specifically in terms of information requirements, leading to a new theory of democratic information.

In contrast, it is too easy to regard protection against an Orwellian development of the ISH as an obstacle to the full exploitation of the 'information revolution' - a roadblock on the superhighway. Privacy protection as a rule of the road may indeed present a necessary bar to dangerous vehicles. The criteria for judging 'roadworthiness' may be disputed, and are at the heart of the contentious politics of data protection. Whilst privacy is highly valued, it is balanced against the consumer or public service benefits promised by the ISH; sometimes needed goods can only arrive on dangerous lorries. However, a more sophisticated construction - seen in several documents - makes some degree of privacy protection a precondition of success in that it enhances the acceptability and legitimacy of ISH applications, just as speed limits and clear lane markings help to organize, rather than impede, the flow of motorway traffic for safe journeys. Beyond this, although more speculatively, the enhancement of privacy could be an achievable ISH goal insofar as the security technologies and systems in the infrastructure, including encryption and privacy technology, advance privacy protection beyond what was possible earlier on.

As with 'Athens', if the superhighway is not to terminate at 'Orwell', it will require a constituency of support for privacy values, as well as a treatment of these values as a robust ideology for - not against - the information age or technology itself. This involves deeper and wider understanding of ICTs and the ISHs, and to some extent this can only come with use. The advent of ISHs are likely to boost the development and globalization of regulatory policy machinery, including a repertory that includes laws, regulatory agencies, organizational self-regulation, and individuals' protective techniques (Bennett 1992, Industry Canada 1994b, Raab 1993). At the moment, the satisfaction of these conditions is uneven within and among countries.

# CHAPTER 14

# Democracy and Datacoupling

Victor J.J.M. BEKKERS and Hein P.M. Van DUIVENBODEN[1]

*Tilburg University, PO Box 90153, 5000 LE Tilburg, The Netherlands*

**Abstract.** Transparency and communication are two characteristics of information and communications technologies which will strategically influence the organization of democratic society. Transparency between government and citizens can be accomplished by coupling databases in which personal data is stored. The mutual relationship between data coupling and a number of democratic and legal principles calls for a new generation of regulation.

## 1. Introduction

In the 1970's and 1980's the emphasis in the way information technology was applied in private and governmental organizations was on the capacity of computers to undertake calculation. Computers could process more information, in a speedier, more detailed and more standardized way. In the 1990's it is clear that there are two other important developments, in the way information technology is used. First, computers, PC's and databases become more integrated, and this improves the exchange and comparison of data. This integration enables people and organizations to get a better, more detailed, insight into the way sectors of the economy and society, function, including social security and health care, consumer and product markets and all kinds of private and (quasi) public organizations function. In this way transparency is increased. The second development is that a communications revolution has taken place within the world of information technology. There has been a synthesis of information and communications technologies. The hype which surrounds the digital or electronic superhighway is a reflection of this communication revolution, a revolution which connects and integrates all kinds of infrastructures, so that free exchange of speech, pictures and text can take place. Time and space are no longer obstacles in the way of communication between people (see Bekkers 1993, 1994).

Transparency and communication are, therefore, two characteristics of information and communications technologies (ICTs) which will strategically influence the organization of democratic society, the functioning of government and the role of

---

[1] The authors wish to thank Mr I. Horrocks for his comment on an earlier version of this chapter.

the citizen as a client and a voter. Not only will society and government become more transparent, so too will the citizen. One of the ways this transparency is accomplished, is by coupling and integrating all kinds of databases and records in which personal data is stored.

Our intention is to explore and to illustrate the relationship between data coupling and a number of democratic and legal principles, including legal equality, legal security, the rule of the law and the principle of checks and balances. On the one hand data coupling has important consequences for the operationalization of these principles, but on the other hand, these principles influence and sometimes restrict the way in which databases are coupled.

In paragraph two we describe some of the principles of democracy and the Rule of Law ('Rechtsstaat') which are at stake. In paragraph three, we will explore the concept of transparency and the phenomenon of data coupling, and discuss the techniques which are used to increase the transparency of government and citizens. Paragraph four will explore the importance of data coupling for the democratic principles which we describe in paragraph two. But as we have already said, this is only one side of the relationship between coupling and democracy. Thus in paragraph five we describe and illustrate the other side of this relationship: the way in which democratic principles foster and limit the operation and extent of coupling. Finally we draw some conclusions about the implications for democracy of the citizen who becomes more and more 'transparent', and pose the question, has the state itself become more 'transparent' too?

## 2. Some Democratic Principles

Lyon states that 'societies that claim to be democratic imply by that term that there is a degree of involvement by the citizens in the political process. Governments thus claim to be responsive to citizens, who are viewed as political equals' (Lyon 1994, 116). To establish and maintain a generally accepted degree of involvement of citizens in all kinds of political and policy processes, it is important to ensure a level of public support. Such public confidence can exist ony if citizens can rely on law and public policy, and on the correct implementation of norms which are laid down in them. Therefore, decision making must be in accordance with known, uniform laws, and must, as far as possible, eliminate arbitrary and capricious behavior. Furthermore, it is necessary to provide an opportunity to excercise the right to appeal, if there is to be assurance that proper procedures are in fact being followed (see Clarke 1992). This is the idea of the 'Rechtsstaat'.

This idea is operationalized in at least four related principles, which complement each other. The first is the principle of legal equality. This means that all cases which are the same in their nature and characteristics should be dealt with in the same way. This principle forbids discrimination in general.

The second principle is that of legal security. Government actions which affect citizens should be based on existing laws and regulations so that in the end these actions are predictable. People can also refer to these laws and regulations in their own actions and should be able to have trust that the law is being executed.

Another principle refers to the Rule of Law. The actions of governmental organizations with respect to citizens should be based on certain competencies, which are laid down in laws and regulations.

The last principle we distinguish is the principle of checks and balances. In order to protect citizens from arbitrary execution of power by the state power should be divided between separate institutions. This separation of powers can be safeguarded if these institutions control each other and keep each other in balance. The classical idea of the division of powers is the distinction between legal power, its execution and the judiciary. In more decentralized or federalized states, the idea of checks and balances is used to balance the power of central government institutions (the federation) and decentralized government institutions (the states). The final aspect of the idea of checks and balances refers to the relationship between government and citizens. Citizens should be protected against capricious actions by the government. Government actions should be controlled and counterbalanced. For instance, citizens should be able to control government. A necessary condition is that government is, to some extent, transparent. Legal requirements like a Freedom of Information Act should create this transparency and at the same time protect the citizen.

## 3. Datacoupling and Transparency

One of the capabilities of modern information and communications technologies is the increased opportunity to combine all kinds of data within and between the databases which are used by a great number of government organizations. This capability particularly applies to the large number of personal records in which all kinds of data on citizens are stored. This data is increasingly being used to support an effective formulation, implementation and evaluation of policy programs and other government initiatives. Government organizations, policy sectors, and the processes within them become more and more transparent.

Transparency has two sides: from the perspective of government and from the perspective of the citizen as a voter and as a client. From the perspective of governmental organizations transparency enables politicians and policy makers to get a better and more detailed insight into the outcomes of governmental actions, the interdependencies between them, and the target or client groups involved. From the perspective of the citizen a more transparent government, with a legal framework that safeguards this transparency, makes it possible to judge - earlier and better - the behavior of politicians and civil servants. It also enables citizens and pressure or interest groups to formulate their own policy and alternatives on government proposals.

The coupling of different data bases is very much contributing to transparant administrations. Within the literature three forms of datacoupling are identified that moreover exist in several combinations (OTA 1986). The first one is 'Computer Aided Front End Verification'. In its most simple and present form this is the checking of the reliability of data: is the information given by a citizen valid? For example, when a person applies for a social benefit social security agencies are likely to seek confirmatory data from other sources than the person concerned. Those other sources can be found within the organization itself but also in the computers of other organizations - like the Taxation Office or municipalities. This kind of coupling can be seen as an ex ante form of coupling: the exchange of data is triggered by a specific transaction with a specific person. In that way, the person whose data is involved has been identified prior to the coupling activity - which is not always the case with other forms of coupling.

The second is 'computer matching' which can serve two goals. Firstly, to search for people or characteristics of people where the data is stored in more than one register, where this data should only have been stored in one register. Secondly, to search for people whose data is missing or is incomplete in a register. For example, when social security agencies try to detect fraud and abuse they are likely to compare a large number of personal data stored in their own databases with a large number of data stored in the registers of the Taxation Office. Thus people can be traced who receive a benefit unlawfully by cheating on their income; the comparison of data then shows that the same person is registered in one database too many or that the combination of his data provides contradictory information. Because computer matching aims at identifying people in stead of verifying data of already identified people matching can be seen as an ex post form of coupling; the coupling activity is sort of a 'fishing expedition' and not a search for confirmatory data prior to specific transactions with specific persons.

The third form of datacoupling is 'computer profiling'. Profiling aims to combine data from different databases, or data within one and the same database. For example, to build up a consumer profile, or a comprehensive personal profile, as in the case of criminal profiles. This is also a form of ex post coupling: the search aims at identifying a profile of a certain group of people instead of aiming at confirming data of people that are already identified for a specific purpose.

Whereas ex ante coupling deals with the data of people who are already identified by the coupling agencies ex post coupling deals with the data of people who are not yet identified. As a result, computer matching and profiling have a different impact on democratic principles from verification. In this chapter we will not discuss those differences in detail. We will discuss the relationship between coupling and democracy in a more general sense, because there is a tendency to combine different forms of datacoupling. In this way we will attempt to focus on recent developments and the near future relationship between coupling and democracy.

The implications of using datacoupling to improve transparency are ambivalent. On the one hand it opens the gateway to new opportunities, but, on the other hand, it gives rises to threats.

Opportunities for government are:

1. To improve insights into the causes of societal and policy problems and the links between them. More variables can be taken into account.
2. To obtain better and earlier insights into the outcomes of policy programs which have been or are being implemented. Here the feedback process is being improved.
3. To improve better insights into certain characteristics of targeted groups, for which government programs are being developed.

Opportunities for citizens are:

1. To improve their capacity to formulate competing proposals and analysis in order to strengthen their influence on the agenda management process.
2. To get a better and earlier understanding of the policy process and the effects of the policy programs being implemented.

Threats for the government are:

1. Transparency is often based on aggregated, quantitative ('hard') data. Therefore a partial picture of policy fields is being constructed which does not represent life in all its details and nuances. Information has a certain bias and the transparency which is achieved is imperfect and insufficient (Bekkers 1993, see also chapter fifteen). Kraemer and Dutton (1982) refer to his threat as 'the automation of bias'.
2. Coupling leads to the construction and creation of 'digital persons' (see Clarke 1994) or 'digital problems', which do not represent actual persons or problems. They are too artificial. Government could therefore select inappropriate policy problems (and solutions) or policy target groups.

Threats for the citizen are:

1. Achieving transparency through datacoupling leads to the creation of new information, for which citizens have not given their permission. They surrendered the information for other purposes. This is a threat which is referred to in the literature as a threat to 'Informationelle Selbstbestimmung' (Bull 1985). The citizen has no understanding of the way personal information is being used.

2. Transparency leads to a more detailed picture of individuals and target groups, which can influence the right to privacy. The so-called 'Gläserne Bürger' (Snellen *et al.* 1989) is being created, which can be more easily followed and controlled. In a more negative way we can speak of 'data surveillance'. The domain of data surveillance will increase, if governments operate in more policy fields then those implied by the 'caretaker state'. There is a correlation between the growth of the welfare state and the demand for data surveillance because, in the welfare state, people and groups demand more of the state, such as subsidies and social benefits.

We have illustrated above the ways in which these opportunities and threats may become reality, how datacoupling will affect the citizen in a democracy, and some of the legal and constitutional principles which are designed to protect his position.

## 4. The Importance of Datacoupling for Democratic Principles

In the introduction to this chapter we said that the relationship between some democratic principles and datacoupling is mutual. In this paragraph we explore one side of this relationship. What does coupling of personal data mean for principles of legal equality, legal security, the Rule of Law and the idea of checks and balances?

One of the goals of coupling is to facilitate legal equality. Often coupling is used to attack fraud and the abuse of social benefits. But data matching can also be used in other ways. A social security agency can match its own records with other records, for example tax records, so that it can identify people who are eligible for benefits but who are not currently claiming those benefits. Clarke (1992) stresses that this effect of data coupling is the sole direct advantage for people whose data is hold on public records. The quality of services can be improved for all those who have a right to them.

But the opposite is also true. Coupling can be a threat to legal equality. For instance, in the Netherlands matching of data is used to detect fraud and abuse of tax payments and social benefits. The amazing results of coupling activities by local social security agencies generates much attention in the media and in the political world. One of the results has been that over 30% of benefit recipients have abused social security regulations (NRC Handelsblad 1993). These results have had a profound impact on the fraud detection policies of the Public Prosecutor. Priority was given to fraud detection in the social security sector. Other types of possible fraud, like fraud with taxes, was given much less attention. Social benefit recipients are, as a result, a bigger target of the Prosecutors search for abuse than, for instance, tax evaders. Therefore, frauds of the first category have considerably more chance of being prosecuted than frauds of the second category (Roording 1994).

Legal security is another principle which is affected by the use of datacoupling. A relevant concept which can be used to gain insights into this relationship is the idea

'Informationelle Selbstbestimmung'. Datacoupling often leads to the creation of new information. Citizens do not give their permission to use their data, when it is needed to establish new information. This affects the principle of legal security in the following way. For the purpose of executing legal rules citizens supply personal information, but this information is then used for other reasons and purposes than those which are outlined in the original Rule of Law. No legal foundation is available. Nowadays, in the Netherlands, government agencies use all kinds of anomalies and lacunae in laws and rules to extend the exchange of personal data, to improve fraud detection and cut public expenditure. In this way, national health services are obliged to give personal data to social security agencies, in order to detect fraud. This data is very interesting because it is updated every month. Originally, employers were obliged to give this data, to allow the daily functioning of the health insurance system, but now the data is also used in another policy field. The citizen is never asked whether they agree to the use of their data outside its original context. Last year, for instance, four Dutch social security agencies were given access to various databases belonging to industrial insurance boards, in order to detect fraud and abuse of social benefits. Two agencies went beyond their authority when they used data belonging to these boards to identify formal spouses who should be contributing to the social benefits of their ex-partners. The director of the Registration Chamber, the Dutch Data Protection Commissioner, stated that this unauthorized use of personal data was due to the lack of clarity of the Dutch Privacy Act (NRC Handelsblad 1994). As a result, registered citizens cannot rely on governmental organizations to use the data only for the purpose for which they provided them.

On the other hand, the success of data coupling also depends on the quality of the data which is stored in registers. Verification and matching of personal data can improve the quality and the topicality of the data and databases. Furthermore, this improvement can also lead to a more effective and a more efficient implementation of law and policy. There is a tendency to use the automated Dutch population registers as the one and only valid input for other records within government. Till now, every agency has defined its registered name, address and other basic data in its own way. Sometimes disputes are the result of divergent ways of registering data. More and more, these basic data are compared with each other. In cases of doubt, the municipal population register is decisive. For the citizen this has the advantage that disputes about these basic data will occur less often (Bekkers *et al.* 1994).

Coupling has also implications for the Rule of Law. There must be a legal foundation for matching and verifying data, and this sets the conditions under which data may or may not be used. A general and legally accepted principle relating to data exchange is the right of people to know if and how they are registered, how the registered data is used, and by whom. An interesting example occurred last year. The Netherlands was anticipating and influenza epidemi. The Inspector of Health Care tried to diminish the number of influenza casualties (especially elderly people and people with heart diseases) by compelling pharmacists to use their up to date medical registers to provide family doctors with appropriate information. In this way, doctors could approach potential influenza patients and persuade them to accept an injection. The Dutch privacy protection agency said that the privacy of those people was at stake, because there was no legal foundation for this particular exchange of data (Registratiekamer 1994).

The increasing opportunities and growing importance of, datacoupling by use of modern information technology requires a legal framework. Till now, many of these activities have occurred in a twilight zone. In Australia and the United States, guidelines and legislation have been formulated to regulate data matching. In 1990 a Bill was passed in Australia, authorizing the Department of Social Security to conduct a series of large scale computer matching programs, and in 1988 the United States Computer Matching and Privacy Protection Act became effective (Clarke 1992). Those guidelines and laws reflect the importance of the Rule of Law.

The principle of checks and balances specifies the division of power in a society, in order to prevent unfair and capricious behavior towards citizens. It has many aspects. It relates to Montesquieu's theorem of the Trias Politica; the division between legislative, administrative and judiciary powers, the relation between central and decentral government, and the relation between government and its citizens. Datacoupling affects the power relations between all those parties. It can redefine or strengthen the position of these parties, because access to and use of information are powerful resources in the interactions between them.

Our example is restricted to the changing relationship between government and citizens. If government uses computer matching techniques, the total number of people contained in two or more registers is being compared. Whether matching takes place primarily for administrative purposes, or because of a desire to uncover fraud, the whole 'population' of the register is treated as potential frauds. So, the position of registered citizens vis à vis government is being weakened and subjected to more or less capricious behavior. There is no check on governmental computer matching by citizens. Clarke (1992: 48) states that 'computer matching is therefore in conflict with democratic standards relating to arbitrary interference. There is no justification for the handling of any one person's data, other than that the person is a member of a population which is known to contain miscreants'. This observation becomes more significant if one looks at the results of computer matching operations. Recently, the results of a computer matching program in the Rotterdam social security agency showed how ineffective datacoupling can be. In order to detect social benefit fraud, the agency checked their own records against those in six other databases. After verifying 1750 potential cases of fraud only two of them turned out to be 'hits'. The director of the agency stated that 'moral panic' had resulted in a general tendency to couple all kinds of personal records and that his organization now had to cope with a 'mission impossible' (Binnenlands Bestuur 1994). Furthermore, the results of this mission makes questionable the justification for using such a large amount of data without the knowledge or consent of registered citizens.

## 5. The Importance of Democratic Principles for Datacoupling

The democratic principles described earlier influence also the extent and the nature of datacoupling. They can, for instance, limit the way in which records are coupled or data matched.

The first principle is that of legal equality. When data is coupled in order to detect fraud or abuse, the determination of guilt is in the hands of government. Government should verify 'the hits' obtained by matching or profile operations in order to prove that fraud or abuse has actually taken place. The requirement that 'guilt that be proven' concerns everybody, and therefore restricts computer matching or profiling operations by government. However, there is a growing tendency that government need not to prove a person's guilt, but, rather, that the accused must prove their innocence. But, in that case, the principle of legal equality is under pressure. The degree to which somebody can prove that he or she is innocent, can for instance depend on the legal or financial resources that he or she can mobilize. It is known that people who are wealthy or of better education, are more likely to be able to prove their innocence. As we pointed out in the previous paragraph, many people who are registered in governmental databases such as social security, education (grants), or housing, are people who are mostly dependent on governmental benefits. Therefore it is likely that they are less competent than people who are more financially independent.

The principle of legal security also influences the nature and degree of datacoupling. This principle points to the obligation of government to inform the people who are registered in a database that an alteration in their records will take place, especially if this alteration infringes the position and the rights of the registered. So, when, as a result of datacoupling operations, government agencies change the amount of, or the qualifications for, the award of benefits, the registered citizens should be notified before coupling operations take place that the results will lead to changes. The National Ombudsman of the Netherlands has recently complained about the behavior of the Dutch Housing Department, because the department changed housing subsidies retrospectively as a result of a data matching operation with the Tax Administration. According to the Ombudsman, it was improper not to inform registered people in advance that alterations in their position could take place as a result of the coupling operations. According to the Ombudsman their legal security and status was threatened (Van Duivenboden 1994).

The Rule of Law is also a principle which should be taken into account when data or records are coupled. For instance, the Rule of Law deals with regulations regarding the protection of privacy and freedom of information vis à vis national security. The registration of data should take these legal norms into account. Specifically, norms regarding privacy and national security should act as constraints on coupling activities. On the one hand, privacy regulation can limit the flexibility of police investigations and protect the privacy of the citizen, but, on the other hand, regulations regarding matters of national security will facilitate these investigations, but could at the same time violate the privacy of the citizen. In the Netherlands, but in other countries as well, there is a debate about the use of electronic surveillance methods in the fight against organized crime. As with data coupling, a legal framework for the use of these methods does not exist. There is little discussion and there are hardly any guidelines governing intrusion into privacy as a result of national security considerations. Lyon points out that 'national security' is often used to create a twilight zone, in which coupling operations can take place. It is therefore worth asking how far the (coupling) policies and priorities of security agencies are subject to democratic accountability (Lyon 1994).

The last principle to be discussed is the principle of checks and balances. In the Netherlands there has been for some decades a debate about centralized or decentralized registration of basic characteristics of citizens. This is the so-called 'population' register which contains data about name, address, birth, nationality a.s.o. The discussion focused on the question whether a centralized database would endanger citizens' privacy and infringe the right of the municipalities who actually gathered this data and were therefore seen as their owner. In the end, decentralized registration was chosen, in which the municipalities kept their autonomy with respect to storing and processing data. The division of powers between the central and decentralized government was therefore maintained. The principle of checks and balances also played a role in the decentralized registration, because a decentralized organization would have given more guarantees for the privacy of citizens. It was argued that a centralized database could more easily facilitate data coupling with other databases so that government surveillance could increase (Bekkers *et al.* 1994).

## 6. A Transparent Citizen in a Transparent State?

The increased opportunities of datacoupling make the citizen more and more transparent. Because citizens are registered in all kinds of (quasi) government databases they leave all kinds of *digital footprints* behind. Coupling of data makes it possible to trace a person more easily and to reconstruct his behavior. At the same time these databases function in the context of the democratic 'Rechtsstaat'. Principles of the 'Rechtsstaat', especially the principles of legal equality, of legal security, the Rule of Law, and of checks and balances', influence the nature and the degree of coupling operations. In this chapter, we have argued that there is a twofold relationship between these democratic and legal principles and datacoupling. First, datacoupling has an impact on the degree to which citizens appeal to these principles, but we saw that this impact is ambivalent. Datacoupling could, in principle, threaten the way in which these principles were applied, but on the other hand it could also enhance the execution of these principles. Secondly, we argued that these principles are also important for the nature and the degree of datacoupling, because they contain guidelines for the organization of coupling processes.

However, when we look at the practices we describe in paragraphs four and five, we notice that the citizen becomes more and more transparent but that the state or government organizations do not become more transparent. Transparency is therefore defined in a very narrow sense, from the perspective of the state, in order to detect fraud and abuse. Datacoupling to enhance justice in the provision of government services and benefits is not well developed. Here is a chance for government to influence its legitimacy in a positive way.

But, above all, the transparency of the citizens to the state lacks a proper legal framework. Some regulation exists, but very often government is very inventive in using all kinds of arguments and anomalies in existing regulations and policies to increase and improve its surveillance of the behavior of citizens. One of the reasons for this lack of regulation is that most of the laws and regulations were established in a period in which coupling of databases was not yet so advanced technically as it is now. Therefore principles like legal security, legal equality, the Rule of Law and checks and balances, have not been considered. In the 'information age', this is a situation which needs to be recognized and rectified, if the public's faith in government is not to be further undermined.

# CHAPTER 15

# Digitalizing Decision Making in a Democracy: for Better or for Worse?

Wim B.H.J. Van de DONK

*Tilburg University, PO Box 90153, 5000 LE Tilburg, The Netherlands*

Odette M.T. MEYER

*Association of Dutch Polytechnics & Colleges,*
*PO Box 123, 2501 CC, 's-Gravenhage, The Netherlands*

**Abstract.** In this chapter, the authors present a conceptual approach that could help investigate and interpret the meaning of informatization for democracy. Their focus is on decision making processes. With respect to the democratic nature of political decision making processes, they introduce the concept of functions of political decision making. The focus of their analysis is not primarily directed towards the actors in the democratic arena, as it has been, for instance, in the second chapter of this volume. Rather the crux of this chapter is that informatization is affecting the functions that these actors perform by affecting information properties, aspects of information processing and information behavior in democratic decision making practices. Two explorative case studies are developed to demonstrate that certain ICTs facilitate the transfer of functions from the classical domain of elected politicians or representative bodies to the bureaucratic apparatus. Such developments beg the question of to what extent these processes can still be considered democratic. A related question is whether the information that is used in democratic decision making processes deserves more explicit political attention when these processes are 'digitalized'.

## 1. Introduction

Since the earliest stages of information technology development, expectations have been high, with many people convinced that ICTs could help improve the quality of human decision making (Van de Donk 1993). Indeed, for many kinds of decision making processes, impressive improvements in the speed and quality of decision making have been realized.

Advances in this technology has further raised expectations. A variety of applications have been introduced to support a kind of decision making which seems to contradict the rigid logic of computers: that is the political decision making. In this chapter, we will explore whether it is reasonable to expect that the use of ICTs in the political decision making processes will, in one way or another, fundamentally affect these processes. In particular, we will try to answer the question of whether informatization will influence the democratic nature of these processes.

In addressing these questions we have developed an analytical approach that suggests a new vocabulary to describe and analyse the relationships between information, informatization and democratic political decision making. This analytical approach is detailed in the second paragraph of this chapter[1].

Paragraph three illustrates the line of reasoning which we have developed by presenting two explorative case studies on two important types of decision making processes in a democracy: agenda building and allocative decision making. In both case studies, we investigate the consequences of a specific application of informatization: transaction systems in the case study of political agenda building and relational databases and spreadsheets in the case study regarding allocative policy making. Finally, in paragraph four, we make some concluding remarks.

## 2. Informatization and Political Decision Making in a Democracy: An Analytical Approach

### 2.1. Introduction

The majority of discussions on the relationship between ICTs and democracy focus on the meaning of ICTs for the functioning of focal actors such as representative bodies and political parties, or focal procedures such as campaigning, voting, and elections. Although (as many other chapters in this book have shown) these aspects deserve attention, it is important not to forget that informatization may also have a profound effect on the 'daily life' of democracies. After an intensive and exciting period of 'electioneering and campaigning', elected candidates become politicians holding a variety of administrative responsibilities. As such, they will participate in different degrees of routinized decision making processes, which from a democratic point of view are no less important than the previous campaigning and electioneering. Whether or not a certain political system is democratic cannot only be determined by merely looking at constitutional arrangements, institutional arrangements, voter turnout and the degree of responsive representation. It is equally important to look at the various decision making processes that characterize the daily routine of modern democracy. It is, therefore, both interesting and important to question the meaning of informatization to the processes that make up political decision making. As we will show in paragraph three, ICTs often play an important role in these processes.

---

[1]  For a more extensive discussion of our approach we refer to Van de Donk and Meyer, 1994: 230-242.

As we have stressed in the introduction to this chapter, we will concentrate on the meaning of informatization for political decision making processes. In this paragraph, we develop an analytical approach to aid the study of the relationships between information, informatization and political decision making. This approach is represented schematically in Figure 1.

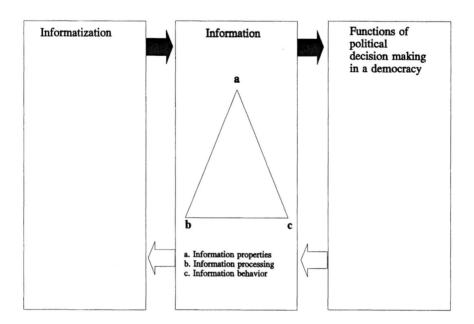

Fig. 1:     Global overview analytical approach

## 2.2.   Political Decision Making in a Democracy

In order to address our main hypothesis an explicit concept of democratic political decision making is required. Such a conception can be found by looking into the functions (or: capabilities, see Almond and Bingham Powell 1966) that political - decision making processes have to fulfil in democratic political systems. We distinguish the following functions:

a. Authoritative selection and neglect of problems in society: (authoritative) allocation of attention and allocation of pleasures and pains in a society;
b. Establishing and maintaining a balance between different interests in society;
c. Creation of institutions, organizational structures and processes for political decision making;

d. Preserving the existence and legitimation of the political system.[2]

It is apparent then that political decision making has to fulfil several functions (see also Almond and Bingman Powell 1966, Sharkansky 1970, Davies and Lewis 1971, Kuypers 1980: 180). The fact that these functions are fulfilled in a political system does not automatically mean, that this system can be considered democratic. Each of these functions can be fulfilled, in one way or another, by one or more actors or institutions (professional politicians, bureaucrats, pressure groups, individual citizens).

Different models of democracy[3] advocate specific sets of normative specifications of how, and by whom, these functions *should* be fulfilled. Some models of democracy promote a more important role for the citizenry, some others suggest that most of the functions should predominantly be carried out by representative bodies.

We identify, at least, three possible ways in which informatization could bring about more or less fundamental changes in regard to the functions previously mentioned:

1. Informatization could alter the way in which the functions of democratic political decision making are fulfilled. Certain applications of ICTs could, for instance, facilitate a deliberative or epistemic mode of democratic political decision making (see chapter 3);
2. Informatization could influence the relative importance of each of the functions in the total mixture of functions. Some functions could be strengthened, whilst others could be weakened as a consequence of informatization;
3. Informatization might also impact the types of actor and/or institutions that predominantly fulfil certain functions.

Depending on the model of democracy used to evaluate the changes in these dimensions, it can be seen that informatization has contributed to the strengthening or weakening of the democratic nature of decision making processes.

It is not intended in this chapter, to use the concept of function as a normative concept of democracy. Rather the concept is utilized as an analytical tool to investigate and interpret the role of informatization in democratic decision making arena's. Although still at an exploratory stage, we think that they can help us to describe and explain what is happening. We also believe that they contribute to a critical comparison and examination of research results, and of any statements in the debate about the relationship between democratic politics and informatization.

> We could critically examine any claim that democratic politics is disappearing,
> or is becoming obsolete due to informatization by investigating whether or not

---

[2]   One could consider function four to be served by each of the first three ones.
[3]   See chapter three and four of this book.

the functions of democratic political decision making are still fulfilled. Such an examination could bring us to the conclusion that a certain function of democratic political decision making (for example the balancing of different interests in a certain society) that used to be fulfilled by (elected) politicians is now predominantly carried out by the bureaucratic apparatus that has procured itself with sophisticated allocation models and sophisticated databases. Democratic politics, we would argue, has not disappeared, but changed its manifestation. A further question then would be whether this kind of politics could still be considered to be democratic according to the various normative models of theories of democracy.

To come to statements of this kind it is important to investigate empirically whether informatization is affecting the functions of democratic political decision making. This chapter attempts to illustrate the theoretical and empirical value of our approach by using it to explain empirical observations (see paragraph 3). Prior to our case study discussions it is essential that some key assumptions of our approach are classified.

### 2.3. *The Role of Information*

A second important characteristic of our conceptual approach is that we think we can investigate the way informatization is affecting democratic decision making processes by expressing the way informatization is affecting the role of information[4] in these processes. Our conceptual scheme illustrates (see Figure 1) three aspects that are determining the role of informatization:

a. Aspects of information-properties (e.g. reliability, accessibility, transformability of information)[5];
b. Aspects of information-processing (e.g. possibilities of combination, integration, control and speed of information-processing);
c. Aspects of information behavior of the various stakeholders (e.g. selection, rejection).

Of course, these aspects are also important in a situation without any informatization. However, we are convinced that the introduction and wide spread adapation of informatization forces us to (re)consider them in a more explicit manner. We think that studying the impacts of informatization on political decision making

---

[4]    Although it is common in most of the literature on information planning and systems design to make a distinction between 'data' as merely consisting of pure symbols and 'information' as consisting of data to which a meaning is attached by a receiver, we will use the term information in both ways throughout this chapter.

[5]    See Van de Donk and Meyer (1994) for a more detailed explanation. We defined (in a rather pragmatic and inductive way) six clusters of information-properties and the way they are likely to be affected by certain applications of ICT: quantity, availibility, storability and collectability (i); accessability, timeliness and suppressability (ii); transformability and processability (iii); contextuality (iv); reliability (v) and transferability (vi).

requires explicit attention to the role of information. All 'first-order'(or: initial) effects of informatization, we hypothesize, will regard one of these aspects. Some of them such as increased accessability, could be, *sui generis*, important for the democratic nature of decision making. Some other effects, for example the facilitation of information behavior that concentrates power in representative bodies, could be seen as second-order (or: further) effects. An evaluation of these effects (first- and second-order) with respect to the democratic nature of political decision making processes, will, of course, depend on the model of democracy one adopted (see chapter two and three).

Although informatization is likely to have impact on all three of these information-aspects, it is, however, also very likely that the various applications of ICTs will primarily affect one of these aspects. Moreover, we suggest that the key aspects are in fact highly interdependent. Consequently, initial effects on information properties could, eventually, influence aspects of information behavior (as a 'second-order' effect).

## 2.4.  Informatization

The first box of the scheme illustrated at Figure 1 also requires explanation. As outlined in the overview, informatization can be seen to be primarily an independent variable. Informatization can also be seen as the outcome of political decisions. This is reflected in the diagramatic scheme by the arrows pointing left. We argue that informatization is neither an autonomous development with unavoidable consequences, nor a mere instrument in hands of actors who use ICTs as a means of achieving their goals. Although the debate continues (Winner 1993, Kraemer and King 1994), we feel that informatization must be understood as a process in which technological and social systems interact and evolve (see Kling 1987b, Van de Donk 1993, Snellen 1994). Once shaped however, concrete ICT applications are likely to have autonomous influence in a restricted period of time.

The concept of informatization (compared to industrialization) refers to a series of phenomena that can be related to the widespread adoption of ICTs. This includes the introduction of ICT applications such as spreadsheets and telefaxes, the development of special 'information policies' and/or the assignment of special officers and departments in this field (see the definition of informatization that has been developed by the Tilburg/Rotterdam research programme 'Informatization in Public Administration', Frissen 1989).

It is thus reasonable to argue that all these phenomena can be considered relevant to the democratic decision making processes. We argue however, that informatization is too heterogeneous a concept to be used in empirical research as many different applications exist. In order to be able to do empirical research, this general heterogeneous concept has to be boiled down to concrete empirical phenomena such as certain applications, like networks, or a certain information policy. It is thus logical that

that some applications tend to support, more than others, certain aspects of democracy.

## 3. Two Explorative Case Studies

### 3.1. Introduction

This section of the chapter presents two explorative case studies concerning democratic political decision making: political agenda building and allocative policy making.

### 3.2. Political Agenda Building: the Use of Transactional Information Systems in the Policy Towards Minorities in Amsterdam[6]

#### 3.2.1. Political Agenda Building: the Allocation of Attention

Before presenting the case study in more detail, it is important first to clarify the concept of political agenda building. This concept refers to the process by which government or governmental authorities come(s) to the conclusion or admit(s) that certain problems have to enter the political agenda as problems about which (binding) political decisions are required. Emphasis is put on the way social phenomena are labelled as problems and on the way these problems are constantly being defined and redefined in the political process, since a once chosen problem definition will to a large extent determine the way in which the problem is actually dealt with by government. Furthermore, the realization of the dominance of a certain problem definition means that other aspects of the problem get less or no attention and are thus (partly) excluded from the agenda (Edelman 1988). Political agenda setting is therefore seen not only as a process of selection and rejection, but far more as an ongoing process of transformation.

An essential democratic value of the political agenda building processes is highlighted by the ways in which equal access to the political decision making arena is allocated, warranted and realized. A further element that is central to the concept of democracy can be derived form this first one. Namely the issue of whether the different, and often conflicting opinions and interests, are well represented in public debate. Crucial to the democratic nature of political agenda building is the flexibility of the political agenda itself. To what extent do new interests find their way on to the agenda, or is the agenda resistant to new interests that are not yet institutionali-

---

[6] This material derives from (first) empirical observations made during a research project which continues by the second author. We will therefore confine ourselves to suggesting possible interpretations as 'informed guesses'.

zed? Furthermore, an important democratic quality is the way in which 'minorities' are being treated by 'majorities'.

### 3.2.2. Some Background Information about the Case Study

During the sixties and seventies, large groups of immigrants from Marocco, Turkey and some Southern-European countries, came to the Netherlands to work in the heavy industry. A large part of them ended up in Amsterdam. At that time there was a shortage of Dutch labourers for unskilled and heavy work. Many enterprises, confronted with this situation, actively enlisted men from these countries. This policy was supported by the Dutch government and also by the local authorities of Amsterdam, who wanted to prevent a serious economic collapse which could result from the labour shortage.

Additionally, before the independence of Surinam, large groups of Surinam and Antillean people, the so called 'citizens from the former Dutch overseas territories', came to the Netherlands with the majority taking residence in Amsterdam.

As these groups stayed longer in the Netherlands, it became clear that they, as a group, had become relatively deprived, when compared to other Dutch population groups. Moreover, their presence led to growing tensions in the Dutch society.

From that time onwards (1982), the Amsterdams local authorities promoted a coordinated policy towards the ethnic minorities. This policy was based on the conviction that these new groups no longer had to be treated as 'guests' (the Dutch for foreign worker translates to 'guest worker') but as fellow citizens who had rights to opportunities for integration in the Dutch society. A special bureau was created to support the coordinating tasks of the alderman of the ethnic minority policy. Despite this policy being given a certain degree of political priority, it constantly had to fight its way into the different sectoral policies, such as the housing and education policy. A recurring topic of debate (brought forward as complaints by representatives of minority groups) in this respect has been that, once policy intentions are established, they are not at effectively implemented.

A delicate matter in this particular case study is to preserve a balance between the different interests at stake, namely the 'new' immigrants (those from the former Dutch colonies), versus 'established' interests (native inhabitants).[7] Important interests are at stake, and in times of economic regression and high unemployment, some gain from resolving the issue while others are forced to surrender privileges.

Also relevant is the way in which the process of decision making itself is structured. For instance are the minorities involved in the process in such a way that they are, or do they at least feel that they are actually able to influence the decision? Some authors state that the formal right to participate highlights far better the actual

---

[7]   But what is still 'new' and 'native' in the context of second and third generations?

(non)participation in allocations of power. In this sense, participation can be highly symbolic (Edelman 1977).

The issue of integration of minorities is of great importance to very existence of the political system. If minorities are excluded from equal participation, the result may be a sharp division between the different population groups ultimately resulting in the disintegration of the political system.

### 3.2.3. Political Agenda Building and Transactional Information Systems

Since 1988 the position of minorities in central policy fields in Amsterdam is being reported on a permanent basis with the help of so called 'transactional' information systems which are available within the municipality.[8] Several query languages and statistical devices are applied to re-use, on an aggregated level, the information that is already present in these systems.

In 1988 it was generally felt, especially by the bureau which coordinated the policy towards minorities, that valuable information on the position of minorities already exists in the various offices of the municipality. This information however, was not available when it was required, if retrievable at all, it remained fragmented. The alderman who was responsible for the coordination of the policy towards minorities, commissioned the 'Information project on minorities'. The statistical office, which was assigned to the Information project, was responsible for bringing data together, primarily on four topics: demography, housing, education and labor. From this point onwards information on the position of minorities has been published annually, by re-using data which was a by-product of different administrative processes.

Without the adoption of ICTs this would have been an impossible and time consuming, expensive job. Technically it was not simple to match the different information systems, and much of the data still had to be processed manually. It would, however, have been virtually impossible to compare more than 700.000 (Amsterdams population) personal index cards by hand with a similar number of cards from a housing card tray! The information that is produced in this way is being used during the process of formulating and defining what in fact is the 'minority problem'.

---

[8]   By transactional information systems we are referring to automated information systems in which different parts of government collect and register a wide variety of data on persons and objects during different implementation processes. On the basis of the collected data government decides on individual, unique cases (as in the case of a citizen searching for a residence).

## 3.2.4. Empirical Observations

One important impact of ICTs for the process of agenda building is that it has enlarged the possibilities to store for longer periods of time larger quantities of data. Furthermore this data is more readily available. This can influence the way in which social problems are and can be put to the fore. Any problems which already exist in the data when held in databases can be compounded. It has become possible to show the magnitude of the problem, for example minorities which make up 20% of the population are confronted with relative deprivation when compared to the native inhabitants, and also to demonstrate that the problem has existed for many years. Here it can be seen that certain elements of the agenda are already 'filed' in the information systems. Moreover, the information stored in databases appears to make it easier to draw attention to certain problems in a more permanent way. For example, in this case it became an easy and routine task to produce yearly and two-yearly reports on the position of ethnic minorities. Deteriorations in their position were monitored and received immediate attention. Where improvements were measured, they were attributed to the effectiveness of the policy, and the figures were used as an argument to give less priority to the problem.

This case study demonstrates the importance of the accessibility of information. In a situation where representatives of ethnic groups have access to the transactional information systems, they have an important instrument for articulating and formulating their demands towards government. On the other hand however, when they are not permitted to have access, they appear to be more dependent on the government which is actually producing the information, and which presents the information in a way that suits its own purposes. In the case study so far representatives of the ethnic minorities have never had access to the transactional systems. Furthermore, until now, they have never asked for it, at least not in a direct way. When on one occasion they were asked to give their opinion, almost accidentally, on a small change in the composition of one of the general policy databanks, they felt passed over, since until that moment they were unaware of what exactly had been happening.

ICTs have drastically enlarged the possibilities of transforming data into new kinds of information. In this instance indicators are produced on the housing positions of all inhabitants of Amsterdam which show that minorities live in overcrowded situations and that their average occupancy rate is significantly higher than the native Dutch citizens. Related to the Dutch housing averages, the indicators clearly illustrate that minorities are still being confronted with a relatively high housing shortage. Furthermore, the indicators show that the average waiting period for a house is much higher for minority groups than for the native inhabitants. Finding a house on the housing market thus proves to be much easier for the native inhabitants than for the minorities. Ultimately then, the production of these indicators has made the issue of minority deprivation, its magnitude and its seriousness, less subject to discussion.

Due to the enlarged capability to transform data to be used in the process of agenda setting, the importance of being registered becomes more crucial. Discussions about the need to register someone's ethnic background illustrate this very well. Since it became common knowledge that the minorities were 'statistically' disappearing, the second and third generation of ethnic minorities cannot be traced in the official registers because they have Dutch nationality and/or they were born in the Netherlands and/or their parents were born in the Netherlands, the registration of ethnic background became a topic of debate. Those in favor of registration claim that without this data no policy can effectively be developed and implemented. Others, mostly representatives of the ethnic groups, state that the argument that the correct data are not available serves as an excuse for postponing adequate measures.

In the case of the policy towards minorities the data was not collected for the sole purpose of policy formulation. Rather, it was created during several implementation processes as a by-product of these processes. 'Ethnicity' was in fact not registered at all during these processes, but was later added from the population register. If, as in the case of the policy towards minorities, the policy problem is being formulated with help of re-used information, the question of whether, and if so how, this will influence the ways in which the problem will be defined, becomes highly relevant. Although the data can be re-used in a different context, it is highly questionable whether any kind of aggregation and combination will be allowed, regardless of the perspective one holds on a certain problem. New information can only be generated within the boundaries of the databases that are available. To illustrate this, it is useful to examine the ways the different stakeholders of the policy have evaluated the computerized information. The coordinating office for the policy towards minorities felt strongly inclined to use the information in their negotiations with the individual municipal institutions. Figures, preferably as up to date as possible, were needed to convince the municipal institutions of the deprivation of minorities and therefore of the necessity to take appropriate actions. Representatives of the advisory board for minority groups however criticized the one-sidedness of the information. According to them deprivation was, when observed on the naked eye, already clear enough and did not need repeated statistical proof. Although the data shows deprivation, it did not give any insight into the causes of it. Discrimination accounts for an important part of the minorities deprivation yet this is invisible in the data. As a consequence of this, representatives of minority groups hold the opinion that minorities are held responsible for their own deprivation. Dutch norms and values leading to deprivation cannot be easily brought up for discussion. Representatives of minority groups feel for instance that in Dutch education teaching activities are insufficiently geared to the ethnic child. As the data only shows that, measured by way of comparing the age of children to their grade, ethnic children perform less well at schools than Dutch children, it becomes easier to place the blame on the minorities and distract attention from the content of lessons. The use of computerized information thus seems to strengthen certain perceptions on societal problems and facilitates them reaching the agenda, whilst on the other hand others are weakened.

The reliability of information is of great importance to the process of political agenda building. ICTs enhance the reliability of information and, therefore, the likely 'authority' of particular kinds of information in the political agenda setting process, namely computerized information. Computerized information from transactional information systems, compared to other kinds of information, has two striking advantages. Firstly, computerized information appears to have been created in a disinterested manner (which in fact is not the case). As a result, it is often seen to be above political parties. Secondly, from the use of computerized information, conclusions can be drawn about the entire population. No longer is it necessary to be confined on samples of the population, in the case of the minorities it became possible to map the position of all inhabitants. This made the information less subject to discussion. Computerized information has the tendency to 'disqualify' other kinds of information used in the political agenda building process. A less extreme impact may be that certain actors will lose their monopoly on articulation, since the databases became a powerful source in their own right. It is for instance conceivable that a representative of the minority groups, who used to gather information from his/hers own circle of acquaintances ('this job creation plan doesn't work: I don't see people getting jobs and if they get a job they are out after some months again') will again and again be confronted with the conclusions derived from the data produced by the transactional system, showing that the program has helped many people.

ICTs have increased the transferability of information enormously. This is of relevance for the scale at which a certain problem is being handled. For example, in the Netherlands information on ethnic minorities is being collected at the national level, with the help of the transactional systems from the municipalities. The transfer of this data can only take place in a meaningful way when the definitions are standardized, for example what do we mean by 'minority'? Only then it will be possible to combine and compare the data. However, the ongoing need for standardization and uniformity which follows from the 'need' to communicate between different administrative databases (integration, coupling etc.) will possibly result in the dominance of more 'uniform' information concepts than are used currently in the agenda setting process. This may result in a certain 'ossification' which may eventually cast a doubt on the democratic quality of the agenda seting process.

### 3.2.5. *Informatization and the Democratic Nature of Political Agenda Building*

Since we only have some preliminary empirical observations available, it is difficult to give adequate and well grounded answers to the question of whether ICTs, by affecting properties and processing aspects of information, will influence the democratic nature of political agenda building processes. Yet, by way of explorative, theoretical analysis we hope to be able to throw some light on this matter.

The introduction of transactional information systems and the re-use of the data in them in the political agenda building processes is likely to affect the ways in which problems are/can be articulated and selected. The articulation of problems, currently carried out by different stakeholders, may take on another form. Instead of consulting different stakeholders, government may simply use the databases for articulating the needs of society. The need for active participation, for instance to pressure groups, is diminished since all government needs to know about its citizenry and the problems they are facing, is already, be it passively, held in the computer and has only to be retrieved and presented. Government may then become a more 'closed system' in which the needs and wants of society are being translated and formulated by (parts of) government itself with the help of its information systems. The image of government as a 'mental fortress' may arise. In the long term, this will have a negative affect on the democratic nature of the political process since the active involvement of stakeholders legitimizes the process regardless of the quality of decisions made. Decisions are often more easily accepted if stakeholders have the impression that their views have been heard. This quality of an agenda setting process then can be considered vital to the functioning of a democracy.

With respect to the selection of problems: if agendas are already passively stored in databases, this would imply that information systems perform a selective function as well, although of course not for all problems. This immediately raises further questions: which proportion of the agenda is pre-structured or ossified by the information systems? Whose interests are served if these systems are actually selecting devices? What does it mean for the interests that are not reflected by the systems? Most transactional information systems are the result of former agenda building processes, (for example the housing register in the case of the ethnic minorities reflects the way in which the problem of housing shortages has been resolved from the sixties onwards) and are realized in a mainly technical-bureaucratic setting. It is likely that they reflect the techno-bureaucratic structures of the past, in particular operational interests. This may diminish the democratic representation of opinions and interests in the debate, and may hinder equal access to the decision making arena.

A further issue is whether the information systems undergo fundamental changes in their design or whether they are merely marginally adapted over time. If they are only marginally adapted and are in fact playing an important role in defining emerging problems, they might well be strongly biased towards stabilizing the existing agenda. As such, they serve as a mechanism for constantly reproducing existing agendas. New problem definitions and ways of looking at societal problems for which data do not yet exist may face greater difficulties in coming into existence and/or perhaps will receive less serious attention. This could have a negative effect on the existence of the political system itself in that it is not possible to identify adequately new developments which in turn could make it more difficult to respond adequately to new problems. Furthermore, if information systems are strongly biased towards the existing political agenda and 'non-registered interests' are permanently excluded from the agenda, the effect may be to alter the delicate balance between 'established' versus 'new' interests in society. This in turn may influence the ways in which 'minorities' are treated by 'majorities'.

If information in governmental information systems is indeed becoming an essential and decisive commodity in the agenda building process then this could affect the democratic nature of the system profoundly even to the extent that information production itself is structured according to democratic principles of the political system.

### 3.3.    Informatization and Allocative Policy Making

### 3.3.1. Introduction

This section discusses some empirical observations made by the first author when studying allocative decision making in six Dutch regional governments. Although only some regional governments utilized ICTs, all were responsible for allocating budgets to homes for the elderly.[9]

### 3.3.2. The Allocation of Pleasure and Pain

Whereas the first case study regarded the allocation of attention, this study focuses on the allocation of *pleasure and pain*: budgets, and budget cuts. Decision making about allocation (distribution and re-distribution) is, qua procedures and qua outcomes, very much related to the basic values of a democracy, notably equality. Apart from the precise outcomes, the processes that result in these outcomes can also be considered part of the democratic apparatus. Although different models of democracy will suggest different norms, it is generally the case that those who have a legitimate interest to participate in the decision making process should realistically be able to do so. As such, decision making about allocation is also related to decisions regarding the selection of problems. The prevailing outcomes thus represent the balancing of competing interests and the legitimation of a certain democratic political decision making structure.

---

[9]    The empirical observations that are discussed here are made by the first author in the context of a comparative case-study in which six regional governments (large and small, informated, non-informated and increasing/decreasing budgets) are compared. In the governments that were informated, a comparison was made between the period before and after the introduction of ICTs. Besides this, these governments were compared with non-automated governments.

### 3.3.3. Some Background Information about the Case

Since 1985, Dutch central government has allocated a budget to seventeen responsible governments that enables them to subsidize the homes in their territory. For some of the regions the annual budget is growing slightly, where as others are confronted with important budget cuts.

The homes, most of which are exploited by non governmental associations, are subsidized by the state because the majority of residents cannot afford all the costs themselves. Each of the governments is responsible for making decisions about the way in which the total budget will be allocated among the houses. Some of them intensively use ICTs to develop, determine, implement and evaluate these policy decisions.

### 3.3.4. Applications of ICTs that are Used in the Allocative Decision Making Process

In most cases, a decision support system was installed on a minicomputer. These systems consist of software programmes for registration, calculation and support for operational transactions. They are used by the civil servants (financial inspectors) for preparing, implementing and evaluating allocative decisions. Frequently spreadsheet-programmes, installed on personal computers became increasingly important. Most of these spreadsheets used data that could be downloaded from a minicomputer which stored the information (per budget-year) on the homes in a database. This data could then be integrated and coupled in order to produce detailed historical overviews, analytical comparisons and long-range estimates. The data is collected from the documents that the homes have to submit each year, such as the annual budget proposals and annual accounts. For preparing and making allocative decisions, informated governments can use the data that is available in the fully digitalized 'dossiers'.

### 3.3.5. Empirical Observations

In some cases, the use of ICTs has clearly increased the quantity of information that is demanded from the allocatees. But in informated governments, greater quantities of data are effectively used for preparing and deciding about allocative policies. In particular the availability of information has been directly affected by the fact that the data are now stored in computers. However only certain kinds of information are more readily available, notably financial data is now easily accessible. Information is still collected manually. In order for ICTs to be able to store, compare, and analyze it, the instructions about how and what data has to be collected became more important and more explicit. In many cases, budget-information systems were developed in order to facilitate exactly this kind of development. Since 1985, each of the governments has become fully responsible for the budget regarding homes for the elderly, which was in many instances nearly half as big as the governments' annual budget. Computer systems were developed with straightforward 'managerialist' goals: control, control and no surprises!

Before these systems were implemented, budget proposals were handled manually by financial inspectors, who could, certainly in the bigger governments, hardly control each other with regard to the criteria they used to approve or disapprove the budget proposals. 'Negotiations' and 'Decibels', and sometimes even a good dinner or wine could help arrange special attention. Since the allocation algorithms are now stored in the computer, the policy discretion of officials has been reduced. The decisions they make are registered and controlled immediately by the system, which is programmed to refuse 'impossible' budget decisions. The interactions of the financial inspectors with the traditional 'dossiers' that were previously somewhat secret, are now controlled and registered by the computer system. Informated governments, have become more transparent to accountants, colleagues, superiors, politicians and in some cases also to the governors and/or managing directors of the homes for the elderly. The allocation of the budgets is done with help of refined and complex allocation formula's which are calculated by the computer. Negotiation and political discussion about the formula is restricted to the time before they are captured within computer programmes.

These practices not only reduce the discretion of the individual bureaucrats, but also of their political masters, who cannot interfere in the allocation of budgets for individual houses without disturbing the allocation policy. When the formula is approved upon, 'ad hoc' adjustments immediately tend to corrupt the logic and consistency of the policy.

With regard to the qualitative part of the information, such as reports on quality of service in the homes, made by visiting inspectors, an increased availability is only observed in those cases where the inspectors decided to 'objectify' the information they gather by storing it in computers. By collecting and storing their observations systematically in computers, they improve the chance of 'their' information being used in the decision making process. Inspectors can thus be seen to be trying to 'imitate' the success of their financial colleagues, who utilize the information to control the houses.

Moreover, the visiting inspectors are considered by their financial colleagues, who have become more powerful in the department because they are controlling the information systems, as 'advocates of the houses', who are mostly presenting ambiguous, information that is subjective, non-controllable and non-comparable. By imitating the information-behavior of their financial colleagues the inspectors try to prevent their further marginalization in the decision making process.

The financial data in the computers could now be used as objective and reliable, reflecting the new first-order evaluation criterion: responsible budget behavior. The financial inspectors and their political masters are thus able to convincingly reject the claims for extra money that were supported by the visiting inspectors.

> For example a memorandum that a visiting inspector wrote to the responsible politician. The visiting inspector claimed that the meal variety could increase when a new kitchen was arranged. The memo was commented upon by financial colleagues: when they want a new kitchen they should be very well able to find the money themselves. They claimed that the money that the home said was needed for a new kitchen could easily be found if they reduced the amount of money the home spent on food per resident when compared to another home in the region.

In most cases, the enhanced detail and analysis of available information, enabled a more sophisticated refinement of allocative policies. In informated governments one generally sees the development of new indicators and complex algorithms that are used to construct the claim an allocatee can formulate towards the allocating government. In some cases, however, a refinement of the allocation formulas in that direction is frustrated by the zero-sum character of the total budget. Collecting more information about the increasing need of extra care, which almost certainly will lead to a claim for extra employees, is in one government effectively blocked by the responsible politician, who did not have the financial means to honour the claims that would automatically follow from other houses. Thus political dangers existed in using the data to formulating problems for which there was no money for solutions. The association that represents the interests of the houses is trying to introduce a new information system that could 'prove' that the amount of extra daily care should be taken in as a parameter.

In some other cases, however, further refinements are warmly supported by the politicians. Especially by those who realized important budget cuts via the effectiveness of spreadsheets and 'print-out politics' (Nathan 1987). The impressive calculations were deliberately used to gain the confidence of the houses, which usually did not think of critical examination of the assumptions that were underlying the re-allocation proposals or budget-cuts. The huge data bases, containing very detailed financial data of the houses over several years, were apparently hiding many possible ways to tighten financial control. In informated governments, these data were used to calculate some arithmic means, for example the cost of gardening per square meter, which 'revealed' the 'norms' that could be applied generally.

By uniforming standards for certain expenses, those governments provided themselves with effective guarantees against overspending. In order to be able to develop new allocation systems and policies, they used the data for a thorough comparative analysis of the financial differences between the houses. Both bureaucrats and politicians motivated and legitimated these re-allocations by referring to the striking inequalities the computer-output 'showed' them.

Some other incentives for policy-renewal such as scaling up the size of homes, inter-home cooperation, and capacity reduction are translated into the formulas that are used for allocating budgets. In doing so, informated governments are making much more policy-rich allocations. They are trying actively to enforce some policy developments by expanding the allocation formulas within policy parameters.

Because these exploitation budgets turn out to be a very powerful policy instrument, who pays, determines, these governments tend to be more successful in integrating new policy problems into existing policy frameworks.

The information systems are very useful and reliable instruments for monitoring and evaluating developments in the policy field. They 'inspire' both politicians and civil servants to complementary rules and policies which in most cases (further) reduce the autonomy of the houses. Politicians and civil servants in informated governments are more pro-active policy makers than those without ICTs capabilities. In informated governments, the allocative policies are much more often adapted and changed.

Both politicians and bureaucrats, of course, realize that the acceptance of a new allocation policy is most likely to be accepted when most of the influential allocatees get somewhat more. Moreover, the amount of houses that will be confronted with an important decrease in their budget, must be as small as possible. Re-allocation formulas can be programmed in such a way that they will do just that. As a result of the increased processability of the financial data that is stored in the databases, the data can be easily and quickly analyzed, processed and presented. The number of alternative scenarios, for re-allocations, for realizing budget cuts etc., that are developed and discussed is much higher in informated governments than in governments that do not use computers. Informated governments are much more successful in getting their re-allocation proposals accepted as they are much more able to develop complicated formulas for transitional periods.

Whether such scenarios are in fact developed and used for policy making seems, however, to be very closely related to other characteristics of the regional government. Politicians and bureaucrats who are confronted with budget cuts do more intensively seek new reallocations than those who see their budget increasing. Moreover, those who do use computermodels to underpin retrenchment proposals, are much more successful in defending them when in discussions with representative bodies, individual homes, judiciary procedures and towards organized interest groups.

In one non-informated regional government that was studied, the responsible politician who was confronted with a serious budget decrease, could only think of writing letters to central government stating that the budget-cut was unrealistic and unfair. A coalition with the homes was quickly established and a common protest-manifestato was organized. When, later, the budget-cut became inevitable, the politician was confronted with the opposition against the budget-cut he had earlier organized himself. Negotiations with each of the homes separately were needed in order to realize the inevitable retrenchment of budgets. If asked to use a military metaphor to describe the way the budget proposals were discussed in this region, when compared with the ways the budgets were decided upon in the informated governments, we would suggest guerilla-warfare versus mass retaliation.

The use of information systems has radically enlarged the accessibility of the information about the individual houses. The information was, before the use of information systems, 'hidden' in the annual documents these houses delivered in order to apply for subsidies. The individual dossiers that were, before the introduction of ICTs, only present in the traditional suspension files, now are rapidly accessible. The data stored is more reliable, complete and accurate than the previous tables and statistics that produced in an ad hoc manual fashion. Now, standard reports are available instantly. This seems to have changed the mere concept of 'knowing' the financial situation of a home. Now that its data is stored in a data base, they are automatically 'known' in relation to comparable data of other homes. In most cases, the data of an individual home is accessible in many forms. Both standard reports as well as additional 'questions' can be formulated and answered very quickly. In one of the informated governments, the responsible politician studied those reports regularly and intensively, and 'invited' those houses that showed some weakness in their financial situation for an, as he called them, 'educational conversation' at his office.

> A colleague in another government suggested to one of the houses that was overspending a reduction in gardening expences (that were far above the computed average) could be achieved by replacing some of the flowerbeds with less expensive lawns.

Generally then, one can see that informated governments are more actively intervening in the policy field, and that they are using the information systems to prevent financial problems from escalating. Most of the information systems also have algorithms that automatically calculate all the budgets for each of the individual homes. Prior to the computers existence the control and calculation work for each of the dossiers was done manually, often taking five or six months. In informated governments, the number of civil servants that are required to prepare and implement allocative decision making is significantly lower than in non-informated governments, with the civil servants in informated regional governments spending much more time on long-term financial policy making. Additionally they are also more often involved in the development of policies and planning. This involvement is mirrored in the policy documents of informated governments: the financial constraints and considerations, even in governments that may expect a budget increase, have a dominant position, and their calculating powers are also used for presenting (graphically) long-range estimates and clear accounts of the financial situation that are very difficult to reject for members of regional parliaments. Critical remarks about the information that is given by politicians in the representative bodies of informated governments are nearly non-existent. In non-informated governments the opposite is true.

Informatization facilitates a transparency in the relative position of all individual allocatees, and therewith a reduction of their power vis à vis the government. Moreover, the possibilities for defining and defending a 'common position or interest' of and by those allocatees proves to be difficult, if not impossible. In one government that was studied, the financial civil servants deliberately forwarded (confidentially) the detailed figures and outcomes of a re-allocation proposal for each of the individual houses, regarding a new situation that resulted from a proposed re-allocation of the total budget, to the association that was founded to defend their common interests. The president of that association studied this detailed information, but was unable to find a common interest. This was because the detailed information did not support any of the slogans that normally were used to mobilize support against the re-allocation proposals.

Some civil servants effectively used the spreadsheets for political calculations. In one government, the computer was explicitly programmed to realize the re-formulation of the allocation formulas in such a way that exactly 50% of the housed gained, while the other half saw its subsidy decreasing. Furthermore, the programme was asked to realize the re-allocation in such a way that most of the houses (80%) was winning or losing only 3% when compared to the existing budget. Some graphical software was used for a 'harmless' presentation of the figures.

### 3.3.6. Informatization and the Democratic Nature of Allocative Decision Making

The allocation function of democratic political decision making seems to be strengthened by ICTs. With help of computerized allocation models and huge data bases, political decision makers appear to become more pro-active and sophisticated allocators in both a technical and political-democratic sense. Technically, the allocations become more sophisticated in that a lot of factual data, which has become more important now than 'decibels', are at the disposal for those who are developing the allocation models. A multitude of indicators can easily be taken into account, expected outcomes of new allocation policies can be thoroughly analyzed, so that the consequences of (re)allocation proposals can be calculated for specific, politically relevant group of homes. A democratic and political sophistication of the allocations is brought about by the fact that now all kinds of interests can be easily and actively looked for, recognized, selected and secured by bringing them in the allocation algorithms. Alternative algorithms that show all kinds of consequences for all kinds of minority interests, such as small houses, large houses, Catholic houses, houses in little municipalities, houses in big cities can be calculated before deciding between alternatives.

It is, from a democratic point of view, very interesting to see that in 'informated' allocative decision making processes, the political and democratic considerations of balancing interests and selection of problems, are taken up and often initiated by bureaucrats, who have access to and know how to use the modern tools. Informatization has made it possible for them to expand their political roles, while the role of elected politicians has become formalized and restricted in both time and content. In this case, representing a decision making process in the 'daily life' of democracy, we see that informatization facilitated an increasing role of the bureaucratic apparatus (see also chapter four).

At present, none of the homes representatives have the possibility to use the system to produce their own alternatives. By defending the monopoly of the use of these systems, politicians and bureaucrats effectively defend their power to decide. Developments in the field can be monitored and controlled with the help of computer analysis. Clearly, this has influenced both policy making needs and capacities. Most of the politicians who were interviewed stressed that financial information systems were important for them in several ways. First of all, they are convinced that they helped them to control effectively and efficiently the huge amounts of money that they had become responsible for. Secondly, they offered a variety of possibilities to *enrich* the allocation models, via pro-active policy objectives they chose to resolve or prevent problems which they wanted to give special attention. Thirdly, the information systems proved an effective instrument to successfully defend their financial policies against their colleagues, against the lobby by individual homes, their associations and even against the judges who were called in by the homes in judiciary procedures. In a way, the politicians of the 'NINTENDO generation' seem to have become the 'Masters of the Information Universe'. This begs the question of whether they are really the masters.

They also have become highly dependent on the information systems and those who maintain them. A lot of the functions previously performed, such as integrating interests, deciding about possible exceptions, are now predominantly performed by those who operate the information system. Some of the functions are transferred radically into the system. Elected politicians see their role diminished. Some of them reported that this *'Political Process Reengineering'* is in fact an unintended and irritating by-product of increased political control. In some cases, they deliberately arranged escapes from the algorithmic discipline of the computer systems. Alternatively, some of the consequences of using these systems are welcomed in so far as they support the political calculus. Politicians in informated governments in many ways have lost their relatively autonomous position towards the executive apparatus, which has strengthened its power base in the arena. In those cases where financial bureaucrats and politicians collaborated, they both profited from the situation. Together, they gained or regained almost absolute power vis à vis the policy field. The new law was helping them in doing so, but informatization appeared as the crucial facilitator.

Whether or not these developments can be considered as a precursor for a more techno-autocratic style of allocative political decision making remains to be seen. Some indicators point in that direction: representative bodies such as municipal and regional councils are not able or willing to challenge the information on which the proposals being discussed are based. Furthermore it is interesting to see that informated governments do not use as often as their non-informated governments advisory bodies and representative committees etc. to gain suggestions or agreement on their policy proposals. Politicians tend to become more priggish. Informated governments tend to *proclaim* their policies, whereas non-informated governments found themselves pulled into a difficult and complex negotiations ('implementation-guerilla') with the other actors in the policy arena. Instead of pushing general policies, the non-informed governments have to negotiate with each of the houses separately, often further increasing the differences between them. On the other hand, these differences could also be regarded upon as the (desired) outcome of complex implementation processes that allow for variation, made-to-measure solutions and (experimental) renewal of policies in the field of care for the elderly. In these processes, policy making and policy implementation are intertwined.

In informated governments, one generally observes the opposite. Instead of a fragmentation of power in a pluralistic manor, one sees the strong centralization and concentration of decision making power in the policy arena. These developments are, often gradually, eroding or contradicting traditional democratic decision making practices. Governments that use computers are more often doing so at the expence of advisory and/or consensus-forming bodies, which represented the key actors of the arena. Almost all the homes for the elderly are administered by non-governmental organizations. The political, religious and cultural history of the Netherlands, often referred to as 'verzuiling', or pillarization, has always recognized a relatively strong autonomy of the social associations and institutions that were active in policy fields like welfare and health care. It is interesting to note that informatization tends to excavate the administrative and political autonomy of these organizations, which have become more dependent on the state. Their capacity for a 'informational self-determination', or: 'organizational privacy' is decreasing. Informatization has strongly facilitated that process by enabling a further standardization in the way these organizations work, a process that is facilitated by an increased transparency. Those who value some form of societal democracy such as the Toquevillian model of democracy, or those who stress the importance of pluralism, checks and balances, will hesitate to consider these developments as a contribution to the democratic nature of political decision making.

Informatization has largely contributed to the fact that the decision making process has become much more structured and organized. Furthermore, policy formulation tends to become more clearly separated from implementation. The influence of elected politicians and representative bodies is more restricted in time and scope, whereas the implementation stage is being immunized against political interventions. Bureaucrats have trained their political masters not to disturb the existing allocation regimes.

ICTs certainly improved the technical sophistication of the allocative policies. But their technical sophistication also increased their political effectiveness. In some cases, traditional actors and methods have been replaced, primarily bureaucrats as opposed to politicians, and print-outs instead of pork-barrel politics, are predominantly fulfilling the functions of democratic political decision making. In some cases, notably in those governments who had to realize severe budget cuts, politicians deliberately identified themselves almost completely with such an infocratic form of political decision making (Zuurmond 1994), because they realized that the political costs of every other strategy were likely to be much higher, if not too high. Practically all politicians, who had to realize severe budget-cuts in other, non-informated governments, are ex politicians.

## 4. Digitally Decision Making in a Democracy: for Better or for Worse?

At the beginning of this chapter, we proposed an analytical framework that could help us to find an answer to our main questions: whether it is likely that informatization is affecting political decision making and whether this would influence the democratic nature of these processes. Preliminary analysis of empirical observations suggest that the concepts we developed can indeed help us to systematically explain what is happening. It is, however, also clear that further empirical research is needed in order to find out whether some generalizations can be made about the impacts of informatization with regard to the democratic nature of the political decision making processes.

The explorative case studies presented in this chapter suggest that it is too early to consider ICTs as technologies that will unconditionally strengthen democracy. By focusing on its role in the daily life of political decision making processes, we have shown that informatization does not seem to generally increase the democratic nature of political decision making. In some cases we may even observe the opposite. In particular in those cases where informatization is 'ossifying' current perspectives or preventing new ones from reaching the political agenda, it is difficult to see informatization as a major facilitator of democratic life. In those cases where informatization tends to reduce the influence of elected officials and to excavate the autonomy and participative power of societal organizations, it is much more contributing to a 'technosphere' than to a 'demosphere' (Fielder 1992).

These observations do not, however, lead to the conclusion that informatization will always diminish democracy and that it is anti-democratic in its very nature. The case study observations are made in the context of rather specific applications of information technology: huge administrative databases and spreadsheets. Perhaps these applications are more 'Orwellian' than other ones. The impact of large information systems on processes of political agenda building is likely to be different from the impact that easily accessible public information systems would have.

The different impacts on democratic life of different applications of ICTs can be explained by the fact that they have different effects on the information aspects we previously discussed. Different applications will, for instance, tend to facilitate different patterns of different degrees of democratic information behavior.

Several observations made in this chapter as well as in other parts of the book suggest that a systematic assessment of the potential effects on democratic aspects of organizations and decision making processes could be helpful to defend or improve current democratic practices. The case study on political agenda building for instance, suggests that the production and processing of information in a decision making process as such deserves explicit attention in both the theory and practice of democratic politics. In regard to the autonomy of societal actors vis à vis the state apparatus, a systematic approach should be taken to information as information relations are power relations.

Some applications are designed to achieve results that contradict the strenghtening of democratic aspects. The information systems that were used for making allocative policies in the field of care for the elderly people have been built with a predominantly managerial and control-oriented perspective.

This 'bias' was - in this case - rather explicitly reflected in the goals of the actors who controlled the introduction and development of the applications of ICTs. This explicit strategy perhaps accounts for most of the decrease of influence and autonomy of the societal actors in this policy field.

But where does that 'bias' come from in the first place? In order to '(...) fully grasp the way in which a major new technology can change the world (...) it is necessary to consider both the manner in which it creates intrinsically new qualities of experience and the way in which new possibilities are engaged by the often conflicting demands of social, political and economic interest in order to produce a 'choice'. (...) To narrow down all discussion of technological change to the play of these interests overlooks the essential power to reorder the rules of the games and thus our experience as players.' (Zuboff 1988:389).

The precise role that was and will be played by ICTs - determining, facilitating, or both - with regard to the impacts in the domain of political decision making is - in a more general sense - thus often difficult to reconstruct. Some comparable research in other policy fields, however, suggests an important determining role of the technology involved. 'The inherent characteristics of the more common applications of ICTs *imply* a greater - *both horizontally and vertically* - transparency: more qualified, and more topical information can be processed and analyzed, which explains why administrations are better able to achieve selectiveness and efficiency, which in turn can improve the effectiveness of guidance and control.' (Zeef 1994: 270, *italics wd/om*). The impact of the more 'common' applications of ICTs, as Zeef calls them, on information properties, aspects of information processing and information behavior leads - generally speaking - to a more effective and encompassing power of the state. In some cases, such an increase of guidance and control may certainly affect the democratic nature of political decision making processes. Bureaucracy and - many applications of - ICTs may form a very effective coalition that, especially in those cases where this coalition is not confronted with any democratic 'opposition'[10], can become a serious threat for some rules and experiences that - in one way or another - are reflected in the ancient ideal of a democratic polity.

---

[10] See the chapter of Pratchett in this volume

# General Bibliography

Abele, P. et al. (1991). *PROMPT - Postlauf und Registratur in öffentlichen Verwaltungen - Möglichkeiten partizipativer Technikentwicklung.* Universität Kassel, Forschungsgruppe Verwaltungsautomation.

Abramson, J.B., F.Ch. Arterton and G.R. Orren (1988). *The Electronic Commonwealth. The Impact of New Technologies upon Democratic Politics.* New York: Basic Books.

Ackroyd, C., K. Margolis, J. Rosenhead and T. Shallice (1980). *The Techology of Political Control.* London: Pluto Press.

Albeda, W. (24 januari 1992). Mozaïek-democratie. *NRC Handelsblad*, p. 7.

Alexander, K. (1995). *Democracy Online: An Evaluation of the 1994 California Online Voter Guide Project.* Sacramento CA: Californian Voter Foundation

Almond, G.A. and G. Bingham Powell (1966). *Comparative Politics: a developmental approach*, Boston: Little, Brown.

Anderson, Ch.W. (1993). Recommending a scheme of reason: Political theory, policy science, and democracy. *Policy Sciences*, 26, 215-227.

Ankersmit, F.R. (1990). *De navel van de geschiedenis.* Groningen: Historische Uitgeverij.

Armstrong, R. (1988). *The next Hurrah: the Communications Revolution in American Politics.* New York: Beech Tree Press.

Arrow, K. (1963). *Social Choice and individual welfare.* New York: Wiley.

Arterton, Ch. (1984). *Video Politics.* Lexington MA: Lexington Books.

Arterton, F.Ch., E.H. Lazarus, J.W. Griffin and M.C. Andres (1984). *Telecommunications, Technologies and Political Parties.* Washington DC: Roosevelt Center for American Policy Studies.

Arterton, F.Ch. (1984). *The News Strategies of Presidential Campaigns.* Lexington MA: Lexington Books.

Arterton, F.Ch. (1987). Representation, Information Technology and Democratic Values. *Report to the Office of Technology Assessment*, Washington DC, May.

Arterton, F.Ch. (1987). *Teledemocracy: Can Technology Protect Democracy?* Newbury Park CA: Sage Publications.

Arterton, F.Ch. (1988). Political Participation and Teledemocracy. *Political Science Quarterly*, 21, 620-627.

Arterton, F.Ch. (1994). *Teledemocracy: can Technology protect Democracy?* New York: Sage.

Association for Computing Machinery (1994). *Codes, Keys, and Conflicts: Issues in U.S. Crypto Policy.* New York: Association for Computing Machinery.

Baecker, R. (ed.) (1993). *Readings in Groupware and Computer-Supported Cooperative Work.* San Mateo California: Morgan Kaufmann.

Bangemann, M. et al. (26 May 1994). *Europe and the global information society. Recommendations to the European Council.* (Report for the European Council, written by the High-Level Group on the Information Society. Brussels: The European Commission.

Barber, B.R. (1984). *Strong Democracy: Participatory Politics for a new Age.* Berkely: University of California Press.

Barber, B.R. (1988). *Pangloss, Pandora or Jefferson? Three scenario's for the future of technology and democracy.* In: R. Plant, F. Gregory, and A. Brier (eds.) *Information Technology: The Public Issues.* Fullbright Papers volume 5. Oxford: Alden Press, 177-190.

Barnouw, E. (1982). Historical survey of communications breakthroughs. In: G. Benjamin (ed.) *The Communications Revolution in Politics.* New York: Academy of Political Science, 13-23.

Barrington Moore, Jr. (1984). *Social orgins of dictatorship and democracy. Lord and peasant in the making of modern world.* Harmondsworth: Penguin Books.

Basse, M. and O. Jørgensen. (1993). *Kommunal forvaltning.* Dansk Kommunalkursus: Grenå.

Becker, T.L. (1981). Teledemocracy: Bringing Power Back to the People. *The Futurist,* 15(6), 6-9.

Beers, A.A.L. (1992). Openbaarheid van bestuur in het computertijdperk. *Computerrecht,* 3, 101-117.

Beers, A.A.L. (1992). Public Access to Government Information towards the 21st Century. In: Korthals Altes W.F. et al. (1992). *Information Law towards the 21st Century.* Boston: Kluwer Law and Taxation Publishers, 177-214.

*Befolkningen i Kommunerne 1. januar 1994.* Danmarks Statistik: København, 23. årgang, April

Bekkers, V.J.J.M. (1993). *Nieuwe vormen van sturing en informatisering.* Delft: Eburon.

Bekkers, V.J.J.M. (red.) (1994). *Wegwijs op de digitale snelweg.* Amsterdam: Otto Cramwinckel.

Bekkers, V.J.J.M., G.J. Straten, P.H.A. Frissen, P. Tas, J. Huigen and S. Luitjens (1994). *De gemeentelijke basisadminstratie: een tussentijdse beoordeling van een interorganisationeel informatiseringsproject.* Tilburg: Katholieke Universiteit Brabant.

Bellamy, C. and J.A. Taylor (1994). Introduction: exploiting IT in public administration: Towards the information polity. *Public Administration,* 72(1), 1-12.

Bellamy, C. and J.A. Taylor (April 1994). *New public management in the information polity: towards theoretical development.* Paper to joint sessions of the European Consortium of Political Research, Madrid.

Bellamy, C., I. Horrocks and J. Webb (1995). Exchanging Information with the Public: from One Stop Shops to Community Information Systems. *Local Government Studies,* forthcoming.

Benjamin, G. (1982). Innovations in Telecommunications and Politics. In: G. Benjamin (ed.) *The Communications Revolution in Politics.* New York: Academy of Political Science, 1-12.

Benjamin, G. (ed.) (1982). *The Communications Revolution in Politics.* New York: Academy of Political Science.

Bennett, J.M. (1983). Computers and Citizen Participation in Politics and Government. In: A. Mowshowitz (ed.) *Human Choice and Computers.* (2 parts). Amsterdam: North-Holland.

Bennett, C. (1992). *Regulating Privacy.* Ithaca and New York: Cornell University Press.

Bennett, C. (1994). *The implementation of Privacy Codes of Practice: Research Plan and Timetable.* Canadian Standards Association Committee to Develop a Model Privacy Code, June 23.

Berelson, B., P. Lazarsfeld and W. McPhee (1954). *Voting.* Chicago: University of Chicago Press.

Berkman, R. and L. Kitch (1986). *Politics in the Media Age.* New York: McGraw Hill.

Betts, M. (28 August 1989). Gerrymandering Made Easy in 1990. *Computerworld,* 23, pp. 1-18.

*Betænkning* (1968). Statens refusioner af kommunernes udgifter. København: Statens Trykningskontor.

*Betænkning* (1993). Redegørelse om aktivitetsbestemte tilskud, forenkling af udlignings- og statstilskuddets fordeling. Københaven: Statens Information.

*Betænkning* (1994). Fornyelse og effektivisering i den kommunale sektor (1994), nr. 1268, med bilag, April. København: Statens Information.

Beyer, L. et al. (1990). Registratur und Postlauf in öffentlichen Verwaltungen, *Werkstattbericht* Nr. 80 Fallstudien. Universität Kassel, Forschungsgruppe Verwaltungsautomation.

Beyer, L., H. Bielefeld-Hart, K. Grimmer (1991). Die Zukunft der Schriftgutverwaltung als technikgestützte qualifizierte Assistenz. *Deutsche Verwaltungspraxis,* Year 42(9).

Binnenlands Bestuur (11 november 1994). Vergelijken van bestanden in fraudebestrijding is doorgeslagen. *Binnenlands Bestuur,* 15(45), p. 17

Bjerkness, G., P. Ehn, and M. Kyng. (eds.) (1987). *Computers and Democracy: a Scandinavian Challenge.* Avebury: Aldershot.

Blakely, S. (1985). Computers alter the way congress does business. *Congressional Quarterly,* 13, 79-82.

Blundell, J., R. de Silva and L. Macchiavello (11 February 1994). The shape of things to come. *Local Government Chronicle.*

Bobbio, N. (1987). *The future of democracy.* Cambridge: Polity Press.

Boelscher, A. (1993). *Imaging.* München: R. Oldenburg Verlag.

Bogumil, J. (1987a). Chancen einer Gegenmacht? Computer in Umweltpolitischen Gruppen. *Wechselwirkung,* 35-39.

Bogumil, J. (1987b). Computereinsatz in den Gewerkschaften. Den erste Schritt zur politischen Modernisierung? *Gewerkschaftliche Monatshefte*, 4, 35-39.

Bogumil, J. and H.J. Lange. (1991). *Computer in Parteien und Verbände*. Opladen: Westdeutscher Verlag.

Borgmann, A. (1988). Technology and Democracy. In: M.E. Kraft and N.J. Vig (eds.) *Technology and Politics*. London: Duke University Press, 54-73.

Bouwman, H. en N. Jankowski. (1989). *Interactieve media op komst*. Amsterdam: Otto Cramwinckel.

Breman, I.W. (1983). De documentaire automatisering bij het parlement. *Informatie*, 25(4), 13-19.

Brinckmann, H. and S. Kuhlmann (1990). *Computerbürokratie*. Ergebnisse von 30 Jahren öffentlichter Verwaltung mit Informationstechnik. Opladen: Westdeutscher Verlag.

Broder, D.S. (8 July 1987). The Amazing New High-Speed Dial-a-President Machine. *The Washington Post*, p. C19.

Broder, D.S. (30 August 1987). Electronic Democracy. *The Washington Post*, p. 7.

Brunnstein, K. (5 Oktober 1973). Mehr Demokratie durch Computer? *Die Zeit*.

Brunnstein, K. (1985). Representative Democracy and Information and Communication Technology: The Malady, the Cure, its Effect. In: L. Yngström, R. Sizer, J. Berleur, and R. Laufer (eds.) *Can information technology result in benevolent bureaucracies?* Amsterdam: North-Holland, 113-123.

Bull, H. P. (1984). *Datenschutz oder Die Angst vor dem Computer*. München: Piper.

Burnham, D. (1985). The Rise of the Computer State. In: Smithsonian Institution (ed.) *High Technology and Human Freedom*. Washington D.C.: Smithsonian Institution Press, 141-146.

Burns, A., R. Hambleton and P. Hoggett (1994). *The politics of decentralisation*, London: Macmillan.

Calhoun, G. (1986). Comments on Democracy in an Information Society. *The Information Society*, 4(1/2), 115-122.

Campbell, A., P.E. Converse, W.E. Miller and O.E. Stokes (1960). *The American Voter*. New York: Wiley.

Carpentier, M. (1994). Editorial. *I & T Magazine*, 1-2.

CCTA. (1994). *Information Superhighways: Opportunities for public sector applications in the UK*. London: HMSO.

Chandler, J.A. (1991). *Local Government Today*. Manchester: Manchester University Press.

Charter 88 Trust (1994). *Ego-Trip*, London.

Chartrand, R.L. (1968). Congress seeks a Systems Approach. *Datamation*, 14, 46-49.

Chartrand, R.L. and J. Borell (1981). The legislator as a user of information technology. *Congressional Research Service Report*, (81-187 SPR).

Chartrand, R.L. (1982). Information Support for Congress: The Role of Technology. In: F.W. Horton and D.A. Marchand (eds.) *Information Management in Public Adminstration*. Arlington: Information Resources Press, 316-343.

Chaum, D. (1992). Achieving Electronic Privacy. *Scientific American*, 267, 96-101.

Clarke, R. (1992). *Computer Matching in Government Agencies: a Normative Regulatory Framework*. Working paper, August. Forthcoming in *Informatization, Infrastructure and Policy*, 1(1).

Clarke, R. (1994). The Digital Persona and Its Application to Data Surveillance. *The Information Society*, 10, 77-92.

Clement, A. (1986). Comments on "Democracy in an Information Society". *The Information Society*, 4, 109-114.

Crick, B. (1982). *In Defence of Politics* (Second Pelican edition). London: Penguin Books.

Cochrane, A. (1993). *Whatever happened to local government?* Buckingham: Open University Press.

Cohen, J. (1989). Deliberation and democratic legitimacy. In: A. Hamlin, P. Pettit (eds.). *The good polity*. Oxford: Blackwell.

Cohen, J. and A. Arato (1990). Politics and the reconstruction of the concept of civil society. In: A. Honneth et al.(eds.). *Zwischenbetrachtungen im Prozess der Aufklärung*. Frankfurt am Main: Suhrkamp.

Coleman, D. (ed.) (1993). *Proceedings of Groupware '93*. San Mateo: Morgan Kaufmann California.

Collingridge, D. and H. Margetts (1994). Can government information systems be inflexible technology? The operational strategy revisited? *Public Administration* 72(1), 55-72.

Commissie-Duyvendak (1993). *Duurzame Democratie*. Amsterdam: GroenLinks.

Commissie-Van Kemenade (1991). *Een partij om te kiezen*. Amsterdam: PvdA.

Commissie-Van Laarhoven (1991). *Politiek dicht bij mensen*. Den Haag: CDA.

Commission of the European Committees (1993). *Growth, Competitiveness, Employment - The Challenges and Ways Forward into the 21st Centrury*. COM, 93, final, Brussels, 5th December.

Commission of the European Communities (1994). *Europe's Way to the Information Society - An Action Plan*. Communication from the Commission to the Council and the European Parliament, and to the Economic and Social Committee and the Committee of Regions, COM (94) 347 final, Brussels, 19th July.

Conseil d'Etat (1988). *Administration et nouvelles technologies de l'information. Une nécessaire adaptation du droit*. Paris: Documentation Française.

Coombs, R., D. Knights and H. Willmott (1992). Culture, control and competition: Towards a conceptual framework for the study of information technology in organizations. *Organization Studies*, 13(1), 51-72.

CORDIS (1994). Bangemann Report: Europe and the Global Information Society. *RTD NEWS Watch*, nos. 2729 and 2730.

Dahl, R.A. (1956). *A preface to democratic theory*. Chicago: University of Chicago Press.

Dahl, R.A. (1982). *Dilemmas of a Pluralist Democracy*. New Haven: Yale University Press

Danziger, J.N., W.H. Dutton, R. Kling, and K.L. Kraemer (1982). *Computers and Politics. High Technology in American local governments*. New York: Colombia University Press.

Danziger, J.N. (1986). Computing and the Political World. *Computers and the Social Sciences*, 2, 182-200.

Davies, M.R. and V.A. Lewis (1971). *Models of Political Systems*. London: Pall Mall Press.

Deetman, W.J. (1995). Digitaal uit de bocht? In: *Christen-Democratische Verkenningen*, 2/95, 54-55.

Delden, P.J. van en W. Roelfsema (1989). *Overheidsautomatisering en dienstverlening*. 's-Gravenhage: VUGA.

Department of Trade and Industry (1990). *Competition and Choice: Telecommunications Policy for the 1990s*, Cm 1303.

Department of Trade and Industry (1991). *Competition and Choice: Telecommunications Policy for the 1990s*, Cm 1461.

Depla, P.F.G. en P.W. Tops (1992). Technologie en politiek. De betekenis van informatie- en communicatietechnologie voor politieke partijen. *Socialisme en Democratie*, 49(9), 383-389.

Depla, P.F.G. en K. Schalken (1992). Nieuwe technologie: kans of bedreiging voor politieke partijen? In: Frissen, P.H.A., A.W. Koers en I.Th.M. Snellen (red.) *Orwell of Athene? Democratie en informatiesamenleving*. Den Haag: SDU, 339-344.

Depla, P.F.G. (1995). *Technologie en de vernieuwing van de lokale democratie. Vervolmaking of vermaatschappelijking?* Den Haag: VUGA

Dewey, I. (1927). *The Public and its Problems*. London: Allen & Unwin.

Dewey, I. (1939). *Freedom and Culture*. New York: Putnam.

Dijk, J.A.G.M. van (1991a). *De netwerkmaatschappij. Sociale aspecten van nieuwe media*. Houten: Bohn Stafleu Van Loghum.

Dijk, J.A.G.M. van (1991b). Teledemocratie: Mogelijkheden en Beperkingen van Nieuwe Media voor Burgerschap. *Beleid en Maatschappij*, 3, 142-149.

Ditlea, S. (1986). Automation in the White House. *Datamation*, 32(16), 77-80.

Dizard, W.P. (1982). *The Coming Information Age. An Overview of Technology, Economics and Politics*. New York: Longman.

Doctor, R. (1992). Social Equity and Information Technologies: moving toward information democracy. *Annual Review of Information Science and Technology (ARIST)*, 27, 43-96.

Donk, W.B.H.J. Van de (1990). De Opkomst van de Surveillance Bureaucratie? Kanttekeningen bij de toepassing van beslissingsondersteunende expert-systemen. *Bestuur, Maandblad voor Overheidskunde*, 144-147.

Donk, W.B.H.J. Van de (1990). Harmonieuze coalities of weerspannige verhoudingen? Een verkenning van de verhouding tussen politici, wetgevingsjuristen en informatici bij synchrone wetgeving en systeemontwikkeling. In: *Recht doen door wetgeving. Opstellen over wetgevingsvraagstukken aangeboden aan mr. E.M.H. Hirsch Ballin.* Zwolle: W.E.J. Tjeenk Willink, 307-321.

Donk, W.B.H.J Van de, P.H.A. Frissen en I.Th.M.Snellen (1990). Spanningen tussen wetgeving en systeemontwikkeling: De Wet Studiefinanciering. *Beleidswetenschap*, 4, 3-20.

Donk, W.B.H.J. Van de en P.W. Tops (1992). Informatisering en democratie: Orwell of Athene? In: Frissen, P.H.A., A.W. Koers en I.Th.M. Snellen (red.) *Orwell of Athene? Democratie en informatiesamenleving.* Den Haag: SDU, 31-74.

Donk, W.B.H.J. Van de and P.W. Tops (1992). Informatization and Democracy: Orwell or Athens? A review of the literature. *Informatization and the Public Sector*, 2(3), 169-196.

Donk, W.B.H.J. Van de (1993). Informatization and Public Policymaking. Some preliminary remarks on a possible conceptual framework for assessing and interpreting empirical observations, *VIIth conference of EGPA's permanent studygroup in informatization in public administration.* Strasbourg, 7-10 September.

Donk, W.B.H.J. Van de and O.M.T. Meyer (1994). Information, Informatization and Political Decision Making. An Exploration of Novel Means and New Conditions in Political Decision Making Processes. *Informatization and the Public Sector*, 3(3/4), 229-264.

Dorsen, N. and S. Gillers (1974). *None of your business. Government Secrecy in America* New York: The Viking Press.

Downs, A. (1957). *An economic theory of democracy.* New York: Harper.

Downs, A. (1967). A Realistic Look at the Final Payoffs From Urban Data Systems. *Public Administration Review*, 27 (September), 204-210.

Dryzek, J.S. and D. Torgerson (1993). Democracy and the policy sciences; a progress report. *Policy Sciences* 26, 127-137.

Ducatel, K. (1994). Transactional telematics in the city. *Local Government Studies*, 20 (1), 60-77.

Dugger, R. (11 November 1988). Democracy in the Computer Age. *The Texas Observer.*

Duivenboden, H.P.M. van (1994). Achter de schermen van de overheid: recht en beleid inzake koppeling van persoonsregistraties. In: A. Zuurmond, J. Huigen, P.H.A. Frissen, I.Th.M. Snellen en P.W. Tops (red.) *Informatisering in het openbaar bestuur: technologie en sturing bestuurskundig beschouwd.* Den Haag: VUGA.

Dunleavy, P. (1991). *Democracy, Bureaucracy and Public Choice: Economic explanations in political science.* Hemel Hempstead: Harvester-Wheatsheaf.

Dunleavy, P. (1980). *Urban Political Analysis.* London: Macmillan.

Dutton, W.H. (1982). Technology and the Federal System. In: G. Benjamin (ed.) *The Communications Revolution in Politics*. New York: Academy of Political Science, 109-120.

Dutton, W.H. (1982). Computer Models in the Decision-Making Process. *Information Age*, 4, 86-94.

Dutton, W.H., J. Steckenrider, and D. Ross-Christensen (1984). Electronic participation by citizens in U.S. local government. *Information Age*, 6(2), 78-97.

Dutton, W.H., J.G. Blumler and K.L. Kraemer (1987). *Wired Cities*. Boston: G.H. Hall.

Dutton, W.H. (1989). Looking Beyond Teledemocracy: The Politics of Communications and Information Technology. In: A.A. Berger (ed.) *Political Culture and Public Opinion*, 79-96. New Brunswick: Transaction Publishers.

Dutton, W.H. and K. Guthrie (1991). An Ecology of Games: the Political Construction of Santa Monica's public electronic network. *Informatization and the Public Sector*, 4(1), 279-301.

Dutton, W.H. (1992). Political Science Research on Teledemocracy. *Social Science Computer Review*, 10, 505-522.

Dutton, W.H., J.A. Taylor, C.A. Bellamy, C. Raab and M. Peltu (1994). Electronic Service Delivery: Themes and Issues in the Public Sector. *Policy Research Paper*. No. 28. Programme on Information and Communication Technologies. Economic and Social Research Council. Uxbridge: Brunel University.

Duverger, M. (1964). *Political parties. Their organization and activity in the modern state*. London.

Eckstein, A. (1993). Objectives and Priorities for DG XIII (interview with Martin Bangemann), *XIII Magazine*, 10 (May), 3-6.

Edelman, M. (1977). *Political language: words that succeed and policies that fail*. New York: Academic Press.

Edelman, M. (1988). *Constructing the political spectacle*. Chicago: University of Chicago Press.

Ekos Research Associates (s.d.). *Privacy Revealed*. Ottawa: Ekos Research Associates Inc.

Electronic Privacy Information Center (EPIC) (1994). *Privacy Guidelines for the NII*. Report 94-1. Washington DC: Electronic Privacy Information Center.

Ellis, C.A., S.J. Gibbs and G.L. Rein (1991). Groupware: Some issues and experiences. *Communications of the ACM*, 34(1), January, 38-58.

Ellul, J. (1992). Technology and democracy. In: L. Winner. (ed.) *Democracy in a technological society*. Dordrecht: Kluwer.

Elstain, J.B. (1982). Democracy and the Qube Tube. *The Nation*, 7-14.

Equifax (1990). *The Equifax Report on Consumers in the Information Age*. Atlanta: Equifax.

Estlund, J. Waldron, B. Grofman, S.L. Feld (1989). Democratic theory and the public interest: Condorcet and Rousseau revisited, *American Political Science Review* 83, 1317-1340.

Etzioni, A., K.C. Laudon and S. Lipson (1975). Participating Technology: The Minerva Communications Tree. *Journal of Communications*, Spring 1975, 25-64.

Eulau, H. (1977). *Technology and civility. The Skill Revolution in Politics.* (Hoover Institution Publ. 167). Stanford CA: Stanford University.

Europe, The Information Society (1994). *Europe*, no. 6260 (n.s.), 26 June. Brussels: Agence Europe.

Everson, D.H. (1982). The Decline of Political Parties. In: G. Benjamin (ed.) *The Communications Revolution in Politics.* New York: Academy of Political Science, 49-60.

Everts, G.T. (1990). The Electronic Commonwealth. Bookreview. *Michigan Law Review*, 87, 1393-1400.

Faber, S. (1985). Parlementaire informatievoorziening. In: E.M.H. Hirsch Ballin en J.A. Kamphuis (eds.). *Trias Automatica. Automatisering in wetgeving, bestuur en rechtspraak.* Deventer: Kluwer, 51-54.

Farnham D. and S. Horton (1993). *Managing the new public services.* London: Macmillan.

Fielder, J. (1992). Autonomous Technology, Democracy and the NIMBY's. In: L. Winner (ed.) *Democracy in a technological society.* Dordrecht: Kluwer.

Fineman, H. (27 February 1995). The Brave New World of Cybertribes. In: *Newsweek*, pp. 30-33.

Fischer, F. (1990). *Technocracy and the politics of expertise.* London: Sage.

Flaherty, D. (1989). *Protecting Privacy in Surveillance Societies.* Chapel Hill, NC: University of North Carolina Press.

*Folketingstidende 1992-93.* Lovforslag nr. L 219. 'Tillæg A,' spalte 7585.

Forester, T. (ed.) (1980). *The Microelectronics revolution.* Oxford: Basil Blackwell Publisher.

Forester, T. (ed.) (1985). *The information technology revolution.* Oxford: Basil Blackwell Publisher.

Forester, T. (1993). Megatrends or Megamistakes? What ever happened to the Information Society? *The Information Society*, 8, 133-146.

Frantzich, S.E. (1982). Communications and Congress. In: G. Benjamin (ed.) *The Communications Revolution in Politics.* New York: Academy of Political Science, 88-101.

Frantzich, S.E. (1982). *Computers in Congress: The Politics of Information.* Beverly Hills: Sage Publications.

Frantzich, S.E (1989). *Political Parties in the Technological Age.* New York: Longman.

Friedland, E.I. (1971). Turbulence and Technology: Public Administration and the role of information-processing technology. In: D. Waldo (ed.) *Public administration in a time of turbulence.* New York: Chandler Publishing Company, 134-150.

Friedrichs, G. and A. Schaff (eds.). (1982). *Microelectronics and Society: For Better of For Worse*. A Report to the Club of Rome. Oxford: Pergamon Press.

Frissen, P.H.A. (1989). *Bureaucratische cultuur en informatisering. Een studie naar de betekenis van informatisering voor de cultuur van een overheidsorganisatie*. 's-Gravenhage: SDU.

Frissen, P.H.A. (1991). *De versplinterde staat. Over informatisering, bureaucratie en technocratie voorbij de politiek*. (Oratie Katholieke Universiteit Brabant). Alphen aan den Rijn: Samsom H.D. Tjeenk-Willink.

Frissen, P.H.A. (1992). Informatization in Public Administration: Introduction. *International Review of Administrative Sciences*, 58(3), 307-310.

Frissen, P.H.A. (1993). Sturing, informatisering en voorlichting. In: Roon, A.D. de en R. Middel. *De wereld van Postbus 51. Voorlichtingscampagnes van de rijksoverheid*. Houten: Bohn Stafleu van Loghum, 264-269.

Frissen, P.H.A., S. Zouridis, A.A.L. Beers, P.H.H. Zeef en W.A.J. Gooren (1994). *Een ambivalente openbaarheid? Verslag van een exploratief onderzoek naar de werking van de nieuwe Wet openbaarheid van bestuur*. Tilburg: Katholieke Universiteit Brabant.

Frissen, P.H.A. (1989). The Cultural impact of Informatization in Public Administration. *International Review of Administrative Sciences*, 55(4), 569-577.

Frissen, P.H.A. (1994). The virtual reality of informatization in public administration. *Informatization and the Public Sector*, 3(3/4), 265-281.

Fyvel, T.R. (1985). Orwell as Friend and Prophet. In: Smithsonian Institution (ed.) *High Technology and Human Freedom*. Washington D.C.: Smithsonian Institution, 161-168.

Færch, H. (1994). *Informationsteknologi til politikerne*. Afdelingen for Innovation, Kommunedata, Maj 1994.

Gallouedec-Genuys, F. (1980). *Une informatique pour les administrés?* Paris: Editions Cujas.

Game, C. and S. Leach (1993). *Councillor recruitment and turnover: an approaching precipice?* Luton: Local Government Management Board, 23.

Gau, J.A. (1980). Le rôle de l'informatique parlementaire. *Actes du Colloque International Informatique et société*, (V). Paris: Documentation Française, 109-113.

Gemeente Amsterdam (1993). *Rapportage Bestuurlijke vernieuwing in Amsterdam*. Amsterdam.

Gemeente Amsterdam (1994). *Publieks Informatie Gemeente Amsterdam (PIGA)*. Projectbeschrijving. Amsterdam.

Gibbs, D. and B. Leach (1992). Telematics and Local Economic Development: The Manchester HOST Computer Network. *Paper to the PICT National Conference*. Newport, Wales, March.

Ginzburg, M.J. (1981). Key Recurrent Themes in the Implementation Process. *MIS Quarterly*, 5, 85-113.

Godwin, R.K. (1988). *One Billion Dollars of Influence: The Direct Marketing of Politics*. Chatham NJ: Chatham House Publishers.

Gore, A. (1991). Infrastructure for the Global Village. *Scientific American*, 265, 108-111.

Graaf, J. de (1992). Diskette 'De Gemeente' en 'De Provincie'. Het succes van voorlichting per computer. *COMMA*, 9, 16-18.

Graham, S. (1992). The Role of Cities in Telecommunications Development. *Telecommunications Policy*, April.

Gray, C. (1994). *Government beyond the centre: Sub-national politics in Britain*. London: MacMillan.

Grémion, P. (1980). Le technicisme démocratisant. *Actes du Colloque International Informatique et société*, (V). Paris: Documentation Française, 115-118.

Grewlich, K.W. and F.H. Pedersen (eds.). (1984). *Power and participation in an information society*. Brussel: European Commission.

Griffiths, A.P., R. Wollheim (1960). How can one person represent another? *Aristotelian Society* XXXIV, 187-224.

Grodsky, J.A. (1990). The Freedom of information act in the electronic age: the statute is not user friendly. *Jurimetrics Journal*, Fall, 17-51.

Grofman, B., S.L. Feld (1988). Rousseau's general will: a Condorcetian perspective. *American Political Science Review*, 82, 567-576.

Grudin, J. (1991). CSCW Introduction. *Communications of the ACM*, 34(12), 30-34.

Grudin, J. (1988). Why CSCW applications fail: Problems in the design and evaluation of organizational interfaces. In: *CSCW'88, Proceedings of the Conference on Computer Supported Cooperative Work*. ACM: New York, 85-94.

Gurwitt, R. (1988). The computer revolution: Microchipping away at the limits of government. *Governing*, 1, 34-38, 40-42.

Guthrie, K. (1991). *The politics of citizen acces technology: The development of public information utilities in four cities*. (Unpublished dissertation). Annenberg School for Communication/University of Southern California.

Guthrie, K. and W.H. Dutton (1992). The Politics of Citizen Access Technology: The Development of Public Information Utilities in Four Cities. *Policy Studies Journal*, 20, 574-597.

Gyford, J., S. Leach and C. Game (1989) *The changing politics of local government*. London: Unwin-Hyman.

Haan, I. de (1993). *Zelfbestuur en staatsbeheer*. Amsterdam: Amsterdam University Press.

Haan, I. de en J.W. Duyvendak (1993). Democratie, referendum en volksinitiatief. In: Ph. van Praag, jr. (red.) *Een stem verder. Het referendum in de lokale politiek*. Amsterdam: Het Spinhuis, 25-40.

Habermas, J. (1981). *Theorie des kommunikativen Handelns*. Frankfurt am Main: Suhrkamp.

Habermas, J. (1985). *Der Philosophische Diskurs der Moderne.* Frankfurt am Main: Suhrkamp

Habermas, J. (1992). *Faktizität und Geltung.* Frankfurt am Main: Suhrkamp.

Hager, B.M. (1978). Computers Help White House Lobying. *Congressional Quarterly Weekly Report,* 11 February, 366.

Hattery, L.H. (1962). EDP: Implications for Public Administration. *Public Administration Review,* 22, 129-130.

Held, D. (1987). *Models of democracy.* Cambridge: Polity Press.

Hickman, L. (1992). Populism and the cult of the expert. In: L. Winner (ed.) *Democracy in a technological society.* Dordrecht: Kluwer.

HMSO (1993). *Open Government.* CM 2290. London: HMSO.

HMSO (1994a). *Optical Fibre Networks.* Trade and Industry Committee, Third report. House of Commons, Session 1993-94, HC 285-I (Report). London: HMSO.

HMSO (1994b). *Optical Fibre Networks.* Trade and Industry Committee, Third report. House of Commons, Session 1993-94, HC 285-II (Memoranda of Evidence). London: HMSO.

Hoff, J. and K. Stormgaard (1991). Information technology between citizen and administration. *Informatization and the Public Sector,* 1(3) 213-235.

Holderness, M. (3 March 1994). Are these Men a Threat to Free Speech? *The Guardian,* p. 17.

Hollander, R. (1985). *Video Democracy: the Vote-from-Home Revolution.* Mt. Airy MD: Lomond Press.

Holvast, J., H. van Dijk en G. Schep (1989). Privacy Doorgelicht. *Onderzoeksrapport,* no. 71. 's-Gravenhage: SWOKA.

Holzman, D.L. (1986). Comments on "Democracy in an Information Society": Computers and Common Sense. *The Information Society,* 4, 101-108.

Hood, C. (1976). *The Limits of Administration.* London: Wiley.

Hood, C. (1991). A public management for all seasons? *Public Administration,* 69(3), 3-19.

Horrocks, I. and J. Webb (1994). Electronic Democracy: a policy issue for UK local government? *Local Government Policy Making,* 21(3), 22-30.

Howell, D. (1985). IT and relations between government and the public. *Catalyst,* 1, 75-85.

Hudson, H. (1986). New communications technologies. *International political science review,* 7(3), 332-343.

*Independent Television Commission News Releases,* February 1994 - July 1994.

Industry Canada (1994a). *The Canadian Information Highway: Building Canada's Information and Communications Infrastructure.* Ottawa: Ministry of Supply and Services Canada.

Industry Canada (1994b). *Privacy and the Canadian Information Highway: Building Canada's Information and Communications Infrastructure*. Ottawa: Ministry of Supply and Services Canada.

Information Infrastructure Task Force (1993). *The National Information Infrastructure: Agenda for Action*. Washington DC: Information Infrastructure Task Force.

Information Infrastructure Task Force (1994). *Principles for Providing and Using Personal Information*. (April 21 draft). Washington DC: Information Infrastructure Task Force.

Jones, P. (29 April 1994). Council Seats to Fall by a Third. *The Scotsman*.

Kamp, J. en M. Kerres (4 februari 1992). De huidige parlementen zijn museumstukken. (Interview met Alvin Toffler). *NRC-Handelsblad*, pp. 13-14.

Kapor, M. (1991). Civil Liberties in Cyberspace. *Scientific American*, 265, 116-120.

Keane, J. (1991). *The Media and Democracy*. Cambridge: Polity Press.

Kevenhörster, P. (1984). *Politik im Elektronischen Zeitalter. Politische Wirkungen der Informationstechnik*. Baden-Baden: Nomos Verlagsgesellschaft.

Kirchheimer, O. (1966). The transformation of the Western European party systems. In: J. La Palombara and M. Weiner (eds.). *Political parties and political development*. Princeton: Princeton University Press, 177-200.

Kling, R. (1982). Social analyses of computing. *Information Age*, 4, 25-55.

Kling, R. (1986). The Struggles for Democracy in an Information Society. *The Information Society*, 4(1/2), 1-7.

Kling, R. (1987). Computerization as an Ongoing Social and Political Process. In: G. Bjerkness, P. Ehn, and M. Kyng (eds.). *Computers and Democracy. A Scandinavian Challenge*, 117-136. Aldershot: Avebury.

Kling, R. (1987). Defining the Boundaries of Computing across Complex Organizations. In: R.J. Boland and R.A. Hirschheim (eds.). *Critical Issues in Information Systems Research*. John Wiley & Sons, 307-362.

Koch, Hal. (1945). *Hvad er demokrati?* København: Gyldendal.

Kock, T., H.M. Loerakker, G.W. Rijnja, A. Timmermans, H. Strooij-Sterken en J.C.M. Veenman (1994). *Jaarboek overheidscommunicatie 1994*. 's-Gravenhage: VUGA.

Koole, R.A. (1992). *De opkomst van de moderne kaderpartij. Veranderende partijorganisatie in Nederland 1960-1990*. Utrecht: het Spectrum.

*Kommunal Årbog 1994* (1994). 65. årgang. Redaktion T. H. Mikkelsen. Vedbæk.

*Kommunale Finanser 1990* (1991). København: Danmarks Statistik.

*Kommunalstatistisk Årbog 2/92* (1992). Kommunernes Landsforening, Kommuneinformation.

KoopA ADV (1992). *Kooperationsausschuss ADV, Bund/Länder/Kommunaler Bereich, Leitaussagen zur Informationstechnik in der öffentlichen Verwaltung*. Fulda.

Kraemer, K.L. and W.H. Dutton (1979). The interests served by technological reform. The case of computing. *Administration & Society*, 11(1), 80-106.

Kraemer, K.L. and W.H. Dutton (1982). The automation of bias. In: J.N. Danziger et al. (ed.) *Computer High Technology in American Local Government and politics.* New York: Columbia University Press, 170-193.

Kraemer, K.L. and R. Kling (1985). The Political Character of Computerization in Service Organizations. *Computers and the Social Sciences,* 1(2), 77-90.

Kraemer, K.L., and J.L. King (1987). Computers and the Constitution: a Helpful, Harmful or Harmless Relationship? *Public Administration Review,* 47(1), 93-105.

Kraemer, K.L., S. Dickhofen, S.F. Tierney and J.L. King (1987). *Datawars. The Politics of Modeling in Federal Policy Making.* New York: Columbia University Press.

Kraemer, K. L. and J.L. King (1994). Social Analysis of information systems: The Irvine School 1970-1994, *Informatization and the Public Sector,* 3(2) 163-182.

Kraft, M.E. and N.J. Vig (eds.). (1988). *Technology and Politics.* Durham: Duke University Press.

Kuypers, G. (1976). *Grondbegrippen van Politiek.* Utrecht: Het Spectrum.

Laffin, M. and K. Young (1990). *Professionalism in local government.* London: Longman.

Lapham, L.H. et al. (1985). *High Technology and Human Freedom.* Washington DC: Smithsonian Institution Press.

Lasswell, H.D. (1936). *Politics. Who Gets What, When, How.* New York: McGraw Hill.

Lasswell, H.D. (1971). Policy Problems of a Data-Rich Civilization. In: A.F. Westin (ed.) *Information Technology in a Democracy.* Cambridge MA: Harvard University Press, 187-197.

Laudon, K.C. (1977). *Communications technology and democratic participation.* New York: Praeger Publishers.

Laudon, K.C. (1980). Informatique et démocratie: l'expérience Américaine. *Actes du Colloque International Informatique et Société,* V, 135-142.

Laudon, K.C. (1984). The possibilities for participation in the democratic process: telecommunications, computers and democracy. In: K.W. Grewlich and F.H. Pedersen (eds.). *Power and participation in an information society.* Brussel: European Commission, 153-168.

Laudon, K.C. (1986b). The Dossier Society (Comments on Democracy in an Information Society). *The Information Society,* 4(1/2), 87-90.

Laudon, K.C. (1986). *Dossier Society: value choices in the design of national information systems.* New York: Columbia University Press.

Leach, R. (1994). *Reorganising for enabling?: restructuring local government for an altered role.* Paper to the PAC Annual Conference, University of York, September.

Lenk, K. (1976). Partizipationsförderende Technologien? In: K. Lenk (Hrsg.) *Informationsrechte und Kommunikationspolitik.* Darmstadt: Toeche/Mitler.

Lenk, K. (1982). Information Technology and Society. In: G. Friedrichs and A. Schaff (eds.). *Microelectronics and Society: For Better or For Worse*. A report to the club of Rome. Oxford: Pergamon Press, 273-310.

Lenk, K. (1990). *Neue Informationsdienste im Verhältnis von Bürger und Verwaltung*. Heidelberg: Decker und Müller.

Leonard-Barton, D. (1988). Implementation Characteristics of Organisational Innovations: Limits and Opportunities for Management Strategies. *Communication Research*, 15(5), 603-631.

Licklider, J.C.R. (1983). Computers and Government. In: L. Dertouzos and J. Moses (eds.). *The computer age: a twenty-year view*, 87-126. Cambridge MA.: MIT Press.

Liedtke, B.H. (1990). Ein kommunales Auskunfts- und Beratungssystem. In: Lenk, K. (ed.) *Neue Informationsdienste im Verhältnis von Bürger und Verwaltung*. Heidelberg: Decker und Müller, 55-78.

Lindsay, A.D. (1935/1951). *The essentials of democracy*. London: Oxford University Press.

Local Government Commission for England (1993). *Renewing local government in the English Shires: a progress report*. London: HMSO.

Løgstrup, G. (1990). Frikommuneprojektet - ved halvvejen. *Juristen*, (72)8.

Lowi, Th.J. (1980). The Political Impact of Information Technology. In: T. Forester (ed.) *The Microelectronics Revolution*. Oxford: Basil Blackwell Publisher, 453-472.

Lowi, Th.J. and D. Lytel (1986). Making It a Real Revolution (Comments on Democracy in an Information Society). *The Information Society*, 4(1/2), 91-99.

Luker, K. (1984). *Abortion and the politics of motherhood*. Berkely: University of California Press.

Lynn, P. (1992). *Public perceptions of local government*. Department of the Environment, London: HMSO.

Lyon, D. (1993). *The Electronic Eye*. Cambridge: Polity Press.

MacBride, R. (1967). *The Automated State. Computer Systems as a New Force in Society*. Philadelpia: Chilton Book Company.

MacKenzie, D. Wajcman, J. (1985). *The social control of technology. How the refrigerator got its hum*. Buckingham: Open University Press.

Macpherson, C.B. (1977). *The life and times of liberal democracy*. Oxford: Oxford University Press.

Magleby, D. (1984). *Direct Legislation: Voting on Ballot Propositions in the United States*. Baltimore MD: John Hopkins University Press.

Malbin, M. (1982). Teledemocracy and its Discontents. *Public Opinion*, (June-July), 57-58.

Malone, Th.W.J., J. Yates, and R.I. Benjamin (1987). Electronic Markets and Electronic Hierarchies. *Communications of the ACM*, 30, 484-497.

Marien, M. (1985). Some Questions for the Information Society. In: T. Forester (ed.) *The Information Technology Revolution*. Oxford: Basil Blackwell Publisher.

Markus, M.L. (1994). Finding a Happy Medium: Explaining the Negative Effects of Electronic Communication on Social Life at Work. *ACM Transactions on Information Systems*. 12(2), April, 119-149.

Martin, J. (1978). *The wired society*. Englewood Cliffs: Prentice-Hall.

Masuda, Y. (1985). Parameters of the post-industrial society. In: T. Forester (ed.) *The Information Technology Revolution*. Oxford: Basil Blackwell Publisher.

McCarthy, T. (1991). *Ideals and illusions*. Cambridge Mass.: The MIT Press.

McLean, I. (1986). Mechanisms for democracy. In: D. Held and C. Pollitt (eds.). *New forms of democracy*. Milton Keynes: Open University Press.

McLean, I. (1989). *Democracy and New Technology*. Cambridge: Polity Press.

Meadows, R.G. (1985). Political Communications Research in the 1980's. *Journal of Communications*, 35.

Mellors, C. (1978). Governments and the Individual - Their Secrecy and His Privacy. In: J. Young (ed.) *Privacy*. New York: Wiley, 87-112.

Meyer, O.M.T. (1994). Informatisering en politieke agendavorming: de agendavormende waarde van informatiesystemen. In: A. Zuurmond, J. Huigen, P.H.A. Frissen, I.Th.M. Snellen and P.W. Tops (red.) *Informatisering in het openbaar bestuur*. 's-Gravenhage: VUGA, 113-135.

Miewald, R. and K. Mueller (1987). The use of information technology in oversight by state legislatures. *State and local government review*, 13, 17-24.

Miles, I. (1988). *Information Technology and Information Society: Options for the Future*. Paper No. 2. Falmer: University of Sussex, Science Policy Research Unit.

Miller, D. (1983). The competitive model of democracy. In: G. Duncan (ed.) *Democratic theory and practice*. Cambridge: Cambridge University Press.

Miller, D. (1983). Deliberative democracy and social choice. In: D. Held (ed.) *Prospects of democracy*. Cambridge: Polity Press.

Ministerie van Economische Zaken (1991). *Videotextdiensten in Nederland, op weg naar volwassenheid*. 's-Gravenhage.

Ministry of the Interior (1993). *Municipalities and counties in Denmark*. Ministry of the Interior, May.

Montes, F. (1986). Prospects for the Era of Computing (Comments on Democracy in an Information Society). *The Information Society*, 4(1/2), 65-86.

Moore, D.W. (1992). *The Super Pollsters. How they measure and manipulate public opinion in America*. New York: Four Walls Eight Windows.

Morris J. and C. Brigham (1993). Filling the information gaps. *Local Government Chronicle*. December 17th-24th, 11.

Morris-Suzuki, T. (1988). *Beyond Computopia. Information, Automation and Democracy in Japan*. London: Kegan Paul International.

*Mostrups Vejviser for Ravnsborg Kommune* (1994). København: Mostrups Forlag A/S, Marts.

Moscow, V. (1989). *The pay-per society: computers and communication in the information age*. Toronto: Garamond

Moss, M.L. (1978). Interactive Television: Reading PA; research on community uses. *Journal of Communication*, 2, 160-167.

Moukhtarzadeh, N. (1993). *Document Image Processing.* München: Computerwoche Verlag.

Mowshowitz, A. (1976). *The conquest of will: information processing in human affairs.* Reading MA: Addison-Wesley Publishing.

Mowshowitz, A. (1977). *Inside Information: Computers in Fiction.* Reading, MA: Addison Wesley Publishing.

Mulgan, G. (1991). *Communications and control.* Cambridge: Polity Press.

Murchland, B. (1983). Citizenship in a Technological Society: Problems and Possibilities. *Journal of Teacher Education*, 34(6), 21-24.

Nathan, R.P. (1987). The Politics of Printouts: the Use of Official Numbers to Allocate Federal Grants-In-Aid. In: W. Alonso and P. Starr (eds.). *The Politics of Numbers*. New York: Russell Sage Foundation, 331-342.

Neustadt, R. (1985). Electronic Politics. In: T. Forester (ed.) *The Information Technology Revolution*. Oxford: Basil Blackwell Publisher, 561-568.

Nora, S. and A. Minc (1978). *Informatisation de la Société*. Paris: La Documentation Française.

*NRC Handelsblad* (14 september 1994). Rapport-Van der Zwan.

*NRC Handelsblad* (29 december 1994). Oneigenlijk gebruik van sociale bestanden/Ruimte voor eigen initiatief bij koppelen van bestanden.

Orton, B.M. (s.d.). *Media-based Issue Balloting for Regional Planning*. (Dissertation). New Brunswick NJ: Rutgers University, University Microfilms, 80-13,177.

OTA (1986). *Electronic Record System and Individual Privacy*. Washington DC: Government Printing Office.

OTA (September 1987). *Science, Technology and the Constitution* (Background paper). Washington DC: Government Printing Office.

OTA (1988). *Informing the Nation: Federal Information Dissemination in an Electronic Age*. Washington DC: Government Printing Office.

OTA (September 1993). *Making government work: Electronic delivery of federal services*. Washington DC: Government Printing Office.

OTA (1993a). *The National Information Infrastructure: Agenda for Action*. Washington DC: Government Printing Office.

OTA (1993b). *Making Government Work: Electronic Delivery of Federal Services*, Washington DC: Government Printing Office.

Panebianco, A. (1988). *Political parties: organization and power*. Cambridge: Cambridge University Press.

Parry, G. (1989). Democracy and Amateurism - the Informed Citizen. *Government & Opposition*, 24(4), 489-502.

Pedersen, F.H. (1984). Power and participation in an information society. In: K.W. Grewlich and F.H. Pedersen (eds.). *Power and participation in an information society*. Brussel: European Commission, 249-289.

Perritt, H.H. Jr. (1990). Federal Electronic Information Policy. *Temple Law Review* 63(2), 201-250.

Phillips, A. (1994). *Local democracy: the terms of the debate.* London: Commission for Local Democracy.

Pickering, W. (1994). Can Suites Fill Groupware needs. *Datamation*, January 7, 27-28.

Pitkin, H.F. (1967). *The concept of representation.* Berkely: University of California Press.

Pitt, D.C. and B.C. Smith (eds.) (1984). *The Computer Revolution.* Brighton Sussex: Wheatsheaf Books.

Plesser, R. and E. Cividanes (1991). *Privacy Protection in the United States.* Washington DC: Piper & Marbury.

Plant, R., F. Gregory, and A. Brier (eds.) (1988). *Information technology: the public issues.* (Fullbright Papers). New York: Manchester University Press.

*Politiken* (1994). 12. Marts.

Polomski, R.M. (1993). *Der automatisierte Verwaltungsakt: Die Verwaltung an der Schwelle von Automation zur Informations und Kommunikationstechnik.* Berlin: Duncker und Humblot.

Poster, M. (1990). *The Mode of Information. Poststructuralism and Social Context,* Cambridge: Polity Press.

Postman, N. (1992). *Technopoly.* New York: A.A. Knopf.

Pratchett, L. (1994). Open systems and closed networks: policy networks and the emergence of open systems in local government. *Public Administration* 72(1), 73-94.

Prewitt, K. (1987). Public Statistics and Democratic Politics. In: W. Alonso and P. Starr (eds.). *The Politics of Numbers.* New York: Russell Sage Foundation, 261-274.

Price, D.G. and D.E. Mulvihill (1965). The Present and Future Use of Computers in State Government. *Public Administration Review,* 25, 142-150.

Raab, C. (1991). *Can Data Protection be Measured?* Brussels: International Institute of Administrative Sciences, Working Group on Public Sector Productivity.

Raab, C. (1993). *Co-producing Data Protection: the Role of the State, Civil Society and the Market.* Leiden: European Consortium for Political Research, Joint Sessions of Workshops, Workshop on Rebuilding Civil Society: The Politics of the New Welfare Mix.

Raab, C. (1994). Open Government: Policy Information and Information Policy. *The Political Quarterly,* 65, 340-347.

Raab, C. and C. Bennett (1994). Protecting Privacy Across Borders: European Policies and Prospects. *Public Administration,* 72(1), 95-112.

Rallings, M., M. Temple and M. Thrasher (1994). *Community Identity and Participation in Local Democracy.* London: Commission for Local Democracy

Ramaker, J.H. (1992). Nieuwe media en communicatie in de publieke sector. *COMMA,* 5, 14-17.

Rawley Saldich, A. (1979). *Electronic Democracy. Television's impact on the American political process.* New York: Praeger Publishers.

Redcliffe-Maud (1969). *Report of the Royal Commission on local government in England 1966-69.* London: HMSO.

Registratiekamer (1994). *Jaarverslag 1992-1993.* Rijswijk.

Reinermann, H. (1992). *Verwaltungsorganisatorische Probleme und Lösungsansätze zur papierlosen Bearbeitung der Geschäftsvorfälle.* Bonn: Bundesministerium des Inneren.

Rejai, M. (1967). *Democracy.* New York: Atherton Press.

Rhodes, R.A.W. (1988). *Beyond Westminster and Whitehall: The sub-central governments of Britain.* London: Unwin-Hyman.

Rhodes, R.A.W. (1986). *The national world of local government.* London: Allen and Unwin.

Rhodes, R.A.W. (1987). Developing the public service orientation. *Local Government Studies.* May/June, 63-73.

Rich, R.F. (1981). *Social Science Information and Public Policy Making. The Interaction Between Bureaucratic Politics and the Use of Survey Data.* San Francisco: Jossey Bass Publishers.

Ridge, M. (1994). Towards a European nervous system: the role of the Economic Union. *Public Administration* 72(1), 127-134.

Ridley, N. (1988). *The local right: Enabling not providing.* London: Centre for Policy Studies.

Riker, W.H. (1982). *Liberalism against populism.* San Francisco: W.H. Freeman.

Rocheleau, B. (1994). Networks and Bulletin Board Systems in Government: Will They be the Third Computer Revolution? *International Journal of Public Administration,* 17(1), 83-99.

Rodden, T. (1991). A survey of CSCW systems. *Interacting with Computers.* 3(3), 319-353.

Roll, Ch. (1982). Private Opinion Polls. In: G. Benjamin (ed.) *The Communications Revolution in Politics,* 61-74. New York: Academy of Political Science.

Roording, J.F.L. (1994). *Sanctierecht in de belastingen en de sociale zekerheid.* Nijmegen: Ars Aequi Libri.

Rose, C. (1980). L'informatique et l'avenir de la démocratie. *Actes du Colloque International Informatique et société,* (V). Paris: Documentation Française, 81-87.

Rousseau, J.J. (1968). *Du contrat social, 1762;* The social contract (transl. M. Cranston). Baltimore: Penguin Books.

Rule, J.B. (1974). *Private lives and public surveillance: social control in the computer age.* New York: Schocken.

Rule, J.B., D. McAdam, L. Stearns, and D. Uglow (1980). Preserving Individual Autonomy in an Information-Oriented Society. In: L.J. Hoffmann (ed.) *Computers and Privacy in the Next Decade.* Academic Press, 65-87.

Ryan, F.B. (1977). Computing as an Aid to Political Effectiveness. In: T. Oden and Ch. Thompson (eds.). *Computers and Public Policy*, 22-27. Hanover, NH: Darthmouth College.

Sabine, G.H. (1952). The two democratic traditions. *The philosophical review*, 451-474.

Saloma, J.S. (1968). Systems Politics: The Presidency and Congress in the Future. *Technology Review*, 71, 23-33.

Scarbrough, H. and J. Corbett (1992). *Technology and organization: Power, meaning and design.* London: Routledge.

Schendelen, M.P.C.M. Van (1975). *Parlementaire informatie, besluitvorming en vertegenwoordiging.* Rotterdam: Universitaire Pers Rotterdam.

Schick, A. (1971). Toward the cybernetic state. In: D. Waldo (ed.) *Public administration in a time of turbulence.* New York: Chandler Publishing Company, 214-233.

Schiller, H.I. (1986). Comments on "Democracy in an Information Society". *The Information Society*, 4, 123-126.

Schneier, E. (1970). The intelligence of Congress: information and public policy patterns. *Annals of the American Academy of Political and Social Science* nr. 388, March, 14-24.

Schoenmacker, M. en D. Rijkers (1993). Nieuwe media en overheidsvoorlichting. In: Roon, A.D. de en R. Middel. *De wereld van Postbus 51. Voorlichtingscampagnes van de rijksoverheid.* Houten : Bohn Stafleu Van Loghum, 90-99.

Schoenmacker, M. (1994). De zappende burger in het elektronische overheidsbos. In: Kock, T., H.M. Loerakker, G.W. Rijnja, A. Timmermans, H. Strooij-Sterken en J.C.M. Veenman. *Jaarboek overheidscommunicatie 1994.* 's-Gravenhage, 101-108.

Schumpeter, J.A. (1943). *Capitalism, socialism and democracy.* London: Allan Unwin.

Sclove, R. (1992). The nuts and bolts of democracy: Democratic theory and technological design. In: L. Winner (ed.) *Democracy in a technological society.* Dordrecht: Kluwer Academic Publishers, 139-157.

Scott, D. (9 November 1994). Lang Makes Concessions Over Single-Tier Councils. *The Scotsman.*

Segal, E. (1985). Computerizing Congress. *PC World*, 3(11), 144-151.

Seibt, D. (1992). *Informatik in Wirtschaft und Verwaltung gestern-heute-morgen.* Braunschweig: Vieweg Verlaggesellschaft GmbH.

Sharkansky, I. (1994). *The Routines of Politics.* New York: Van Nostrand Reinhold.

Sherman, B. (1985). *The New Revolution: The Impact of Computers on Society.* New York: John Wiley and Sons.

Snellen, I.Th.M. (15 juli 1986). Informatietechnologie bedreigt normale functies van de politiek. *NRC Handelsblad.*

Snellen, I.Th.M. en W.B.H.J. van de Donk (1987). *Some dialectical developments of informatization in public administration.* Contribution to the conference on New technologies in public administration: socio-economic aspects from an interdisciplinary viewpoint. Zagreb, 13-15 November.

Snellen, I.Th.M. (1988). Informatisering in en voor het openbaar bestuur. *Beleidswetenschappen*, 2, 18-32.

Snellen, I.Th.M., C. Balfoort, W.B.H.J. van de Donk, H. Henkes, J.J.M. Stevens, en R.L.N. Westra (1989). *Informatisering in het openbaar bestuur. Indicaties voor politiek-inhoudelijke sturing*. NOTA-studie V11. 's-Gravenhage: SDU uitgeverij.

Snellen, I.Th.M. (1994). ICT: A revolutionizing force in public administration? *Informatization in the Public Sector*, 3(3/4), 283-305.

SOCITM (1993). *IT Trends in Local Government*. Birmingham: Society of Information Technology Managers in Local Government.

Sola Pool, I. de (ed.) (1973). *Talking Back: Citizen Feedback and Cable Technology*. Cambridge: MIT-Press.

Sola Pool, I. de (1983). *Technologies of Freedom. On free speech in an electronic age*. Cambridge MA: Harvard University Press.

Solomonides, T. and L. Levidow (1985). *Compulsive Technlogy*. London: FAB.

Sorokin, L.T. (1990). The Computerization of Government Information: Does it Circumvent Public Access Under the Freedom of Information Act and the Depository Library Program? *Columbia Journal of Law and Social Problems*, 24, 267-298.

*Statistisk Tiårsoversigt 1993* (1993). 34. årgang. København: Danmarks Statistik.

*Statistisk Årbog 1994* (1994). 98. årgang. København: Danmarks Statistik.

Steinbuch, K. (1978). Computer und Politik. *Datascope*, 28, 3-10.

Sterling, Th.D. (1986). Democracy in an Information Society. *The Information Society*, 4(1/2), 9-47.

Stewart, J. and C. Game (1991). *Belgrave paper No 1: Local Democracy - Representation and Elections*. Luton: Local Government Management Board.

Stewart, J. and M. Clarke (1987). The public service orientation: issues and dilemmas, *Public Administration*, 65(2), 161-177.

Stoyles, R.L. (1989). The Unfulfilled Promise: Use of Computers By and For Legislatures. *Computer Law Journal*, IX, 74-102.

Street, J. (1988). Taking Control? Some aspects of the relationship between information technology, government policy and democracy. In: R. Plant, F. Gregory and A. Brier (eds.). *Information Technology: The Public Issues*. (Fullbright Papers, volume 5). Oxford: Alden Press, 1-20.

Street, J. (1992). *Politics and technology*. London: MacMillan.

Székely, I. (1991). *Information Privacy in Hungary*. Budapest: Hungarian Institute for Public Opinion Research.

Taylor, J.A. and H. Williams (1990). The Scottish Highlands & Islands Initiative: An Alternative Model for Development. *Telecommunications Policy*, June.

Taylor, J.A. and H. Williams (1991). Public administration and the information polity. *Public Administration*, 69(2), 171-190.

Taylor, J.A. and H. Williams (1991). Public Administration and the Information Polity. *Public Administration*, 69, 171-190.

Taylor, J.A., H. Williams and B. Mcleod (1993). Telecommunications in Scotland: Auditing the Issues, *Quarterly Economic Commentary*, March.

Taylor, J.A. (1994). Telecommunications infrastructure and public policy development: evidence and inference. *Informatization and the Public Sector* 3(1), 63-74.

Taylor, J.R. and E.J. Van Every (1993). *The Vulnerable Fortress. Bureaucratic Organization and Management in the Information Age*. Toronto: Toronto University Press.

Taylor, P. (6 May 1990). Citizenship Fades Among Disconnected Americans. *Washington Post*, p. 1.

The Cable Television Association (1994). *The Case For Cable*. April.

Thomassen, J.J.A. (red.) (1991). *Hedendaagse democratie*. Alphen aan den Rijn: Samsom H.D. Tjeenk Willink.

Thompson, A.A. (1970). *Big Brother in Britain today*. London: Michael Jozeph.

Tops, P.W. and C.M.B. Kommers (1991). *Informatization and local democracy in the Netherlands: an exploration*. Paper for the EGPA conference on informatization in public administration. The Hague, August 29-31.

Tromp, B. (21 december 1985). De neergang van politieke partijen. In: *het Parool*, p. 21

Trouong, H.A., G. Williams, J. Clark and A. Couey (1993). *Gender issues in online communication*. Bay Area Women in Telecommunications

Turner, J.A. (1986). Comments on "Democracy in an Information Society": the Difficulty of Projecting Impacts from Trajectories of Emerging Technologies. *The Information Society*, 4, 53-64.

Vig, N.J. (1988). Technology, Philosophy and the State: an overview. In: M.E. Kraft and N.J. Vig (eds.). *Technology and Politics*, 8-32. Durham: Duke University Press.

Vintar, M. (1992). Upravljanje s pisnimi gradivi in nove informacijske tehnologijeö, Zveza ekonomistov Slovenije - V. posvetovanje sekcije za raziskovanje informacijskih sistemov, Izlake, 1-6.

Vintar, M. (1992). Organization and handling of written materials in business and public administration under new information technologies. *Proceedings of International Conference on Organization and Information Systems*, Bled.

Vintar, M. (1993). Toward the implementation and use of 'electronic' files in public administration, Decision Support in Public Administration - *Proceedings of the IFIP TC8/WG8.3 Working Conference on Decision Support in Public Administration*. Noordwijkerhout, The Netherlands, May.

Vitalis, A. (1981). *Informatique, Pouvoir et Libertés*. Paris: Economica.

Wasby, S.L. (1989). Technology in appellate courts: the Ninth Circuit's experience with electronic mail. *Judicature*, 73(2), 90-97.

Weeramantry, C. (1983). *The slumbering sentinels*. London: Penguin.

Weingarten, F.W. (1986). Comments on 'Democracy in an Information Society'. *The Information Society*, 4, 49-52.

Weiss, C.H. (1983). Ideology, Interests and Information. The basis of Policy Positions. In: D. Callahan and B. Jennings (eds.). *The Social Science and Policy Analysis*. New York: Plenum Press, 213-245.

Westcott, B. (1993). *IT for Councillors*. The Foundation for IT in Local Government.

Westin, A.F. (1971). Prologue: Of Technological Visions and Democratic Politics. In: A.F. Westin (ed.) *Information Technology in a Democracy*, 1-11.

Westin, A. (1971). *Information Technology in a Democracy*. Cambridge Massachusetts: Harvard University Press.

Westin, A. (1974). The Technology of Secrecy. In: Dorsen, N. and S. Gillers. *None of your business. Government Secrecy in America*. New York: The Viking Press, 288-327.

Widdicombe D., (Chairman). (1986). *The conduct of local authority business: the report of the Committee of Inquiry into the conduct of local authority business*. Cmnd 9797. London: HMSO.

Will, I.C. (1993). *The Big Brother Society*. London: Hasrop.

Willcocks, L. (1994). Managing information systems in UK public administration: issues and prospects. *Public Administration* 72(1), 13-32.

Willcocks, L. and J. Harrow (1992). *Rediscovering public services management*. London: McGraw-Hill.

Williams, F. (1982). *The communications revolution*. Berverly Hills: Sage Publications.

Williamson, O. (1975). *Markets and Hierarchies*. New York: Free Press.

Wilson, D. (1994). Facing up to the democratic deficit. *Local Government Studies*, 20(2), 193-201.

Winner, L. (1977). *Autonomous Technology. Technics-out-of-Control as a Theme in Political Thought*. Cambridge MA: MIT Press.

Winner, L. (1986). *The Whale and the Reactor. A Search for Limits in an Age of High Technology*. Chicago: University of Chicago Press.

Winner, L. (1987). *Political Ergonomics: Technological Design and the Quality of Public Life*. (IIUG dp 87-7). Berlin: International Institute for Environment and Society.

Winner, L. (1988). Do Artifacts have Politics? In: M.E. Kraft and N.J. Vig (eds.) *Technology and Politics*. Durham: Duke University Press, 33-53.

Winner, L. (ed.) (1992). *Democracy in a Technological Society*. Dordrecht: Academic Publishers.

Winner, L. (1993). Upon Opening the Black Box and Finding it Empty: Social Constructivism and the Philosophy of Technology. *Science, Technology & Human Values*, 18(3), 362-378.

Wright, R. (23 January 1995). Hyperdemocracy. Washington isn't dangerously disconnected from the people: the trouble is it's too plugged in. *Time*, pp. 51-65.

Yates, J. (1989). *Control through Communication. The Rise of System in American Management*, London: John Hopkins University Press.

Yngström, L. R. Sizer, J. Berleur and R. Laufer (eds.). (1985). *Can information technology result in benevolent bureaucracies?* Amsterdam: North-Holland.

Young, K. and L. Mills (1983). *Managing the post-industrial city*. London: Heinemann.

Zeef, P.H.H. (1994). *Tussen toezien en toezicht. Veranderingen in bestuurlijke toezichtsverhoudingen door informatisering*. Rotterdam: Phaedrus.

Zolo, D. (1992). *Democracy and complexity: A realistic approach*. Cambridge: Polity Press.

Zuboff, S. (1988). *In the Age of the Smart Machine. The Future of Work and Power*. Oxford: Heinemann.

Zuurmond, A., J. Huigen, P.H.A. Frissen, I.Th.M. Snellen and P.W. Tops (eds.) (1994). *Informatisering in het Openbaar Bestuur*. Den Haag: VUGA.

Zuurmond, A. (1994). From Bureaucracy to Infocracy: a Tale of Two Cities, *Informatization and the Public Sector*, 3(3/4), 189-204.

# II. Index of Items

# Q

# R

# S

# T

# U

# U

# V

# W

## IV. Information about the Authors

**Barbara Bardzki** is a lecturer in the Department of Business Administration, Glasgow Caledonian University, Glasgow, Scotland. She is currently working towards a doctorate on telecommunications infrastructures and innovations in public service delivery.

**Victor Bekkers** is associate professor of Public Administration at Tilburg University (The Netherlands) and participates in the Rotterdam/Tilburg research program 'Informatization in Public Administration'. His main fields of interest are the development of new forms of interorganizational steering, especially in relationship to informatization issues, local government and European policy-making. He was one of the editors of an earlier IOS Press publication on 'European Public Administration and Informatization'.

**Christine Bellamy** is professor of Public Administration at the Nottingham Trent University. Her research interests are in the application of ICTs in British local and central government. With John Taylor, she has convened the UK Study Group on Information, Communication and New Technology in Public Administration. Chris Bellamy is the current Chair of the UK Joint University Council's Public Administration Committee.

**Paul Depla** is assistent professor of Public Administration at the Tilburg University. He participates in the Tilburg/Rotterdam research program on Informatization in Public Administration. Furthermore, he works for the staff of the chairman of the Dutch Labour Party. He has published about local democracy, political and administrative renewal, the political impact of the rise of new media, electoral behavior, and about the Dutch Labour Party.

**Wim van de Donk** is assistent professor of Public Administration in the Department of Law and Public Administration of Tilburg University. He participates in the research program 'Informatization in Public Administration', and is secretary of the permanent studygroup for informatization in public administration of the European Group for Public Administration. He is preparing a PH-D thesis on the meaning of informatization for political decision making processes. (Email: Wim.B.H.J.vdDonk-@KUB.NL)

**Hein P.M. van Duivenboden** is connected to the Department of Public Administration at Tilburg University in the Netherlands. He prepares a dissertation on the
impact of coupling personal data in legal and administration-scientific perspective. He
also participates in research involving an evaluation of the Dutch automation of
population registers and is currently a member of a research group on the evaluation
of the Dutch Privacy Act.

**Arthur Edwards** is assistent professor of Public Administration at the Erasmus
University Rotterdam and participates in the Rotterdam/Tilburg research program
'Informatization in Public Administration'. His recent publications refer to the
comunicative aspects of the relationships between citizens and government.

**Erik Frøkjær** is an associate professor of Computing at the University of Copenhagen. He received MSc degrees in Mathematical Engineering and in Electrical Engineering from the Technical University of Denmark in 1973, and in 1977 a Bachelor
degree in Business Administration. Areas of research include, from the perspective of
understanding computing as a human activity, studies of methods and tools for
systems development, expert support systems, information storage and retrieval, and
usability evaluation methods for interactive information systems. He joined the
university of Copenhagen in 1985 after twelve years as a systems developer and
project manager within the Public Administration, and has maintained a special
interest in the application of information technology in that area.

**Halldór Færch** is head of Department of Innovation in Kommunedata, a data
processing service bureau for the counties and the municipalities in Denmark. He
received a Msc degree from the Technical University of Denmark, Faculty of Civil
Engineering, in Copenhagen in 1969. He has been working with computing as
technical consultant and project manager in Kommunedata, the last 7 years managing
innovative projects such as 'Citizen self-service for the municipalities using videotex'
and 'Electronic information to the municipal board', both two-year projects.

**Ivan Horrocks** BA (Hons) Dip Policy Studies is a research fellow in the department
for Economics and Public Administration, The Nottingham Trent University. He
formely worked for ten years as a community development worker in both local
government and the voluntary sector.

**Helge Korsbæk** MA in economics from Aarhus University, has now retired, but
served as a Deputy Secretary in the Ministry of Finance, Department of Administration, primarily concerned with questions regarding the organization and the efficiency of the Public Administration. He has been chairman of a number of working
groups among others the so-called 'Korsbæk-committee' which in 1970 made

proposals for general changes of the organization of the Danish central administration (Official Report no. 629).

**Odette Meyer** studied Political Sciences at the University of Nijmegen. After her study she has worked as a researcher on the staff of the department of Public Administration at the Erasmus University Rotterdam. She combined this post with a position as consultant and project manager of various informatization projects carried out in the Municipality of Amsterdam. From September 1993 till July 1994 she stayed as a visiting scholar at the Netherlands Institute for Advanced Study in the Humanities and Social Sciences in Wassenaar. She is preparing a thesis about the meaning of informatization for (the realization of) the political agenda. At the moment she is working for the Association of Dutch Polytechnics and Colleges.

**Lawrence Pratchett** is a research fellow in the Department of Public Policy and Managerial Studies at De Montfort University. He has worked for a number of English local authorities as a systems analyst, designing, developing and implementing ICT systems during a period of substantial change in the management and organization of local government. His PhD thesis is on the politics of ICT strategies in UK local government, and has concentraded particularly upon the existence and influence of an ICT policy network which sets the general direction and bounds of such strategies. He has published on a number of issues relation to ICTs in government, including the rise of open systems technologies and their implications for local authorities in the UK. His current research is concentrating upon the impact of local government reorganization on sub-central government relation, and the role of ICTs in developing such relationships.

**Charles Raab** (BA Columbia; M.A. Yale) is Senior Lecturer in Politics at the University of Edinburgh. His research interests include privacy and data protection; information policy, technology and processes in public organizations; electronic service delivery and public access to information. He has edited a collection of papers and published by many articles in leading journals and contributions to edited volumes. With Colin J. Bennett, he is writing a book on British data protection with the help of a Nuffield Foundation grant. Other work in progress includes an encyclopaedia article and papers on information policy. He is planning comparative European research on privacy in health data. He is a member of the European Group of Public Administration's Study Group on Informatization in Public Administration and of a similar United Kingdom-based group. He is co-author of a forthcoming book on police co-operation in Europe, and has co-authored a book and published many other works on education policy, in which he conducts research projects.

**Kees Schalken** is Ph.D. student at Tilburg University. He is preparing a dissertation on Free-Nets and Digital Cities.

**Ignace Snellen** is Professor of Public Administration at the Erasmus University in Rotterdam, the Netherlands. He graduated in Political Science and Law at the University of Amsterdam. As political advisor to the Board of Management of Philips Electronic Industries he wrote a dissertation on 'Approaches to Strategy Formulation' (1975) in the public and private sector. His publications, books and articles, cover a wide range of subjects related to management, policy, planning and control. Since 1985 he has been, together with professor Paul Frissen, head of the research program on Informatization in Public Administration of the University of Tilburg and Erasmus University. He is co-chairman (with Jean-Paul Baquiast) of the permanent study group of EGPA, which regularly organizes conferences on this subject. With professor John Leslie King UC Irvine and professor Brian Kahin, Harvard University, he is chief-editor of the International Journal 'Information, Infrastructure and Policy'

**John Taylor** is Professor of Management at Glasgow Caledonian University, Glasgow, Scotland, with special responsibilities for the development of research in the Faculty of Business. He has published widely on information and communications technology in government and in the business firm. He also has a special interest in UK and European telecommunications policy and its significance in the provision of infrastructure for the delivery of other public policies. He publishes widely, contributing to many international academic journals and books. He has recently co-edited a special issue of the journal *Public Administration* which looked in detail at his core concept of the 'information polity'. He is editing a special issue of the journal *'New Technology, Work and Employment'* on the subject of Business Process Re-engineering, for September, 1995, and is co-authoring a book - Government in the Information Age - to be published in 1996 by the Open University Press.

**Pieter Tops** is professor of Public Administration at Tilburg University. His research topics are local government and information and communications technology.

**Mirko Vintar** is Assistent Professor of Applied Informatics at the University of Ljubljana, School of Public Administration, Ljubljana, Slovenia, currently also Dean of the School of Public Administration. His main research interest is in Information Systems Design Methodologies and Document Management Systems. He has written three textbooks and a book on Analysis and Design of Information Systems and has more than 30 publications in the same field. He is also editor-in-chief of a journal Applied Informatics and Vice-President of the Slovenian Informatics Association.

**Jeff Webb** is an Economist and Urban Planner who has previously worked in British local and central government. He is now Principal Lecturer in Public Policy and Management at the Nottingham Trent University, where he is developing courses for practising managers in local authorities. His primary research interests are in inner city regeneration and urban management. He has recently been working on public policy and management in Poland and Azerbaijan.

**Caroline Wilson** is an Education and Training Officer at Scottish Nuclear in East Killbride, Scotland. Prior to this she was a lecturer in the Department of Business Administration, Glasgow Caledonian University, Glasgow, Scotland, with research interests in the area of Information Technology and Business Process Re-engineering.

**Stavros Zouridis** is a researcher at the Faculty of Law of Tilburg University. He wrote his doctoral thesis on the legal admissibility of automated implementation of law. At the moment he is involved in the evaluation research of the Dutch Act on the Openness of Administration and the Dutch Privacy Act. He also publishes on the subject of local democracy and the implications of information and communication technologies and the electronic highway for the openness of government.

CPSIA information can be obtained at www.ICGtesting.com
Printed in the USA
BVOW081808171111

275950BV00005BA/3/A

9 789051 992199